TRANSFORMING BUYER-SUPPLIER RELATIONS

Also by Jonathan Morris

FLEXIBLE FUTURES: Prospects for Employment and Organisation (*edited with Paul Blyton*)

JAPAN AND THE GLOBAL ECONOMY (*editor*)

Transforming Buyer-Supplier Relations

Japanese-Style Industrial Practices in a Western Context

Jonathan Morris
Lecturer in Organisational Behaviour
Cardiff Business School

and

Rob Imrie
Lecturer in the Department of Geography
Royal Holloway and Bedford New College,
University of London

First published 1992 by
MACMILLAN ACADEMIC AND PROFESSIONAL LTD
Houndmills, Basingstoke, Hampshire RG21 2XS
and London
Companies and representatives
throughout the world

Copy-edited and typeset by Cairns Craig Editorial, Edinburgh

ISBN 0-333-51247-2

A catalogue record for this book is available
from the British Library

Printed by Antony Rowe Ltd, Chippenham, Wiltshire

Contents

List of Tables

List of Figures

Acknowledgements

Although this book has been a collaborative effort, Rob Imrie is responsible for writing Chapters 1 to 3 and, substantially, Chapter 8, while Jonathan Morris wrote Chapters 4 to 7. We wish to acknowledge the Welsh Development Agency for funding the research and the companies for generously participating. We would also like to thank various colleagues at Cardiff for reading the manuscript and offering helpful suggestions. Included are Tod Rutherford, Pete Wells and Sarah Fielder. Finally we wish to thank Louise Jones for her part in the preparation of the manuscript.

1 Buyer-Supplier Relations and Changes in Industrial Organization

1 INTRODUCTION

By the mid-1980s, many commentators on the British economy were in agreement that British industry was in the process of a series of major changes in managerial styles and strategies, industrial relations, and associated working practices. The Treasury's Economic Progress Report (1986) was typical in noting the Government's intent on encouraging the development of 'an enterprise culture and a more flexible and responsive economy'. This political agenda has incorporated a number of enabling measures, including the deregulation of private capital, the privatization of significant parts of the public sector, and the introduction of commercial criteria into residual state sector activities. These changes have occurred alongside a major restructuring of industrial production, work and employment, with the emergence of new forms of flexible economic and labour organization, characterized by a diverse range of new technologies, products, and services (Boyer, 1987; Jones, 1988; Martin, 1988; Wood, 1989).

In particular, a major feature of contemporary industrial change is the restructuring of large corporations (Shutt and Whittington, 1984, Thrift, 1988). While the post-war trend of an increased scale of employment has been reversed, with average plant sizes diminishing, new firm formation rates have risen quickly and there has been a commensurate rise in the numbers of small businesses. These transformations are illustrative of wider changes in multinational corporations (MNCs), including a mixture of forward and backward disintegration, diversification into new product markets, and the development of a much more fluid set of intra-firm and interfirm organizational networks than has hitherto existed. A plethora of research indicates how MNCs are devising a whole host of new product and market strategies (Amin and Robbins, 1990; Castells, 1988; Dunning, 1986). This is occurring in the face of rising Research and Development (R & D) costs, rapidly changing and shortening product life cycles, greater

1

risk of market failure, and the availability of technologies which permit enhanced task and communication integration between constituent parts of industrial organization (Castells, 1988; Dunning, 1986).

In turn, it is argued that these trends relate to the development of cooperative, non-market, relations, characterized by the global diffusion of dynamic networks and industry synergy (Amin and Robbins, 1990). An illustration of this is strategic alliances between large corporations, based on the principle of mutual complementarity between specialists, relations characterized by collaborative marketing and distribution, shared R&D, and co-production (Cooke, 1988; Gordon, 1988). As Amin and Robbins (1990) note, these organizational innovations indicate a significant deepening of oligopolistic behaviour and control, illustrative of more effective corporate integration across vertical, horizontal, and territorial boundaries (1990, p. 12). In this sense, the emergence of new interfirm relationships is partly linked to a 'network' logic dictated by the need to reduce market uncertainty, to control development trajectories, and to share information, communication systems and related production costs.

However, this is not to suggest that the increasing fragmentation of productive systems is the same as a fragmentation of capital and control. As Harrison (1989) notes, the development of new interfirm relationships corresponds to the revitalization of the centralization and concentration of capital. In this way, the tendency is not indicative of cartel formation, but rather a redefinition of competitive market relations (that is, towards heightened forms of competitive pressures). As Amin and Robbins (1990) conclude, these have been elevated to the level of rivalries between global galaxies of firms, or what Gordon (1988) terms 'transnational alliance formations'.

In particular, these trends are underpinned by corporations slimming down for reasons of cost and competitiveness, with vertical disintegration to satellite and subcontract firms (Shutt and Whittington, 1984; Scott, 1988). This takes a number of forms, including the contraction of core activities, from the manufacture of parts and sub-assemblies to maintenance and cleaning and, in some instances, the putting-out of design as well as research and development. As Amin and Robbins (1990) note, these processes of externalization are more complex than a simple choice between 'make' or 'buy', in so far that the development of new interfirm relations involves a distinct quasi-market or quasi-integration formation, characterized by close collaboration and long-term contractual practices.

This is particularly the case with the development of new supplier networks by buyer companies, with a turnaround in past practices based on archaic methods of production control, poor quality and development, and prohibitive pricing systems. This contrasts with the establishment of new practices between particular buyers and suppliers, following a 'network' concept. This is characterized by longer contracts, flexible delivery schedules, collaborative practices, and so on. In particular, new supply practices are increasingly characterized by cooperative, or obligational, relations in contrast to a 'hands-off', or adversarial, system traditionally operated between British companies. While recent changes in buyer-supplier relations are indicative of wider changes in industrial organization as a whole, one intention of this book is to provide an account of the changing nature of interfirm organization by investigating the particular example of buyer-supplier relations in the British economy.

Towards this end, we consider two specific aspects of the changing relationships between buyers and suppliers in this first chapter. In the next section we outline the main dimensions of recent economic change in British manufacturing industry. In particular, we consider the importance of industry's relative neglect of non price competition as a mechanism for levering and controlling both markets and competitive pressures. In this respect, we point to the importance of external supply relations as a key element of competitiveness. The chapter then discusses the changing nature of supply relations in the British economy, by comparing and contrasting old-style 'adversarial' models of industrial linkage, with new forms based on longer term, 'obligational' relationships between buyers and suppliers. We conclude the chapter by outlining the organization of the book.

2 THE IMPORTANCE OF EXTERNAL SUPPLY RELATIONS

The period from the early 1970s has been traumatic for British industry. A wide variety of research has described the various facets of what is now termed 'deindustrialization' or the demise of British manufacturing industry (Massey and Meegan, 1982; Williams *et al.*, 1983; Williams *et al.*, 1989). Williams *et al.* (1989) show that, after five years of economic recovery, British manufacturing output was no higher by 1987 than in 1979, and was 10 per cent lower than in 1973. Further, despite massive rationalization programmes and the scrapping of redundant capacity, labour productivity has grown much more slowly in the British economy than elsewhere in Western Europe since 1979, at a rate of 3 per cent per annum. Similarly, Department of Trade and Industry data shows that the British share of world trade has markedly declined since 1979, with a fall of over two per cent (Table 1.1).

TABLE 1.1 *The UK's share in the volume of manufactured exports (per cent)*

1975	1976	1977	1978	1979	1980	1981	1982	1983	1984	1985
11.2	10.9	11.2	10.7	10.0	9.7	8.9	9.3	9.0	8.9	9.1

SOURCE: DTI, in Williams *et al.*, 1989, p. 72.

TABLE 1.2 *Britain's balance of trade in manufactures (SIC, divisions 5–8, £ millions)*

1980	1981	1982	1983	1984	1985	1986
+3634	+2905	+199	−4849	−6308	−5774	−8239

SOURCE: *Central Statistical office, Monthly Digest of Statistics*, August 1987, in Williams *et al.*, 1989, p. 73.

The relative uncompetitiveness of British manufacturing is also indicated by a growing and chronic deficit in the balance of trade in manufactures (Table 1.2). In particular, a prime cause of the trade deficit has been the sustained inflow of manufactured and semi-manufactured imports, reflected by buoyant domestic demand (Ball, 1989). Others argue that the inflow is an indicator of a more fundamental imbalance, an excessive rundown of domestic manufacturing capacity and the inability of domestic producers to compete in international markets (Williams *et al.*, 1989). As Table 1.3 indicates, investment in 1988 was barely at its 1979 cyclical peak yet, as Ball (1989) notes, overall national income was much higher. On top of this, the decline of uncompetitive British industry has produced major changes in the level and composition of employment, with more than 2.4 million manufacturing jobs lost to the economy between 1970 and 1983.

As Williams *et al.* (1989) argue, there are a number of main elements in the failure of British industry to meet the prevailing standards of international competition. The first they identify is the failure of firm-level

TABLE 1.3 *Manufacturing investment in the UK economy, 1979–88*

Year	1979	1981	1983	1985	1987	1988
Manufacturing Investment (£ bn.)*	10.2	6.6	6.4	8.7	9.1	10.0

* Gross fixed investment excluding leased assets at 1988 prices.

SOURCE: Ball *et al.*, 1989, p. 21.

management decision-making in relation to the character of the product, the nature of the market, and the marketing strategy. This is reflected across the spectrum of British industry, with a plethora of research documenting the simultaneous failure to design and produce the right product ranges and then to market them effectively. Imrie's (1989b) study of an export orientated British clothing manufacturer illustrates the general point. The company's attempt to develop a domestic market was hindered by a general unawareness of the costs in servicing and entering it, and an ineptitude in responding to the additional demand which retailers were generating at that time. In the words of the Managing Director, ' . . . we did not understand the service needs of the retail business, and entered the new markets at grossly inflated and unrealistic prices . . . ' (p. 346).

This also relates to a second feature of decline which is the failure to effectively utilize forms of production techniques which have been successful elsewhere. As Hirst and Zeitlin (1989) note, machinery and technologies are often imported but not the forms of organization and working needed to make them efficient. In this respect, researchers have compared contrasting areas, like Japan and Emilia-Romagna in Italy, with the United Kingdom (Murray, 1987; Sayer 1989). While researchers argue that equipment is integrated into flexible systems of work organization in the Japanese and Italian cases, it is posited that this is singularly lacking in much of British industry where narrow job definitions and short-term managerial goals have inhibited the development of more flexible forms of industrial organization (Hirst, 1989; Tomlinson, 1989).

This relates to a further explanation for the underlying malaise of British manufacturing industry, which Williams *et al.* term 'the British Management Problem'. By this, they mean that within their area of discretion, British managers have consistently tended to take poor decisions about product strategies, technical investment, and marketing policy, characterizing a general ineptitude in their execution of key strategies. As Williams *et al.* (1989) note,

> Before the 1979–83 recession it was possible to blame poor organization of production on the workforce and the unions. But that excuse is no longer plausible. The organization of production inside the factory is now clearly within the prerogative of management. (p. 82)

The key contribution made by Williams *et al.* is in highlighting how and why the efficient organization of production is a crucial prerequisite for manufacturing success. As they illustrate, one of the classic British mistakes is an acceptance that buying-in technology is sufficient to enhance productivity. However, other research clearly shows how British producers lag far behind their international competitors in developing efficient production systems, leading to waste, high cost, and uncompetitiveness (Daly *et al.*, 1985; Hirst and Zeitlin, 1989).

For instance, Daly *et al.*'s (1985) study, of the adoption and utilization of metalworking machinery in British industry, shows the inept ways in which plant and machinery is organized in British plants. Their study is a catalogue of quite common difficulties in British manufacturing, including poorly set-up and badly maintained machinery, characterized by frequent breakdowns; poorly devised plant lay-out with numerous production bottlenecks; a badly trained and supervized workforce with little understanding of the capabilities of the more sophisticated equipment on the shopfloor; and poorly devised systems of quality control which reinforces a high level of product rejects. As Williams *et al.* conclude, these problems associated with the organization of production are typical rather than exceptional across British manufacturing industry.

Williams *et al.* (1989) also point to the importance of non-price factors in foreign competitive advantage. It is clear that British managers have usually been more concerned with price and unit labour costs as factors in competition, and less with superior design, production quality, and high standards of delivery and service. In noting this, Williams *et al.* contrast British manufacturing practices with Japanese industrial organization, emphasizing the Japanese practice of 'no waste' with regard to time as much as to manufacturing materials. As Williams *et al.* argue,

> If production is not organized well then the results include reduced operating profits, poor quality, high cost, and poor delivery performance . . . if the problem of production is not solved, then the result is likely to be a damaging disharmony between the different domains of calculation as productive inferiority compromises the enterprise's ability to achieve market and financial objectives. (p. 83)

This observation relates closely to one of the key organizing principles of production, namely inter-industry linkages and related supply practices. As New and Meyers (1986) suggest, bought-out items can account for 50 per cent of total costs for the average manufacturing firm, so control over supply is a crucial ingredient in overall business success. Similarly, as Turnbull's (1989) research indicates, this proportion can be much higher in particular industrial sectors, such as the motor vehicle industry, given the scope for 'make-or-buy' decisions on a whole range of parts and sub-assemblies. However, as Bessant *et al.* (1984) note, major producers have tended to pay little attention to scheduling and buyer-supplier relations, relegating them to one of the last areas of manufacturing control to be considered in restructuring programmes.

This is particularly problematical for British manufacturers who have tended to ignore the organization of work-flows at the intra-plant scale, and between plants and external suppliers. In particular, British producers have traditionally operated buyer-supplier relations through a system of 'adversarial' contracting, a 'hands-off' process which involves open tendering, with the focus predominantly on price competition. Sako (1989) refers to this form of buyer-supplier relation as 'universalism', whereby the identity of trading partners does not matter as long as the required goods are produced and delivered. In developing this notion, Sako (1989) notes that under this system,

> Suppliers who can deliver the same goods are interchangeable for the buyer, while there is the same duty by the supplier to fulfill commitment whoever is the purchaser. (p. 6)

Illustrations of the adversarial system are cogently outlined in Lamming's (1989) and Bessant *et al.*'s (1984) studies of the British motor vehicle industry. In particular, the system has operated on the basis of closed competition, insofar that new businesses for one supplier could only be won at the expense of another. Further, relationships involved a one sided design effort with little collaboration between buyer and suppliers in the crucial facets of product development. This situation was compounded by relatively little sharing of information between the parties, beyond the supply of basic requirement levels by the buyer and cost structuring by the supplier.

This model was widespread in British manufacturing towards the end of the 1970s, and was driven by price competition, whereby buyers operated a method of open tendering, usually selecting the supplier for the job who could produce and deliver at the cheapest price. The relationship between buyers and suppliers tended to be at arms length, with buyers tightly defining product and process specifications, divulging little information to their suppliers about projected production targets, and tending to give suppliers only selected information about their technologies and processes. In this sense, there was little trust within the relationship. Also, as Figure 1.1 indicates, this lack of trust was compounded by multi-sourcing as a means of ensuring competitive tendering, by playing the suppliers off against each other. As Robinson (1989) concludes, it was quite common for a buyer to drop a supplier at short notice, if offered more advantageous price terms by a competing supplier, a feature which

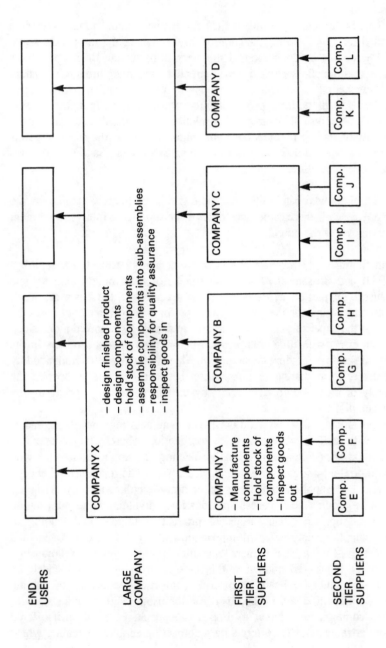

Company X designs all parts of the finished product, buying in components from its suppliers, then assembling sub-assemblies and finally assembling the finished product. As shown, Company X is a manufacturing company, but the same principles would apply, for example, to a retailer such as a supermarket chain.

Companies A, B, C and D actually produce the same components for Company X, as Company X believes that this multi-sourcing arrangement leads to more competitive pricing, by playing the suppliers off against each other. Relations with suppliers are normally short term, as Company X drops a supplier if a new supplier offers a lower price.

Company X inspects some goods in, and has to return a proportion of components to the suppliers as being of low quality, frequently failing to meet the specifications. This costs Company X a lot of money, but even more expensive are the components that slip through, giving a low quality finished product, leading to a poor reputation for X in the market place.

Company X has substantial capital tied up in inventory, as it does not trust its suppliers to deliver on time. The suppliers in turn do not trust Company X. They do not think it is worth investing sufficiently to improve the quality of the components they make, due to the lack of commitment shown by Company X. Relations are best described as "adversarial".

Source: Robinson, 1989

Figure 1.1 Traditional Supply Chain

really brought the adversarial system into disrepute by the end of the 1970s.

Thus, it was quite common for major manufacturers to express disquiet about a number of related practices associated with adversarial-style buyer-supplier relations during the 1970s. Foremost, it was clear that suppliers, particularly in the motor vehicle industry, were building contingencies into their prices, to allow for fluctuations in demand. Further, it was noted that the traditional model of suppliers working to drawings, and generally contributing little to design effort, was largely a waste of their expertise and resource base. This difficulty was compounded by the 'free-for-all', laissez-faire, attitude of buyers towards supply, with minimal concern for control of quality, delivery, or stability of the supply base. As Lamming (1989) aptly notes, British producers,

> had been schooled in the 'old' way: adversarial or at best politely distant communications, based upon the premise that the other party was out to cheat and prosper at your expense. It has not been easy to change such fundamental attitudes: in some cases it has not been possible. . . .   (p. 1)

However, by the mid-1970s, a combination of a profits crisis, the decline in international competitiveness, and difficulties posed by overcapacity, led major British producers to reappraise specific parts of production organization, not the least of which was the adversarial model of buyer-supplier relations. As Lamming (1989) notes, cost pressures on suppliers increased due to material, wage, and energy inflation, at the same time that buyers, faced with declining markets and intensified foreign competition, demanded lower price increases and greater quality. The result of this was not only diminished profits (if not bankruptcy) for suppliers, but poor buyer-supplier relations (Bessant *et al.*, 1984, p. 27). Others point to the inherent limitations of a system driven by price competition, with less regard for quality and reliability of supply. For instance, the Central Policy Review Staff's (1975) report on the British car industry, argued that despite its competitive price structure, inferior quality and unreliable supply had resulted in a net cost disadvantage by the mid-1970s.

The recognition of limitations with the 'adversarial' model has led major British producers to reappraise their relationships with sources of external supply. In particular, the influence of Japanese-type styles of buyer-supplier relations, characterized by the notion of 'obligational' contracting, is increasingly evident in a range of British companies. The 'obligational' model involves a series of close ties between the buyer and the supplier, insofar that trading partners are not all treated as equal, but prioritized. As Sako (1989) notes,

> prioritization is according to the strength of the trading relation with the company to which one is obligated, and these relationships become strengthened on trust and confidence, and possibly affective sentiments which develop over time between trading partners. (p. 7)

In particular, the 'obligational' relationship interacts along several dimensions with the objective of producing high quality, low cost parts and/or services. For instance, while it is expected that suppliers maintain semi-autonomous control over production, buyers are increasingly exercising influence over related supply practices like R&D, investment decisions, and labour utilization. Also, because of the onus on 'heightened inter-dependency' with obligational contracting, there is a greater transfer of managerial techniques and technological expertise between buyers and suppliers. As Turnbull (1989) indicates, the Japanese have worked with this model for years, combining,

> the benefits of vertical integration with the additional market efficiency check of maintaining a clear transaction at each stage in the supply chain. (p. 3)

As large British companies try to redefine relationships with their suppliers along these lines, it is evident that the traditional role of the supplier is moving beyond that of the manufacture of components. As Robinson (1989) notes, suppliers are increasingly being expected to undertake rigorous vendor certification programmes, having to prove to their buyers that they have the capabilities to manufacture high quality components (see Figure 1.2). It is also clear that a greater range of buyers are expecting suppliers to adopt a 'zero defects' policy, providing goods to a defined specification with failure rates minimized to no more than two or three per cent. In turn, this is linked to the wider objective of quality assured supplies, with buyers increasingly requiring their suppliers to have a full quality assurance programme to measure the level of quality and identify problems as soon as they occur.

In line with this is the adoption of a manufacturing philosophy which calls for the uninterrupted flow from raw material to end user, without buffer stocks or bottlenecks. This contrasts with traditional British manufacturing practices, where buffer stocks and inventories were held because of the slowness in tooling changes, the fear of equipment breakdowns,

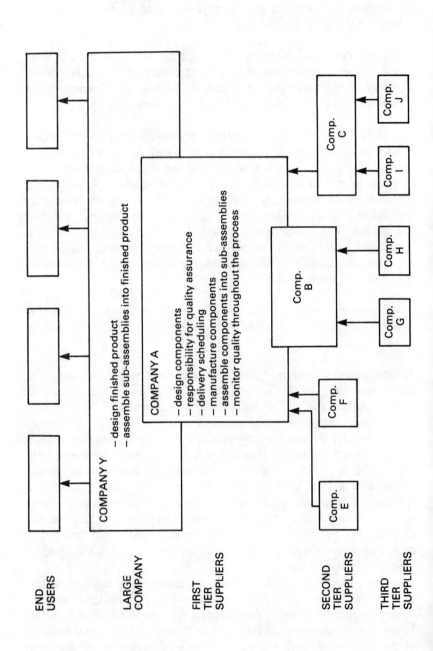

Company Y has moved away from vertical integration and now only designs the finished product, assembling it from bought-in sub-assemblies. Company A has become a "preferred supplier", and collaborates with Company Y on the design of the components, quality management and delivery logistics.

The failure rate of Company A's components has fallen dramatically for a number of reasons: collaboration in the design stage means the component is easier (and cheaper) to make; a quality management programme identifies problems much earlier in the process, and as it is sole supplier of the component, new investment in people and equipment can be afforded, due to the increased value and firm commitments given by Company Y.

Company Y no longer inspects goods in, as it trusts Company A to deliver to the agreed level of quality. Due to the increased level of coordination, Companies Y and A have both substantially reduced their inventory levels.

Companies B and C are still in the supplier chain, but are now second tier suppliers, as Company A has taken over much of Company Y's component assembly. To ensure its own quality, Company A is placing more stringent requirements on B and C, and is working in particular much more closely with B. Company D could not provide adequate quality, and has disappeared from Company Y's supply chain altogether.

Company Y has managed to lower its costs, as well as receiving fewer faulty goods back from its customers.

Source: Robinson, 1989

Figure 1.2   Partnership supply chain

and supplier non-delivery (see Bessant *et al.*, 1984). The adoption of just-in-time (JIT), which this implies, is the key facet of organizational innovation. This system is organized around the notion that costs can be reduced and control enhanced if the exact quantity of (defect free) raw materials, parts and sub-assemblies are produced just-in-time for the next stage of the manufacturing process. As Turnbull (1989) notes, the principle is intended to be extended back to the firm's suppliers and also forward to the final customer, with the aim to match the output of the manufacturing system with the demands of the market.

These changing priorities are all part of the emerging model of buyer-supplier relations, not the least of which is the development of a tiered, preferential, system of supply. As Figure 1.2 indicates, buyers are more concerned with manufacturing control and quality than in the past, and with a diminution in any elements of conflict with suppliers over price. This means that multiple sourcing, based on price competition, is less significant than ensuring that a reliable supplier can manufacture and supply good quality components. In turn, this is creating operational coordination of a largely financially integrated pyramid of suppliers, rather than vertical integration. In this sense, Figure 1.2 is illustrative of a process whereby buyers are not only devolving a greater range of responsibilities to tier 1 suppliers, but creating channels for long term relationships with them (a situation particularly common in the Japanese automobile industry).

In a sense, this development of new buyer-supplier relations is only one of a series of changes in western manufacturing principles, arguably based on an attempt to emulate some of the more positive aspects of Japanese work practices (Graham, 1988; Oliver and Wilkinson, 1988). In particular, Holmes (1988) notes that American and Canadian automobile producers have sought to challenge Japanese competitiveness through a combination of Japanese innovations in production management (that is, soft process technology) with new developments in micro-electronic based 'hard' process technologies organized around flexible automation. In this way, organizational changes in buyer-supplier relations are integrally linked to the wider corporate objectives of reducing unit labour costs, while, at the same time, enhancing the degree of flexibility in the production process (themes expanded at length in Chapter 2).

For instance, Abernathy *et al.* (1983) have argued that a primary impetus for change amongst western producers has been the penetration of their markets by Japanese manufacturers, with the Japanese altering the 'basic contours of competition by introducing new standards of production quality and design. In particular, Ford's 'After-Japan' strategy, in the early 1980s, was a well documented example of how one western producer was attempting to generate an increased awareness of product design and quality as a critical competitive factor (Starkey and McKinlay, 1989). The company's subsequent failure to instill new worker discipline, or develop new forms of organizational control, highlight some of the difficulties in attempting either to emulate or transfer systems of industrial organization from one context to another.

In developing this point, Dickens and Savage (1988) argue that the notion that western producers are undergoing a process of 'Japanization' is confusing in so far as the term only refers to a small sector of Japanese industry and 'to practices and relations associated with particular types of capital' (Dickens and Savage, 1988, p. 60). Further, as Graham (1988) argues, so-called Japanization techniques, like JIT and work team quality control, are similar to concepts like autonomous work groups which were a feature of European companies as long ago as the 1950s. Similarly, a survey by Voss & Clutterbuck (1989) of the implementation of JIT systems in Britain, indicates that British managers do not regard JIT as a practice they have imported from Japan, but more a system that has evolved to tackle many of the rigidities of task specialization and poor inventory control. In this way, Graham argues that the techniques underlying JIT are not wholly new, nor especially Japanese.

Furthermore, Ackroyd *et al.* (1988) argue, in so far that British producers appear to be emulating particular practices associated with Japanese MNC's, in essence, it is more that British capital is responding to the competitive challenge posed by the Japanese and, in this sense,

> the logic of the response is systematic and defensive and is not to be equated with behaviour in institutional settings as such . . . what the British are doing today is not Japanization in any single sense, but attempting to adapt to changed economic conditions without relinquishing established bases of profit, power, and influence. (p. 23)

This observation poses some doubts on the extent to which new organizational innovations are capable of being incorporated into British, and western, manufacturing systems (or, indeed, if it is desirable to do so). For instance, evidence from the United States suggests that the adoption of Japanese-style supply practices is limited by a lack of availability of suitable suppliers and a reservation on the part of buyers to transfer crucial aspects of the production process to their supply network. As Lamming (1989) notes, Ford's contractual relationship with Bendix Electronics for the sole supply of braking systems to its US plants, broke down in 1988, with a consequential return to multiple sourcing. Similarly, the General Motors

Saturn division, gearing up for production in 1990, has argued that a lack of suitable suppliers has limited the degree to which tiers can be created.

These examples are illustrative of some of the potential difficulties manufacturers face in developing buyer-supplier relations of an obligational nature. It is also important to note that there is much contention as to how far suppliers gain any measure of control over products and technologies with their involvement in a system which is apparently orientated towards devolved responsibility (Jones, 1988; Marginson *et al.*, 1988). Research findings, from the International Motor Vehicle Programme (IMVP) International Policy Forum (1989), indicates that despite the wish to involve suppliers in the development process, Japanese car manufacturers in the United States are retaining close control over vehicle technology. While suppliers are being identified earlier in the development cycle, usually without fear of losing the production business after involvement in product development, buyers are still looking towards their own engineering and design for innovations in vehicle specifications. As Lamming (1989) rightly concludes, this faces buyers with a potential conflict, as suppliers grow in expertise, of either limiting the degree of joint development or taking a reduced role in controlling the technology.

Many of these issues relate to the shifting terrain between buyers and suppliers, and the degree to which inter-industry dependencies are being reorganized and redefined. It is clear that stronger vertical relationships are emerging between buyers and suppliers, characterized with the move towards single sourcing and longer term contracts. For instance, a typical buyer in the American motor vehicle industry grants around 60 per cent of its suppliers three to five year contracts in respect of 100 per cent supply of a specific commodity on a particular model (Lamming, 1989). Similar trends are evident in Europe too, reflecting the emergence of forms of commitment and dependence which have the potential for conflicts of interest between competing buyers. Also, as some of our empirical findings indicate in later chapters, large buyers who involve their suppliers in the design stage of production, are not always happy if they then serve competitor buyers with similar services.

At a wider, strategic, level, it is important not to lose sight of the essence of buyer-supplier relations, whether they be based on adversarial, obligational, or some other model of interfirm dependency. At the crux of the relationship remains a system of component suppliers who must compete effectively on the basic features of engineering, including price, quality, and delivery. And, as Lamming (1989) rightly argues, the development of best practice, like zero defects, reduced costs, and product delivery timing, remain goals rather than realities for many British manufacturers.

As later chapters will reveal, such practices remain goals for a wide range of reasons. For instance, Ford's 'After-Japan' strategy highlighted some of the constraints in overturning established industrial relations practices, while other studies note the difficulties involved in breaking down job demarcations and other established work practices in British industry (Jones, 1988). In this sense, the wider socio-institutional and political context, within the confines of both supranational and nation states, is an integral element in our understanding of new inter-industry relations.

3 ORGANIZATION OF THE BOOK

The transformation of industrial organization in Britain has been profound and dramatic since the early 1980s, given the development of new manufacturing systems, new styles of industrial relations, and the adaptation of new frameworks for product development, systems engineering, and marketing. In this first chapter, we have given a flavour of the nature of some of these transformations in the British economy, indicating that a key component is the realignment of buyer-supplier relations and the adoption of new supply practices by segments of British industry. In the rest of the book we consider the extent to which new forms of buyer-supplier practices are being adopted by companies in the British economy. In doing this, we divide the book into seven further chapters.

We begin in Chapter 2 by considering a range of theoretical concepts which have been deployed to explain recent changes in industrial organisation. In particular, we focus on various concepts attached to the notion of the 'flexible firm' and we critically evaluate the theoretical cogency of contrasting versions of what we term the 'flexibilization theses'. The chapter then considers the notion of integration and disintegration in industrial organization, and we provide a critique of the widely held view that interfirm linkages are purely a function of economic transactions, with cost the major factor in the determination of the degree of integration or disintegration between producers. The chapter concludes by discussing the question of why particular forms of disintegration and/or quasi-integration emerge in industrial organization.

Chapter 3 reviews the variety of empirical research to date on buyer-supplier relations. The first part of the chapter discusses the extent to which new forms of supply relations are evolving in western capitalist countries. As Pollert (1988) notes, there appears to be little aggregate evidence to indicate how far new forms of industrial integration and/or disintegration are emerging. However, our review of recent empirical research shows that the emergence of corporate fragmentation strategies, allied to the growth in new forms of supply, is a more substantial part of industrial organization than has hitherto been acknowledged. This is particularly evident from the reporting of our own empirical research in this chapter, based on a postal survey of recent corporate practices.

While there is a correspondence between various pieces of empirical research into the extent of vertical disintegration in the economy, we concur with Pollert (1988), that it is more important to trace some of the key qualitative changes that are occurring between buyers and suppliers. This provides the dominant theme for the main substantive chapters of the book. Chapters 4 to 7 are based on case studies of major corporations, and a sample of their primary suppliers, in the electrical engineering and motor vehicle industries. In particular, the studies are grouped around companies at the 'leading edge' of the development of new forms of work organization, not the least of which is their adoption and utilization of specific types of obligational contracting.

In Chapter 4, we consider the case of the Nissan motor vehicle plant in Sunderland. The chapter outlines the company's supply practices in Britain, and the methods by which it has sought to develop a range of obligational supply relations with British companies. In particular, the case of Nissan is illustrative of the 'new wave' of supply relations in British industry, albeit based on innovations led by foreign investors. In contrast, Chapter 5 considers the case of Lucas Girling, a British manufacturer of braking systems for the motor vehicle industry. This case is illustrative of a 'leading edge' British company struggling to readjust from adversarial supply relations into a new era of assured quality, just-in-time manufacture and zero defects.

We then contrast the motor vehicle industry with two companies in the electrical engineering and electronics industries. In Chapter 6, we outline the case of the Sony Corporation, one of the world's leading innovators of obligational-style contracting. This stands in marked contrast with our final case study in Chapter 7, that of IBM, the world-wide market leaders in a range of computer products. As our study shows, IBM has been somewhat of a laggard in buyer-supplier relations, exercizing tight control over its supply network and only recently starting to develop and adopt practices characteristic of obligational contracting. In the concluding chapter of the book, we synthesize the material presented in the empirical chapters, and we use this to make a number of theoretical and empirical generalizations about the dynamics of buyer-supplier relations. In particular, we generalize between the case studies, and critically compare and contrast our empirical findings.

2 Economic Change, Vertical Disintegration, and Buyer-Supplier Relations: Some Theoretical Considerations

1 INTRODUCTION

Throughout the 1980s, an intense debate has developed around the notion that core sectors of industry have been reorganizing production strategies associated with mass production (Jones and Scott, 1987; Lipietz, 1986; Lovering, 1988; Wood, 1989). In particular, it is argued that new forms of production organization are redefining the utilization of technologies and labour, underpinned by the development of new productive strategies aimed at serving a wider range of variagated and fragmented markets (Kelly, 1983; Marginson *et al.*, 1988; Piore, 1986; Williams *et al.*, 1987). While there is a vigorous debate concerning the meaning, nature and implications of changes in production organization, there is widespread consensus that fundamental changes are occurring in advanced capitalist societies (Cooke, 1989; Hakim, 1987; Handy, 1984; Harvey, 1988). In response to a period of economic turbulence, a number of researchers have attempted to develop key concepts to clarify and explain contemporary changes in industrial organization.

In this chapter, we review these as a prelude to our more detailed, empirical, documentation of transformations in buyer-supplier relations in later chapters. The next section of the chapter considers 'regulation' theory, a notion recently popularized as a means of explaining the apparent break-point in advanced capitalist societies, from mass production to more flexible forms of industrial organization (Aglietta, 1979; Mavier, 1982). We also focus critical attention on concepts attached to the notion of the 'flexible firm', and we critically evaluate the theoretical cogency of versions of what we term the 'flexibilization theses'. The chapter then considers the notion of integration and disintegration in industrial organization, and we provide a critique of the commonly held notion that industrial linkage is primarily driven by economic transactions. We conclude the chapter by discussing the question of why particular forms of disintegration and/or quasi-integration emerge in industrial organization.

2 FLEXIBILITY AND INDUSTRIAL ORGANIZATION: A CRITICAL REVIEW

The idea that capitalism has undergone a 'radical break' with the past is cogently argued by a perspective termed 'regulation', a macroeconomic theory which is primarily concerned with the long term development of capitalist societies (Aglietta, 1982; Clarke, 1989; Lipietz, 1984; Mandel, 1975, 1978). The utility of regulation theory is its periodization of capitalist development around a long-run perspective, and its focus on production as the driving force of industrial organization. At its simplest level, regulation theory is concerned with the nation state and the role of socio-political institutions in supporting, or regulating, particular forms of economic production and consumption. This was clearly evident in postwar Britain up to the end of the 1970s, whereby the welfare state both sustained and underpinned high levels of consumption to enable the expansion of Fordist productive capacity.

A crucial insight of regulation theory is the inability of a regime of accumulation, like Fordism, to sustain itself in the long run, and the inevitability of a transformation in the socio-political modes of regulation or governance. In particular, it is argued that structural tensions in the modes of regulation will undermine the capacity of the system to reproduce itself (Clarke, 1989). These tensions are wide and varied, but might include a disjuncture between the capacity of the system to consume larger proportions of productive output, at a time when the costs of sustaining the process are increasingly borne by the state. As analysis of the crisis of Fordism has indicated, the inability of the state to continue to underpin mass consumption has been a crucial pre-condition for alterations in productive organization since the late 1970s.

In utilizing regulation theory, a number of authors concur that the period of economic history, from the early twentieth century until the end of the 1970s, was dominated by a regime of accumulation termed Fordism. (Aglietta, 1979; Boyer, 1987). Named after the production methods pioneered in Henry Ford's River Rouge car plant in the early twentieth century, Fordism was to become the strategic method of organizing production in capitalist economies. Fordism was based on a number of key elements, including the standardization of the product to realize economies of scale, the use of integrated assembly line production to equalize conveyance times between work processes, and the development of new patterns of worker control.

In particular, the system became associated with three principles of scientific management, or Taylorism, which involved the fragmentation of work tasks, the separation of mental and manual labour, and a general deskilling of jobs. Foremost, the technical division of labour was fragmented into a highly differentiated system of tasks, a process which reduced jobs to routinized, compartmentalized, operations. In this way, labour costs were minimized by the hire of a largely unskilled workforce, while productivity was increased by task simplification. Fordism was also based on separating mental and manual labour, whereby worker autonomy was reduced by concentrating decision making powers and planning functions in the hands of management. The system was also predicated on the deskilling of labour, whereby task simplification was used as a mechanism for eroding traditional craft skills and, consequentially, a method for cheapening the cost of labour.

The development of Fordism was predicated on the real gains made in productivity through mass production, coupled with the rise in real incomes after the Second World War, a rise which facilitated an increase in the rates and levels of consumption. For instance, Ford's '$5 day' in the 1920s was justified on the assumption that a larger wage bill could be offset by major increases in labour productivity, and, far from threatening profits, was integral to the success of mass production. As Meegan (1988) argues, Fordist factories offered the possibility of dramatically increasing the productivity of the workers employed within them, diminishing the prices of the products, and increasing wages without threatening profitability. This system, which was to rapidly expand throughout capitalist economies in the 1950s and 1960s, was also supported by the 'social wages' of the Keynesian welfare state and by state management of capital and labour conflicts (Jessop *et al.*, 1987).

However, by the end of the 1970s, it was apparent that some of the key mechanisms underpinning Fordism were beginning to break down. Foremost, there was the onset of escalating production costs associated with stagnating labour productivity. During the 1970s, a whole host of management-union deals in British industry failed to raise levels of labour productivity, thus bringing into question the Fordist system of economic and labour management. Moreover, international competition began to intensify, and major trade deficits signalled the collapse of both domestic and international markets. British producers were also locked into saturated markets, and were failing to respond in terms of product or process innovation, or of new investment. The effects of these factors led to productivity gains outpacing the levels of mass consumption necessary to absorb output, leading to a crisis of overproduction, productivity, and of profit.

As Clutterbuck and Hill (1981) note, this crisis of production has been associated with a number of changes in work design and employment. In particular, these have been indicative of a fundamental restructuring of work from the Fordist model towards forms of production and work organization which some term neo-Fordist, a perspective which considers the possibilities of transformations within Fordism and Taylorism. Neo-Fordism denotes those processes by which the crisis of Fordism can be overcome, primarily by changes in the spatial division of labour, the task structures of firms, and levels of automation (Wood, 1989, p.3). In particular, neo-Fordism involves reversing the Taylorist division of labour, through processes of job enrichment and other forms of work redesign (Palloix, 1976).

Further, Aglietta (1979) argues that neo-Fordism offers a solution to the contradictions of Fordism by diversifying product ranges and generating a new flexibility involving the transformation to flexible forms of mass production, including the ability for firms to produce in short and medium batches. In contrast, Sabel (1982) uses the term to describe transformations in managerial control over the labour process, and a weakening of rigid management systems characteristic of the Fordist factory. This differs from others who define neo-Fordism as strategies which utilize technologies and internationalization for overcoming the rigidities of Fordism (Frobel *et al.*, 1980). As Wood (1989) notes, the contrasting notions of neo-Fordism attempt to define industrial change in terms of specific development trajectories, although other commentators doubt that Fordism has been wholly eclipsed (Pollert, 1988).

These apparent transformations away from Fordism indicate that restructuring in the 1980s was orientated towards a more flexible, entrepreneurial, economy, with the rigidities of Fordism giving way to a more flexible organization of production and labour. However, other authors argue that the development of a new productive apparatus represents a more radical departure from Fordism, and, far from entering a stage of neo-Fordism, production is increasingly orientated towards 'post-Fordism' or 'a flexible regime of accumulation', whereby a considerable change in the nature of production and consumption, and the relationship between them, is underway. Whereas Fordism, and neo-Fordism to a lesser extent, was concerned with mass production, it is argued that firms in the 1980s and 1990s are developing innovations aimed at serving market niches, so sensitizing production to switches in patterns of consumption.

These changes in industrial production also signal an end to the Keynesian state and a transformation in capital-state relations, and the relationships between the state and labour. As Jessop *et al.* (1987) note, 'flexibility' forms part of a wider socio-political programme of change, with three related objectives. First, it is concerned with extending a neo-liberal strategy to the depressed, low or no growth urban areas and parts of the welfare state. Second, it seeks to undermine Labour's electoral base in the north and peripheral parts of the United Kingdom, by creating the conditions for new alliances to be forged between the working class and what is popularly termed the 'new right'. Finally, flexibility is about significantly altering modes of representation, internal organization and intervention in the state system.

While Jessop *et al.* (1987) provide a wider conception of socio-political flexibility, Cooke *et al.* (1989) argue that the more important manifestations of post-Fordist organization are evident in the ways by which companies have developed a host of new markets, products, product strategies, technologies, and associated labour practices. Compared to periods prior to the 1980s, they argue that new flexibilities are characterized by several features of contemporary industrial organization. Foremost is the vertical disintegration of production, with companies tending to contract out to the market for an increasing proportion of inputs. This is related to an overall tendency for firms to reduce the proportion of semi- and unskilled workers as compared to professionals, with an increasing use being made of part-time and temporary workers (also, see Morris, 1988c). To this end, workers are being required to retrain and develop multiple skills, in contrast to the Taylorist division of labour based on rigid demarcations and little in the way of job rotation.

Moreover, post-Fordist production is also related to investment in 'flexible manufacturing systems', like computer numerically controlled machines tools, which enable large batch and small batch output to be produced interchangeably. In this way, researchers argue that post-Fordist production is one way of developing flexible and responsive forms of volume production, with scale economies sensitized to rapid switches in market demand (Cooke, 1988; Martin, 1988; Rubery *et al.,* 1987). This is allied to a greater concern with quality and consumer satisfaction, a process documented in Chapter 1, whereby Total Quality Control is increasingly being combined with systems like Statistical Process Control and JIT to ensure quality and zero defects. Finally, Cooke *et al.* (1989) point to the tendency for firms to enter into new collaborative relations, as part of a process of expanding market share at a global scale.

As Cooke *et al.*, conclude, to the extent that any or all of the above strategic elements are part of a corporate programme, then the firms involved are engaged in some form of flexible strategy. However, this notion appears to be 'catch-all' and suffers from an imprecision which is characteristic of much of the debate on post-Fordist industrialization. As Wood (1989) argues, the starting point for a reappraisal of the debate must lie with a clarification of the key concepts, and the difficulties in their operational utility. To this end, the next section of the chapter evaluates some of the key concepts to have emerged in the recent debate on post Fordism.

3   THE DEBATE ON FLEXIBILITY: SOME CONTRASTING PERSPECTIVES

Transformations in employment have prompted much speculation about the underlying dynamics of change, and the multiple forms of labour and firm flexibility. It is possible to identify two main contributions to the post-Fordist debate, which both argue that new flexible work practices, and flexible industrial organization, mark a radical break with the past. These perspectives are the 'flexible firm' and 'flexible specialization' theses, which we now outline.

The Flexible Firm

Flexibility in the labour market is a key theme in business and government approaches to employment policy, and has been popularized by Atkinson and Gregory (1986). At the heart of the flexibilization strategy is the break from the conventional, unitary and hierarchical, internal labour market, towards more flexible patterns of working time and labour deployment. It is argued that many companies are now experimenting with new ways of using labour in an attempt to match the volume and nature of demand more closely to the types and levels of labour used. This is partly due to technical change, but has also been stimulated by the uncertainties of the market place which calls for an ability to respond rapidly at minimum cost. As a result, firms have introduced a number of ways of improving productivity through the flexible deployment of labour. These range from the greater use of temporary workers to meet variations in demand, to the increased use being made of contractors and supplementary reserves of labour (especially part-timers). These developments can be categorized in terms of three contrasting types of flexibility.

First, firms are incorporating functional flexibility into their operations. This relates to what workers actually do. Firms with functional flexibility can adjust and use the skills of their employees to match the tasks that their changing workload, production methods, and technology require. Functional flexibility is concerned with the versatility of employees and their ability to work within and between jobs. These workers tend to do the core tasks in the firm, and their job tenures are secured by accepting a degree of functional flexibility. A second type of firm flexibility is numerical whereby the core is surrounded by a cluster of peripheral groups. Their purpose is to protect core workers from numerical employment fluctuations while conducting ancillary, non-essential, activities. Numerical flexibility is achieved in a number of ways, with the most common practices using additional or supplementary labour resources, such as part-time, temporary, short term contract, and casual workers, or to alter the working time patterns of existing labour (Cross, 1986, p.14). A third type of firm flexibility is distancing, whereby firms increasingly subcontract a major element of their work to other firms.

While forms of labour flexibility vary from firm to firm, there is empirical evidence which supports the main propositions of the flexible firm thesis. For instance, a recent report by ACAS (1988) outlines findings from a survey of 584 companies. The research shows that over two thirds of respondents employed part-time workers and were increasing their proportions of contract workers. Further, the survey indicates that 75 per cent of respondents used subcontractors. These findings concur with Imrie and Morris (1988), whose survey of 74 Welsh plants shows that 57 per cent of respondents had increased their use of subcontractors in the last five years. Other research shows that functional flexibility is quite common in specific industrial sectors (e.g. automobiles), with employees often being required to perform upwards of three or four different tasks (Holmes, 1988). Task flexibility is also supplemented by a greater use of flexible working hours, with the ACAS survey showing that the trend towards shiftworking is on the increase.

However, Atkinson's model of the flexible firm is not without its critics. At an empirical level, both Pollert (1988) and MacInnes (1987) question the validity of Atkinson's data. MacInnes claims that Atkinson's study covers too few companies to warrant accurate generalizations. Similarly, Pollert is not convinced by Hakim's (1987) claim that a growing periphery is emerging, a claim based on data purporting to show that a third of the workforce is flexible and not simply a fringe group in the labour market. Moreover, while Pollert acknowledges that work practices are changing, like MacInnes, she points to the limited extent of multiskilling and functional flexibility (LRD, 1986). The LRD study argues that flexible practices are rarely implemented on the shop floor, except in a few highly publicized cases. Indeed Hakim's latest (1990) work suggests that only 35 per cent, of a self-selecting sample of 877 establishments using some type of 'peripheral workers', were doing so as part of a systematic manpower strategy or plan.

While the evidence is inconclusive to reject Atkinson's flexible firm model on empirical grounds, there are a number of conceptual weaknesses with the model. Pollert (1988), for instance, claims the model asserts that a segmentation between a 'core' and a 'periphery' is a new departure from a previously homogeneous internal labour market. However, there is sufficient evidence to refute this notion on both historical and analytical grounds, insofar as fragmented labour markets have always been an enduring characteristic of industrial organization (Bresnen, 1990; Jones, 1988). There are also problems associated with the definition of the core, as Marginson *et al.* (1988) note, it is not just the classification of workers as 'full-time' employees which qualifies them for membership of the core.

A further problem hinges on the assumption that market instability can be overcome solely by inducing various forms of labour flexibility. For instance, Clutterbuck and Hill (1981) assert that, ' . . . many forecasters believe we are on the edge of a shift in attitudes and behavioural patterns comparable to that involved in the transition from the Middle Ages to the Renaissance . . .' (quoted in Pollert, 1988, p. 66). Further, it is mooted that company survival depends on breaking down collective wage labour and developing a 'flexibility of response'. As Handy (1984, quoted in Pollert, 1988) notes,

> Jobs will be shorter . . . jobs will be difficult, more dispersed, and, in many cases, more precarious . . . whether we like it or not (and there are many who don't), the contractual organization is with us, is growing and is likely to grow faster.   (p. 66)

This perspective illustrates the convergence between neo-liberal policies of labour market deregulation, and management policies for labour fragmentation, insofar as the onus for economic recovery is seen as dependent on the regulation and control of labour. As Pollert (1988) notes, the focus on labour is ideological because it takes a restrictive view of the reasons for economic change, choosing to ignore the influence of other key factors like capital concentration, the interplay of financial money markets, and capital flight. Also, some commentators note that the trend towards the flexible firm is more evident in only a small number of industrial sectors, like engineering and automobiles, and not as widespread as proponents of the thesis have suggested.

The Flexible Specialization Thesis

A second way of interpreting the transformation in industrial organization is provided by the Flexible Specialization thesis (FST). Whereas the flexible firm perspective predominantly looks at the development of flexibility within firms, the FST considers the changing relationships between firms. Flexible specialization denotes a phase of capitalist production which heralds a new era of skills, craftwork, and technologically driven manufacturing systems. This seductive image is one of a return to craft labour, dominated by small scale industry using the latest technologies, and operating in diversified world markets. The FST is derived from the work of Piore and Sabel (1984), and is the basis for many of the current interpretations of industrial change in western capitalism. There are a number of propositions to the thesis.

Foremost, it is argued that the dissolution of mass production is giving way to a more fragmented pattern of demand, with quality and design, rather than price, the crucial determinants of production and consumption. In this context, an alternative system of production is seen to be developing, leading to what Piore and Sabel (1984) term, a 'second industrial divide'. This new divide is based on the development of flexible specialization, whereby the new economic leaders are those firms able to respond quickly to market niches and rapid changes in market demand. In turn, this creates opportunities for the development of a new form of craft production made increasingly flexible with the aid of programmable technology. As Pollert (1988) indicates:

> it is both technology and the mass market which previously determined the dynamism of the 'primary' sector, with its capital intensive advantage, and held back the 'secondary' sector, with its low capital investment and inability to use economies of scale . . . (p. 65)

New technology and the fragmentation of market demand appears to be reversing this relationship. In other words, the FST sees the break-up of mass production as signalling the end of the economic dominance of multinationals, and the development of new opportunities for small firms to step in and serve the emerging fragmented markets. In particular, the emergence of economies of scope, industrial deconcentration, and the re-emergence of 'regional economies' built around a network of flexible firms, are key components of change envisaged by the FST.

As Pollert (1988) notes, the political implications of the FST is the acceptance of enterprise capitalism, deregulation and entrepreneurship as the basis for a reinvigorated British economy. Recession and growing unemployment towards the end of the 1970s meant that the small firm became ideologically and politically significant, as a sector which was potentially the basis for economic recovery. Although small firms have proliferated since the early 1980s, research indicates that the birth and death rates of small firms is roughly equivalent (Gerry, 1985). As Gerry (1985) argues, the significance of the small firm is more ideological than material insofar as,

> it has fostered competitive individualism, and obscured the extent of exploitation in this sector with the illusion that the self employed are all independent, profit making entrepreneurs. (p. 3)

This echoes a plethora of small firms research which shows that, far from being a panacea for economic recovery, the small firm continues to be marginal to the mainstream of the British economy, while still exhibiting some of the worst excesses of employment, like low pay and poor conditions at work (Rainnie, 1988). Murray (1987), for instance, cites the example of decentralized production in the Third Italy, a region built on small flexible businesses, and held up as the exemplar of contemporary flexible specialization. He shows that racial, gender, skill, and age divisions are essential to its success, with much of the work unskilled and routinized, with little of the technological sophistication predicted in the FST.

Others similarly cast doubts on various aspects of the FST, both in terms of its empirical validity (i.e. is it descriptively accurate of present trends) and theoretical cogency (MacInnes, 1987). For instance, Pollert (1988) criticizes the FST by casting doubt that mass markets and production are breaking down. She notes that,

> one can look at a whole range of industries which are based on mass and large batch production and continue to sell well to large markets: food, flatpack furniture, DIY goods, toiletries, records, toys, the list covers most consumer goods. (p. 60)

Moreover, one of the keys elements of FST is the role of new flexible technology and its suitability for small firms. Again, Pollert indicates that the major items of equipment for more flexible production, like computer aided design and numerically controlled machines, are very expensive and available only to the larger manufacturers.

This means that the larger companies are those best placed to implement flexible production by using such technology. As a GLC report (1985) concludes, flexible production based on new technologies does not necessarily stimulate artisan, craft and small production units. Further, other researchers have shown that many of the flexible strategies pursued by firms have occurred independently of technology, which casts doubts on the overall significance of a small firm-led regeneration of local economies (Morris, 1988C). It is also questionable as to the extent of major changes in consumer tastes and how far product diversification is stimulating firm fragmentation. As Wood (1989) argues, while niche marketing may be on the increase, there is still overwhelming evidence to support the continuation of mass production.

Some Themes and Issues with the Flexibilization Theses

Running through the debate on post-Fordism are a number of issues which relate to the form and content of work and employment and, in particular, the question of skill composition and development. In this section of the chapter we consider a number of strands of the post-Fordist debate. First, we comment on the extent to which mass production is being dissolved, and how far the power of multinationals is being challenged by small businesses. Second, we then consider how far post-Fordism is transforming skills and worker control, and the extent to which the FST is grounded in contemporary changes in the workplace. Finally, we conclude by making some general comments about the theoretical cogency of the post-Fordist debate.

It is problematical to suggest that the era of mass production has ended. Substantial bodies of research indicate the continued viability of the mass production model, albeit based on modified forms of industrial organization. For instance, research findings by Imrie and Morris (1988) suggest a transformation in the way large firms are organizing mass production, in distinction to the FST. In particular, the research shows that the onus is on flexible systems of production characterized by diversified product ranges, being produced for volume markets. It is also clear that vertical disintegration is a key component of these strategies, insofar as large firms are developing new buyer-supplier relations which involve closer ties between them and their suppliers. These relationships involve the development of preferred supplier status, closer technological collaboration, and "high trust" relations, with the onus on systems of "flexible response" in developing volume flow lines' (Imrie and Morris, 1988). In this sense, it is problematical to doubt the resilience of large firms, or to predict the demise of volume production.

A further issue in the debate on post-Fordism is that skill composition and development is a complex process, and not reducible to Braverman's (1974) deskilling thesis – that is, the long run tendency inherent in capitalism for the deskilling and fragmentation of work. In contrast, elements of the post Fordist thesis argue that the impact of work reorganization is to change the nature of the skills required and/or to extend them rather than a simple deskilling process. It is also argued that workers are central to this, in terms of dictating the pace and direction of changes in the labour process, requiring management to manage by consent – what Burawoy (1979) terms 'the management of consent'. While there is contention about the nature and direction of changes in worker skills, the post-Fordist debate is unequivocal in noting that contemporary work reorganization is creating higher levels of skills and greater control by workers over the labour process. However, this is a contentious claim in a number of ways.

Foremost, as Gough (1986) argues, the FST, extrapolating from traditional craft employment, fails to acknowledge that the technologies which underpin new work organization have the capacity to deskill and degrade work much in the way outlined by Braverman (1974). However, some empirical work indicates that many craft and design jobs have been deskilled into routine operational tasks, with the aid of technologies like CAD-CAM systems. Further, it is difficult to sustain the notion that flexible specialized work, orientated around craft skills, increase the level of worker autonomy and discretion, particularly given that researchers have demonstrated how computerized production control systems are used by management to plan, monitor and control the performance of workers (Gough, 1986).

There is also an underemphasis, by both Braverman and the FST, on the socially constructed nature of skill. Rather, both perspectives are reductionist, in that the transformation of skills is considered more as a technical than a social issue. In contrast, a range of authors clearly indicate the importance of social variables, like the gender division of labour, in determining, and defining, the ascribed nature of skill. For instance, there is an established literature which highlights how the fragmentation of tasks, and the related skill composition of the labour process, are 'gendered' into 'men's work' and 'women's work (Coyle, 1984; Mitter, 1986; Walby, 1986). In a recent study of the pottery industry, management used the gender division of labour as a mechanism for re-categorizing the skill content of particular segments of the labour process (Imrie, 1989a). In this sense, we concur with Meegan (1988) in that one cannot consider skill designation, in the technical division of labour, as simply an outcome of the technological characteristics of the production process.

A related point is made by Wood (1989), who observes that there was considerable flexibility in Fordism, and central to Taylorism was the notion of 'worker disposability' built around forms of numerical flexibility. Further, others argue that flexibility really only represents new forms of worker control, and attempts by management to reassert their dominance over the labour process. The point here is how far the term 'flexibility' extends our understanding of control strategies in the workplace? It is also questionable as to the extent Fordism was ever dominant, and whether industrial production has undergone the radical transformations identified in the post-Fordist thesis. As Williams *et al.* (1987) note, one should question Fordism as a model of the past and

> caution against its use as a central organizing concept as it elides too many differences and establishes an uninformative stereotype . . . (p. 423)

A further point by Wood (1989) concerns the interrelations between different epochs of work and work organization. As Wood argues:

> Any transformation of work is approached in terms of whether it reverses Taylorism or represents an abandonment of Fordism, and a move towards autonomous working arrangements, as exemplified by craft working . . .   (p. 33)

However, new forms of work organization do not necessarily indicate a reversal of previous types of work organization, and it is possible to identify elements of Taylorist organization co-existing alongside new forms of employment and control. Further, Wood (1989) notes that a major problem of the debate is the lack of a comprehensive empirical base. Pollert (1988) concurs with this by adding that there is no systematic data base from which to evaluate various strands of the flexibilization theses. In particular, many of the problematical aspects of empirical work have been ignored. For instance, how does one reconcile one survey which suggests job deskilling, while another shows the reverse? Similarly, what should one make of research which makes generalizations on the basis of single sector studies, and how far can individual case studies be used as illustrations of wider processes of industrial change. As Hyman (1988, p. 54) argues, empirical research has, as yet, covered a very limited range of contexts.

4 INTEGRATION, DISINTEGRATION AND THE ROLE OF THE SUBCONTRACT

Industrial organization, in its widest sense, is characterized by a complex technical division of labour which spans a myriad of firms involved in complex business transactions. Neo-classical economics regards the consequential interfirm linkages as a sub-optimal solution to the uncertainty found in free capitalism. This is a solution which involves the creation of direct economic transactions between firms engaged in complementary activities which are external to 'pure market' transactions. With this assumption, it is argued that linkages permit a degree of market coordination by facilitating an efficient (that is, cost effective) exchange of information and/or materials. These exchanges include information on levels of supply and demand in the economy, the optimum price levels for a product, the technical characteristics of products to be exchanged, and other items connected to exchange relations between firms.

These elements have been formally identified in a brand of analysis termed 'linkage studies' (Keeble, 1968; Marshall, 1980; Moore, 1972). Industrial linkage is defined as occurring when one producer purchases inputs of goods or services from, or sells output to, another producer. Sako (1989) argues that linkages may range from 'tangible' institutional arrangements (like interfirm subcontracting) to more informal or 'intangible' arrangements like personal networks based on high trust and/or exchange of obligations. In particular, these conceptions are concerned with the question of how intermediate forms of governance (like the subcontract) contribute towards industrial competitiveness. As Sako (1989) argues, the price system is never perfect in conveying all aspects of the goods being exchanged and, in this context, other considerations become important. The question, of course, is how do institutions facilitate the coordination of transactions and productive activities within and between sectors?

As Walker (1988) notes, neo-classical economics treats integration as the amalgamation of factories and product lines in which the effect of corporate bulk on prices and competitive behaviour are prime concerns. In this sense, the treatment of linkages is seen in mechanistic terms, as a set of economic relations whereby the firm either choses, on cost criteria, to internalize productive activity (do it all in-house) or purchase the necessary output (by externalizing production). In most of the literature, there is acceptance of the premise that the market economy operates unproblematically in its allocation of goods and services. Industrial linkages are conceptualized as part extension of the rationality of the market economy, enabling the 'smoothing out' of imperfections in market systems by increasing the efficiency of information and material flows.

Neoclassical theory also assumes that firms engage in rational decision-making independent of each other, which implies that firms meet and operate as equals in the market place (Holmes, 1986 p. 82). Clearly this conception is problematic for an understanding of subcontracting because the primary characteristics of a subcontract relationship are that firms meet as unequals in the marketplace (whether through differences in resources, technologies or market power). Friedman (1977) and others show this in a number of empirical studies which outline two important features of the subcontract relationship (Sabel, 1982; Villa, 1981). First, subcontracting relations are complex and differentiated, and are more than economic transactions. Second, they operate according to power differences between firms through the medium of contrasting, yet complementary, production processes.

In contrast, neoclassical theory focuses only on two types of linkages: internal organization through vertical integration or external organization by arms-length transactions between firms regulated by the free market (Friedman, 1977). In this view, the internal operations of the firm is viewed as a rationally operated technical production function, with external (market) relations governed by efficient price fixing markets. In a review paper, Walker (1989) argues that Coase (1937) was the first to challenge the neo-classical position, in conceptualizing firms and markets as alternative, and potentially interchangeable, mechanisms for coordinating production. In particular, Coase was concerned with the question of why the economy derives a particular balance of internal administration and external market exchange.

In going some way to answering this, Chandler (1977) called attention to the internal organization of the large corporation and how it sought to internalize markets by forward integration into sales, and, later, to imitate the market by dividing up and playing off divisions like competing companies. Later authors have come to analyze the potential for market failure and the need to form more fixed contractural relations, a perspective closely aligned to the Transaction Cost school led by Williamson (1975). In this view, the degree of integration of any production system depends on two things. First, the economies of scope between related processes, what Walker (1989) terms 'pieces of the division of labour'. Second, the transaction costs of bringing more processes under the wing of a single firm, or leaving them dispersed among several firms doing business with each other. As the theory suggests, the optimal degree of integration/disintegration depends on items like the relative scales of coordinate proceses and the institutional conditions for enforcing contracts (see Walker, 1989, p. 52).

In developing a critique against transaction costs theory, Walker argues that it is unsatisfactory since it reinforces and reaffirms neo-classical economics. In particular, the basic consideration in relation to transaction costs is economic efficiency, underpinned by the notion that firms are engaged in cost-minimization practices. In this sense, transaction cost theory slightly modifies the neo-classical assumption of 'rational economic actors' by adding the notion of 'self interested behaviour' (or opportunism), and acknowledging that there are limits to perfect knowledge which cause markets to fail in certain circumstances. As Walker notes,

> Not only is the theory of action a thin gruel of free-floating individuals, information and logical chance, the theory of the economy cuts only skin deep.   (p. 53)

In a far reaching critique, Walker (1989) points to a number of major deficiencies with the transaction cost approach to industrial organization. In particular, he argues that the market is seen as being in the realm of commodity exchange, while the firm is consigned to that of administration. However, this analytical distinction is problematical because it fails to recognize that transactions are also structured by the technical and social characteristics of the products and production methods, and that markets are not solely a means of transfering cost, but are also a mechanism for transfering social relations between factory regimes.

Sayer (1989) also echoes Walker in noting that the theoretical exegeses of the transaction costs approach offers a largely unidirectional explanation, from cost patterns associated with markets and production processes to organizational forms, that is disintegration or integration. However, as Sayer argues, cost patterns are also a product of organizational forms and, in this sense,

> organizational forms are to some extent the creator as much as the creature of the patterns of costs distributed across production systems.   (1989, p. 679)

This relates to the wider difficulty of the theory which notes that the fundamental economic problem is one of exchange, thereby reducing production to exchanges between profit-seeking actors and between humans and nature. In this way, efficiency is achieved by the minimization of the factors of exchange, although, as Walker notes,

> People must do a great deal more than touch, barter and trade to produce useful objects: they have to work, to transform nature into new forms. (p. 53)

And it is this transformation, that of nature into products, which offers a more fruitful line of investigation from which to understand some of the dynamics underpinning the organization of production, not the least of which concerns the transformation in the technical division of labour. In particular, the literature notes that the extension of the technical division of labour, through new supply networks, is linked to the development of new productive forces which seek to recreate, and maintain, profitable forms of industrial organization. As Holmes (1986) notes, two themes dominate this discussion. First, the role of flexibility, and, second, the nature of unequal power relations between buyers and suppliers.

In considering the first theme, suppliers often bear the costs of a downturn in demand through an ability to use accumulated resources or to shed (or absorb) fixed costs. That is, buyers can use suppliers as 'economic buffers' in times of economic downturn. However, flexibility can also be achieved in a more dynamic and positive sense (see also the next section). The best instance is the specialist supplier (at the top of the tier) who can enable the buyer to realize economies of scale at the level of individual machines, rather than at the level of individual plants (Sabel, 1982). Moreover, suppliers provide options to buyers by virtue of the large amounts of accumulated skills and processes they possess. In this sense, an extension of the technical division of labour, into a wider supplier network, provides buyers with a means of tapping a resevoir of potential production capacity.

The second major theme concerns the nature of shifting power relations between buyers and suppliers and the implications this has for the stability and development of both parties (a theme which is hardly considered by transaction costs). Holmes (1986) notes that there are clearly some benefits to the supplier from entering a relationship with a major buyer. Such benefits include a guaranteed market for products, assistance in securing raw materials and the technology to carry out the tasks, the provision of managerial and technical assistance, and the possible transfer and accretion of knowledge between the parties. However, the literature has tended to see the relationship between buyers and suppliers as one of 'supplier subservience' to the buyer. In this model, there is a tendency to stereotype the supplier's position as one of outright passivity.

This is exemplified by Friedman's (1977) use of the dual economy thesis which, simply stated, argues that many suppliers (particularly small businesses) occupy the margins of economic activity and remain both peripheral and subservient to (large) multinational corporations. On the basis of unequal resource bases, a dual economy develops which utilizes and reinforces inequities between buyers and suppliers. In this conception, a number of problematical assumptions are made. Foremost, it is assumed that buyers dictate the terms of contracts and freely choose who to contract out to. It is also argued that suppliers have to take what is offered and contracts can easily be broken by buyers without fear of reprisal, legal or otherwise. Thus, suppliers have little bargaining base on which to control the excesses of buyer firms. Finally, it is argued that suppliers have little room for manoeuvre in terms of the content of the product, production, and labour processes.

Although these assumptions accurately describe some forms of buyer-supplier relations, it is problematical to elevate them to a generalization. As Rubery and Wilkinson (1981) observe, buyer-supplier relations are not necessarily based on the subservience of the supplier to the buyer. One obvious example is the specialist supplier who has the technology and skills to innovate and produce. Moreover, supplier firms do exercise degrees of relative autonomy and control through a number of formal and informal networks, as evidenced by a number of European studies (Sabel, 1982; Villa, 1981). These include, first, the ability to control their own specific technologies and skills, particularly if these are scarce commodities; second, the innovativeness of particular suppliers in building up a large volume of customers, thus minimizing their reliance on any one customer; and, third, the willingness of suppliers to enter the design stage of production, volunteering involvement in a process which ultimately shapes the content of production.

However, the significant point about the reductionist conceptions of the suppliers position, with regard to their buyers, is that it proceeds on the basis of insignificant empirical research. Clearly, one can identify the power differentials between buyers and suppliers, but what is less evident are the ways in which power differentials operate in practice. For instance, how do buyers and suppliers negotiate with each other, on what basis and with what effects? What are the bases for power and how is it expressed? However, in terms of explaining the notional ties between buyers and suppliers, we have to go beyond the question of flexibility, or the reductionist idea that suppliers are a passive residue willing and waiting to function as an extension of the technical division of labour. In the next section, we briefly consider some scenarios which more clearly define the transforming relations between buyers and suppliers.

5 THE KEY DETERMINANTS OF VERTICAL DISINTEGRATION

In the last section, we argued that the development of new forms of industrial organization is related to what Walker terms the 'forces of production'. In developing this notion, this section of the chapter critically evaluates some of the key determinants underpinning the development of new forms of buyer-supplier relations in the British economy. Shutt and Whittington (1984) provide a useful starting point by suggesting that supply relations are governed by 'demand risk'. By this, they envisage two situations, one in which a buyer is involved in manufacturing a product for which demand is uncertain or irregular because of cyclical or seasonal variations in demand and, in instances where demand does not exist for continuous mass production. In the former case, the supply network becomes an important instrument in reducing the buyer's production costs in line with output, an adjustment known as 'production smoothing' (Friedman, 1977; Holmes, 1986; Imrie, 1986).

As Berger and Piore (1980) note, cyclical demand patterns force firms into differentiating product demand into an unstable and stable component. The stable component is determined by the level of demand at the bottom of the trough in the cyclical demand curve. That is, each firm can identify a minimum level of demand able to support a minimum scale of output. The unstable component is therefore equal to the difference between actual demand and the stable component of demand (Berger and Piore, 1980). This form of industrial organization is close to the model of 'capacity' subcontracting, whereby suppliers pick up expanded levels of production. This type of industrial organization has been more evident where demand has not been sufficient to warrent mass production techniques. This enables buyers to realize economies of scale by decentralization rather than by centralization, because of the reliance both on cheaper and more skilled labour in subcontracting firms.

This relates more closely to an important element in a buyer's makeup, the nature of its production process and associated technologies. Suppliers are often a strategic mechanism for cutting into the fixed costs of production processes, particularly those parts which operate at an inefficient level. For instance, if the existing technologies of a buyer fail to maintain output and/or increase efficiency, one solution to the problem is to contract work out to firms who have the technologies available to reach and maintain an optimal level of efficiency and output. This type of relationship between a buyer and supplier closely characterizes the formation of a tiered structure, with front-line suppliers operating as key specialists, offering a technical know-how and expertise which the buyer does not possess.

This form of work decentralization is a crucial part of the transition to forms of relational contracting, and can arise in a variety of contexts. For instance, Imrie's (1989b) study of a clothing company's costing exercise, carried out on the efficiency of the existing technologies, concluded that specialist cutting and knitting machines would enable the factory to restore competitive levels of output. However, because of cost constraints, and the availability of local specialist cutting and knitting machines in a small firm, the clothing firm contracted the work out. As Scott (1984) notes, this is an example of a means of collectivizing work tasks so as to avoid the heavy cost penalties incurred in the partial or inefficient use of capital. Moreover, Sheard (1983) notes that the shortage of available capital for investment in technologies can lead buyer firms to seek out plants with the requisite technologies, either for a long or short period.

The role of the specialist supplier has also been seen as a form of 'technological fix', a process lucidly outlined by Mensch (1977). Mensch has called the post-1974 stagnation of the global economy a 'stalemate of technology', one requiring new innovations and technologies to stimulate new waves of growth. The development of new supply relations is cited as a key part of the apparent technological-led growth of global capitalism since the mid-1980s. For instance, it is argued that buyers are increasingly using suppliers to spearhead the initial periods of research and development so that innovation costs are borne by the supplier and not by the buyer (Kaplinsky, 1983). Moreover, many suppliers operate in specific market niches which use specialist skills and technologies. Rather than increase fixed costs (and risk capital expenditure), buyers seeking to expand innovative activity have been known to use specialist suppliers, exploiting their existing skills and technologies without adding to the burden of increased resource expenditure, supervision, and the investment of high levels of risk capital.

In contrast, Gordon *et al.* (1982) stress the importance of control over work organization as a feature in the trend towards vertical disintegration. A number of researchers concur with this by arguing that the utilization of suppliers can act as a means of ensuring wage and labour discipline by segmenting labour into a number of disparate and competing groups (Murray, 1985; Sabel, 1979, 1982; Shutt and Whittington, 1984). For instance, Rubery and Wilkinson (1981) note that off-setting work to suppliers can drive the costs of labour down to a point at which high labour costs are threatened by the relative advantages that supply labour offers to buyer firms. This has been evident in a number of European countries, not the least of which is Italy.

As Mingione (1981) has outlined, successive periods of inflationary wage pressure in the Italian economy has resulted in waves of work decentralization to low-waged areas and low-waged supplier companies. The use of suppliers is important in this respect because it divides the workforce spatially and institutionally (that is, it produces segmented labour markets) which fragments employee efforts to stabilize and increase wages. Further, the process of divide and rule also has the potential to drive down overall wage costs by virtue of passing the work to those suppliers which traditionally pay lower wages than the buyer companies. These forms of control over the content and processes of work also provides a context in which the utilization of an expanded supply network becomes a means of disciplining employees in buyer firms.

For instance, Edwards (1979) notes that cycles of economic growth in buyer firms are often related to new techniques of control by management which are partially achieved by work decentralization. He identifies two roles for the buyer-supplier relation in this context. First, work is devolved to what are largely docile, non-unionized, workers in supplier firms, unable, and often unwilling, to resist changes in work organization. That is, they are more easily controlled than their counterparts in larger unionized plants. Second, the use of suppliers often enables managers of buyers to sidestep militant unions and employee resistance without necessarily conceding any level of control (other than the central coordination of work tasks).

6 CONCLUSIONS

Clearly then, the rationales for the development of buyer-supplier relations are numerous and complex and cannot be reduced into a single monocausal explanatory framework. The relative importance of the factors outlined here will vary from industry to industry and from one buyer-supplier relation to another. What is required at this juncture is more empirical research to show both the conditions and varied circumstances which give rise to different types of buyer-supplier relationships. While our own empirical data will go some way towards this, the next chapter reviews research which has attempted to chart the transformation in buyer-supplier relations.

3 Vertical Disintegration and New Forms of Work Organization: a Review of Empirical Evidence

1 INTRODUCTION

An important trend in recent years is for companies to buy in specialist non-core services which provide openings for the decentralization of work to a host of supplier firms. This takes a number of forms including homeworking, freelance work, and, more commonly, subcontracting. However, what is particularly surprizing in the literature is the absence of any coherent or systematic set of empirical research to indicate the extent or nature of different patterns of productive decentralization. The British Institute of Management (BIM, 1985) made a similar observation about the nature of buyer-supplier relations, in noting that,

> Apart from futurology and some interesting studies of the interplay between the formal, black, and household economy, little research has been done to reveal ongoing trends in this field, and hardly any on the immediate practical implications for those involved.

In view of this, Chapter 3 provides a critical overview of the empirical research which has reported on transformations in buyer-supplier relations. Our focus is primarily related to the two industrial sectors which best exhibit the development of relational contracting ties, that is, the motor vehicle and electronics industries. Our objective is to provide a flavour of the contrasting ways in which old-style adversarial relations are being transformed in two of the more highly disintegrated industrial sectors. This review of previous empirical research will also provide a wider contextual platform with which to view our case study findings presented in subsequent chapters. In pursuing these objectives, we divide the chapter into five. First, we consider the evidence on the extent to which specific features of relational contracting ties have been developed in British industry (with the focus on motor vehicles and electronics). In particular,

40

this section of the chapter considers some of the wider, aggregate, trends.

Second, while acknowledging the importance of obtaining a wider picture of buyer-supplier relations, this part of the chapter reports research which has traced some of the key structural changes between buyers and suppliers. In this sense, we are more concerned with highlighting some of the main inter- and intraorganizational implications of the development of obligational-style contracting. In a third section, we briefly consider the impact that the apparent diffusion of relational contracting ties is having on supplier labour practices. In this way, we focus attention on changes occurring in the labour process. Fourth, we then outline and consider some of the real constraints which are inhibiting the development of relational contracting practices. Finally, we consider some of the key empirical questions that researchers should seek to answer, and we provide an outline of our own research presented in subsequent chapters.

2   CHANGING BUYER-SUPPLIER RELATIONS: A REVIEW OF EMPIRICAL TRENDS

In this section of the book, we wish to outline, and evaluate, a range of research which has been reported on the changing nature of buyer-supplier relations. This review is fragmentary due to the dearth of empirical research completed on the subject. Notwithstanding this, the review gives some impression of the nature and scale of changes in buyer-supplier relations, with two themes of some importance. First, the evidence suggests that buyer-supplier relations are evolving new forms of inter-industry dependency, with suppliers both gaining and losing particular measures of control over their productive capacity and organization (Rawlinson, 1990; Turnbull, 1989, 1991). In this sense, the emerging relationships demand that we rethink the nature of inter-organizational power relations between buyers and suppliers. Second, it is clear that the development of obigational contracting is highly uneven between and within industrial sectors and firms, and part of the task of this chapter is to illustrate this point.

The trend towards new buyer-supplier relations: some evidence from national and sub-national surveys

A useful starting point is provided by Pollert (1988) who notes that while the alleged increase in outsourcing relates most directly to the interest in Japanization, the fragmentation of the corporate sector, and the growth of small firms, there is little evidence, at the aggregate level, of a dramatic increase in outsourcing in the private sector. In noting this, she cites one of the few pieces of research on work decentralization, the Warwick Industrial Relations Research Unit Company Level Survey (reported by Marginson *et al.*, 1988). In particular, the Warwick study focussed on subcontracting as an important form of external economy. In interviews with managers of 106 head and divisional offices, their research shows that 56 per cent of companies had undergone a policy change towards subcontracting. In the majority of cases, the managers claimed that this change had resulted in an increase in the level of subcontracting for the service concerned. In particular, a policy change, leading to an increase in subcontracting of cleaning and catering services, was reported in 30 per cent of the cases.

Further, Marginson *et al.* (1988) also found that 61 per cent of establishment respondents reported no change in the level of subcontracting over the previous five years. Rather, the subcontracting of ancillary activities, like services, was already widespread with 83 per cent of managers reporting that they subcontracted out at least one service, with 39 per cent contracting out three or more services. The study also found little evidence of the widespread contracting out of production related activities. Other research reaffirms the findings of the Warwick study, and further notes the concentration of subcontracting in specific industrial sectors, especially engineering and automobiles (NEDO, 1986; Rubery, *et al.*, 1987). For instance, Rubery *et al.* (1987), reporting a survey of forty manufacturing companies in a range of industrial sectors, indicate that they found little evidence of an increase in subcontracting. In a significant number of cases, they report that firms had actually 'brought-in' production previously subcontracted. Moreover, they note that firms were wary of problems of coordination, design and quality control, because of the growth of subcontracting at a more remote, international, scale.

This observation, however, is contradicted by Rawlinson (1990), who provides evidence on the trend towards increased levels of vertical disintegration in the motor vehicle industry. His analysis of industrial change in Coventry, shows that the development of new production relations between buyers and suppliers is part of a strategy of reversing the trends of huge capital losses and internal inefficiencies that became apparent in the local motor vehicle industry in the late 1970s. In particular, Rawlinson's analysis outlines the shift from capacity to specialist supplier relations, with large buyers increasingly reliant on suppliers to provide goods that they previously made in-house. For instance, Rawlinson relates the story of the BBA takeover of Automotive Products in 1986, which led to the closure of the largest collection of multi-spindle automatic machine tools in Western Europe at the Leamington plant. As a consequence, £13 million per year of batch machinery work was subcontracted into the local economy, compared with £4 million in 1982 (Rawlinson, 1990). As Rawlinson notes, the decision to out-source was based on the comparative costs of buying-in new machinery to replace old technologies, relative to utilizing specialist suppliers with the expertise and capacity to carry out the requisite tasks. The relative cheapness of the latter strategy prevailed in this instance.

In a similar vein, a postal survey by Imrie and Morris (1988) contributes towards the debate on the extent of a shift towards work decentralization. In total, they sent out 150 questionnaires to medium and large sized Welsh plants (that is, plants employing more than 250 employees) questioning them on the degree to which they were utilizing subcontractors and whether or not they were introducing 'best practice', like just-in-time. In total, there were 74 returns, a response rate of 49 per cent. Responses were received from a wide variety of industrial sectors, with 57 per cent of respondents indicating an increase in the volume of work they were putting out to subcontractors compared to five years ago. In particular, this shift was concentrated in metal manufacturing, chemicals, automobiles, and engineering. In the sample as a whole, there was a tendency for firms to concentrate on subcontracting services, reaffirming the findings of Marginson *et al.* (1988). For example, while 38 firms (51%) contracted out some production, 55 (74%) contracted out at least one service.

Table 3.1 is also illuminating in indicating that the majority of plants that were subcontracting some production (68%) were putting out less than 10 per cent of the volume they produced, while only a relatively small proportion of firms (8%) were putting out more than 50 per cent of their volume. When asked why they were subcontracting, reasons of cost and flexibility were cited. In this way, subcontracting relieves the operator of the need to maintain an in-house capability across a diverse range of activities, many of which have a high degree of technical specialism.

TABLE 3.1   *The proportion of production and service activities contracted out by the sample firms*

proportions of work contracted out (%)	plants contracting out production		plants contracting out services	
	No.	(%)	No.	(%)
1–9	26	(68)	20	(36)
10–24	6	(16)	19	(34)
25–49	3	(8)	6	(11)
50+	3	(8)	10	(19)
TOTAL	38	(100)	55	(100)

Source: Imrie and Morris, 1988.

Further, firms indicated how in-house management and administrative overheads were saved by subcontracting, with operators able to maintain flexibility in responding to external and internal fluctuations.

This concurs with the findings of Rubery *et al.* (1987) who note, from their research, that buyers were putting work out for a wide range of reasons. In particular, companies in their sample were buying-in to extend the range of goods marketed outside the range of their own production capabilities. The reasons for this were cited as enhancement of brand image by adding quality goods to their range, a clear case of supplying goods complementary to the range produced in-house. Further, companies argued that buying-in was a rational tactic in testing the market as a prelude to the possible production, and the supply of goods, for which demand was expected to be short-lived, an instance of risk aversion. Moreover, in distinction to the findings of Imrie and Morris (1988), Rubery *et al.* also note that outsourcing was common in firms where the production of small batches was threatening to disrupt long-run production schedules.

In developing some of these issues, Imrie and Morris's survey also considered the extent to which respondent firms were operating more flexible, 'best practice', systems of production, including just-in-time, single sourcing, and quality assured supplies. Table 3.2 outlines some of the results, showing that 66 per cent of the sample had developed quality assured supplies, especially in the metal manufacturing, engineering, electronics, chemicals, and automobile sectors. Also, 22 of the respondent firms gave an indication of when they had set up quality assured systems. Of these, 77 per cent had done so since 1980, with 36 per cent having done so since 1986. In contrast, just-in-time and daily delivery systems were less in evidence; only 23 per cent of all respondents had set up some form of just-in-time by 1988. A similar number were using single sourcing, while half of the respondents gave some form of technical assistance to their subcontractors.

TABLE 3.2 *Numbers of firms in the sample using new operating methods with their suppliers*

Operations with suppliers	Numbers	% of the sample
Single Sourcing	16	22
Quality Assured Supplies	49	66
Daily Delivery	23	31
Just-in-Time	17	23
Technical Assistance to Subcontractors	37	50

SOURCE, Imrie and Morris, 1988.

Respondents were also asked to what extent they made use of local subcontractors. While it has been argued that the economies of agglomeration and scale will lead to a clustering of subcontract work, generating localized patterns of interfirm linkages, in contrast, others note that spatially diffuse patterns are more common (see Holmes, 1986; Morris, 1988c). The results from the survey show that 84 per cent of the respondents subcontract some, or all, of their contract work to firms based in Wales. In fact, a high number of firms (45%) subcontract at least 75 per cent of contract output to Welsh based firms, although the survey gives no indication of the value of local contracts. There is also a tendency to concentrate subcontracting at a local level, evidenced by the high proportion of respondents who use subcontractors within a twenty mile radius. Overall, 76 per cent of respondents use local firms to carry out a proportion of contract work, and 32 per cent subcontract 75 per cent or more of the available contract work to firms within a twenty mile radius.

In summary, aggregate data on the utilization of a wider supply base is inconclusive, although the evidence suggests that many non core activities are being increasingly bought-in. Similarly, where core work is being put-out, it tends to be concentrated sectorally, and related to cost and technical considerations rather than any concern with capacity. Furthermore, while the various studies illustrate multi-responses to production change, and the contrasting styles of vertical disintegration, they also indicate the limitations of elements of the post-Fordist thesis that we outlined in Chapter 2. In particular, many firms seem to use new supplier relations as a mechanism for casting off 'dead-weight' and non-essential activities, rather than utilizing suppliers as a central core part of their production processes. If this is the case, then it would seem to go against the conventional wisdom, that new forms of industrial organization are increasingly characterized by a web of new inter-industry dependencies.

New relations between buyers and suppliers: the development of obligational contracting?

While data from several sources indicates some shift to new forms of interfirm organization, we concur with Pollert (1988), that there is a need to trace some of the main qualitative changes that are occurring between buyers and suppliers. In acknowledging this, it is possible to identify a range of research which shows that new, qualitative, relations are emerging between buyers and suppliers. For instance, the move towards forms of relational contracting is evident in numerous industrial sectors, with a clear trend towards the implementation of preferred supplier policies.

One instance of this is reported by the West Midlands Industrial

Development Association (WMIDA) report (1989) which notes that the Ford Motor Company has been cutting its number of direct suppliers from 2500 to 900 in the last ten years, while Austin Rover has embarked on a programme to reduce its supply base from 1,200 to 300 firms. This trend is evident across a wide range of industrial sectors. For instance, as the later case studies illustrate both Lucas and IBM UK are reducing their British supplier bases. Similar evidence is cited by Helper (1989), who also notes that, in the US auto industry, contract length has doubled in the last five years. Her research findings show, that on average, suppliers had 2.5 year contracts in 1989 compared to 1.3 year contracts in 1984.

However, as Wilson and Gorb (1983) note, from their study of 189 firms in London, the trend towards a preferred supplier base has little to do with creating new efficient lines of supply, but more to do with short term, cost minimization, objectives. For instance, there are substantial costs involved in identifying, investigating, and evaluating, and either rejecting or accepting, new suppliers (Wilson and Gorb, 1983, p. 5). In particular, the paucity of published and readily accessible data on supplier firms contributes to high investigatory costs which tend to minimize the attractiveness of developing and maintaining multiple suppliers. The administrative costs of monitoring and maintaining suppliers are also compounded with a multiple supply base, factors which tend to mitigate against its survival. In this sense, single sourcing is, in many ways, a pragmatic response to intensified competition and cost pressures.

Furthermore, as Helper (1989) notes, a key development in buyer-supplier relations is collaboration. This takes a number of forms, including a greater degree of information interchange between companies, the development of joint problem solving, and a diminution in haphazard scheduling. Helper's research shows that there has been an impressive increase in the amount of information which suppliers provide to buyers. The most significant gain is the number of suppliers who provide their Statistical Process Control (SPC) charts to their buyers.[1] Whereas only 16 per cent of her sample did so in

---

[1] Statistical Process Control (SPC), comprises a series of technical and human innovations aimed at continual improvement in manufacturing processes, with the objective of eliminating the special causes of variation from a fixed standard. SPC makes it possible to continuously monitor the process, giving operators responsibilities for checking performance, eliminating errors and compiling measures which, when interpreted, provided a basis for improvement. In particular, different types of SPC systems check for the reintroduction of a special cause of variation, before the process is significantly altered. In this way, SPC is supposed to lead to never-ending improvement.

1984, 91 per cent were providing their charts by 1988. Similarly, a greater range of suppliers (75%) were willing to provide production scheduling information in 1988, compared with five years previously (when only 50% of the sample did so).

An important aspect of new collaborative practices relates to the assistance that buyers are willing to give to suppliers. As our case study material in later chapters will show, the level of assistance from buyers varies considerably. However, as Rubery *et al.* (1987) indicate, levels of technical, personnel, and management assistance all appear to be on the increase. These conclusions are echoed by Tan's (1990) research on buyer-supplier relations in the Singapore electronics industry. Utilizing survey responses from 74 firms, out of a population size of 232 companies, Tan shows that they were all forthcoming with some technical support to their suppliers. Practically all the American and European companies, and some 84 per cent of local companies, gave technical support to local suppliers, ranging from the transfer of sophisticated tools and machines to on-the-job training.

Moreover, a great deal of research has documented the development of new vetting procedures, technical collaboration, partnership agreements, and training policies, as part of the transition to relational contracting. Trevor and Christie's (1989) research provides a clear documentation of the transition to a tiered system of contracting, with buyer firms insisting on internal audits and rigorous vetting prior to giving suppliers preferred status. For instance, an injection moulding company, serving a major Japanese buyer, had to undergo a six month evaluation programme. The evaluation was more concerned with detailed inspections of the company's organization and production methods, less with technical processes and issues. As Trevor and Christie note, the Japanese obsession with control over quality is the central issue at stake with one electronic components company noting that,

> at the beginning every single error that was identifiable was sent back in a little packet with full details of time and place discovered and a segment of information on the remedial action we would be taking to solve the problem.   (p. 23)

A related issue is the extent to which suppliers respond favourably to the changes which leading buyers require them to make. As one company in Trevor and Christie's sample, remarked, 'the quality and delivery demands of the Japanese are seen as entirely beneficial'. Other companies argue that the move towards relational contracting has acted as a catalyst for new practices in quality assurance. Similarly, Tan (1990) notes the importance of buyers evaluating and monitoring supplier performance. In his research, 95 per cent of the sample considered close monitoring of supplier performance important, with 93 per cent carrying out regular checks and evaluations.

Gorgeu and Mathieu (1989) also provide a number of important insights into new organizational practices in buyer-supplier relations in the French automobile and aerospace industries. In interviews with an unspecified number of large buyer companies, and thirty of their suppliers, they show how the development of a relational model is placing new demands on suppliers. For instance, in the French aero-space industry, it is now more difficult for suppliers to receive quality certification than in the early 1980s. Many supplier firms are governed by a system of certification issued by the Department of Weaponry Industry Surveillance (or SIAR). The renewal of contracts (which occurs every three years) poses problems for suppliers, with the audits being much more precise and formalized than they were a few years earlier. Thus, from their survey, 30 per cent of the companies that had obtained a SIAR certification three years ago were at risk of failing to obtain a renewal.

A related study, by Peck (1988), surveyed a wide range of companies in North East England, confirming many of the trends discussed above. In particular, the study indicates that a diverse range of firms, from micro switch producers to manufacturers of pistons and radar equipment, were placing 'quality' issues at the centre of their restructuring programmes. These encompassed not only the performance of suppliers, but also pervading attitudes to management priorities. As the Tyne and Wear survey suggests, the real concern for quality has had a domino effect in so far that the guarantees of quality, which customers increasingly demand, has to be matched by enhancing the quality of production systems and related supplier practices. In particular, the research shows how the efforts to improve quality of supply has formed only one part of a series of interrelated changes which extend beyond purchasing to the wider operations of production.

While these general sectoral trends are evident, it is clear that the most far reaching transformations in buyer-supplier relations are concentrated in particular sectors, and, within these, amongst particular firms and plants. In this sense, the British automotive industry is at the leading edge in developing new supply practices. The report by the WMIDA (1989) shows how component makers are becoming more involved with manufacturers in the overall design of the new vehicle, closely following the long established Japanese model. However, as the report points out, there are a series of major weaknesses with the British supply industry to the motor vehicle industry, not the least of which is undercapitalization, limiting the ability of suppliers to undertake technological change and long-term planning and development.

While this is a crucial issue, much concern also relates to the role of price in buyer-supplier relations and the extent to which non-price criteria are evolving as the basis for 'make' or 'buy' decisions. As Neil *et al.* (1988) argue, the importance of, what they term, 'acquisition cost', as a key component in the buyer's choice between competing contract bids, is increasingly significant in buyer-supplier relations. Their analysis, of buyers and suppliers in the Scottish electronic and mechanical engineering industries, shows that while 'supplier price' has continued to be a main factor in suppliers gaining a contract, there is now a move on the part of some buyer companies towards trying to identify and quantify the full costs of sourcing business with a particular vendor. This concurs with Helper's (1989) investigations which show that every criterion is now more important than it was five years ago in arriving at a decision to contract out. Quality is the single most important criterion in a buyer's selection of a supplier, with price of lesser importance.

However, research by Shapiro (1985) suggests that price is still a key determinant of the form of buyer-supplier relations, and that 'new adversarial' relationships are emerging in which suppliers are being told that they must provide the lowest price, the highest quality, and the best delivery if they are to receive a contract. Rutherford (1990) reinforces this point in noting that one supplier, in his study of the South Wales automotive components industry, was conscious of their buyer's quality objectives while noting that there were still very strong pressures to be price and cost competitive. As Shapiro (1985) concludes, the competitive position has intensified, and the ground rules for contract-qualification have been altered. This is clearly indicated in the range of case studies reported by Trevor and Christie (1988). Their wide ranging analysis of buyer-supplier relations in Britain and Japan reveals the continued importance of price.

For instance, an electronics company they interviewed, involved in supplying Japanese consumer electronics plants, showed that quality and delivery is not the whole story in supplying to the Japanese. On one occasion, extra costs had to be passed on to the Japanese clients, whose policy is to seek price reductions from established suppliers. This 'caused a lot of acrimony', and the supplier admitted that there had been a fall-off in business as a result (Trevor and Christie, 1988, p. 93). Similarly, it is common practice for Japanese buyers to ask suppliers for annual price reductions, with the attitude that it is up to the supplier to manage their factory in such a way as to achieve the requisite price reductions. In some instances, the demands placed on suppliers can be more stringent. A packing case company, in Trevor and Christie's sample, commented that Japanese buyers expect a price reduction every six months. As the managing director argued,

> The company has made some cuts and has attempted to keep prices stable despite some rises in material costs, but has had to ask for the first price rise in three years. The Japanese have reacted with alarm 'it's arms in the air all round' but all but one of the Japanese customers has come to accept the increases.   (Trevor and Christie, 1988, p. 109)

In commenting on the continued importance of costing and price, Wilson and Gorb (1983) note that buyer inertia, a lack of interest in the products or services of suppliers, combined with a reactive buying stance, is reflected in the tendency of buyers to opt for 'value for money' as their primary buying criteria. They argue that such behaviour is still typical across much of British industry, reflecting a deep-rooted conservatism and failure-averse practices. Further, they also note that the policies and attitudes of the large buyers towards their small suppliers varied from the supportive to the obstructive. As they indicate, it was the deliberate policy of two organizations not to take on suppliers who would need to devote their entire production to the large customer.

Rawlinson (1990) also notes that new supply contracts are not necessarily confined to manufacture and service work. His research shows that Jaguar and Massey Ferguson were externalizing a large proportion of their prototype and development work, leading to the development of a dense network of local suppliers specializing in basic research and development. These findings neatly illustrate an emerging facet of buyer-supplier relations, the development of spatial clusters or concentrations of suppliers around buyer plants. As Rawlinson indicates, spatial proximity is a pre-requisite in developing cost-effective buyer-supplier relations where prototype work is involved. The high numbers of modifications which are made to prototype products in the course of their development requires an intensive level of physical interaction between buyers and suppliers. Therefore, spatial clusters or physical proximity is one organizational response towards cutting down development time.

Rawlinson also shows that a supplier's loyalty, in doing the relatively lower paid prototype work, is increasingly being rewarded with buyers giving them a greater proportion of final production contracts than has hitherto been the case. This situation contrasts with the period prior to the early 1980s, when the development firms were often undercut on price by other companies when competing for final production work. As Rawlinson argues, the move towards an integrated, prototype development-final manufacture package is being driven by a number of considerations, including a greater concern with process control, the integration of purchasing, production and marketing, as well as quality assurance.

This concurs with Wood (1989) who notes that these various changes occurring in the workplace represent less a coherent response to intensified competition, and more a series of *ad hoc* responses to the particular circumstances that different companies find themselves in. In this way, while the trend towards new forms of buyer-supplier relations is evident, it also shows some of the limitations of post-fordist theory. For instance, most empirical evidence seems to note how corporations are utilizing suppliers to widen product ranges and intensify volume production, a strategy not wholly consistent with the tenets of the post-fordist thesis. Also, the evidence gathered by researchers is, as yet, only partial, in so far that it represents a series of sectoral and firm-based studies. This makes it difficult to be conclusive about the adequacy of existing theory.

Obligational contracting, industrial relations, and supplier labour practices

It is increasingly evident that the term 'labour flexibility' is often used as a euphemism for 'speed-ups', redeployment potential, and job enlargement, than any major change in the relationships between labour and the technical apparatus of production. In this sense, production flexibilities often depend less on new machines and upgraded skills than on flexible methods of exploiting labour, such as forms of work intensification, the extension of the working day, and the utilization of shift systems. In particular, the development of relational-style contracting is integrally linked to the transformation of labour practices, involving, as it does, new systems of control, job definitions, and new responsibilities.

This echoes Rutherford *et al.* (1989), who argue that relatively little attention has been paid to the complication that the diffusion of relational contracting ties has had on supplier labour practices. In particular, their research indicates that buyer firms are both directly and indirectly influencing the labour practices of first tier suppliers. For instance, in 1987, Rover was forced to intervene in a dispute at A. J. Williams, its sole supplier of door handles for the Metro and window trim for the Cowley-built Maestro and Montego. The supplier had only offered a 2 per cent wage increase to its workforce but, as a strike threatened, Rover forced it to increase its offer to 4.5 per cent to avoid production disruption (Turnbull, 1989, p. 23). Interestingly, such industrial relations concerns on the part of the buyers towards suppliers does not necessarily include anti-unionism attitudes and/or practices. Indeed, one firm visited by Rutherford *et al.* (1989) had unionized its workforce largely due to pressures from unions in the buyer company not to subcontract to non-unionized firms.

The other aspect of this intervention, which is increasingly evident at the level of first tier suppliers, is in the training of production employees and, more indirectly, their recruitment. This is not just due to industrial reasons, but for quality control (in, for example, the use of SPC), and to enhance production efficiency. In the last four to five years there appears to have been the realization, on the part of the first tier suppliers, of the need for a substantial increase in training. In particular, the major motor vehicle assemblers have put pressure on suppliers to take training more seriously. For instance, Ford now demands that SPC training be given to supplier production employees and has sold its interactive training videos to suppliers at reduced rates.

As Rutherford (1990) notes, it is clear that an important impetus in training is pressure being exerted by buyer firms on suppliers. Suppliers to Ford, Nissan, and almost all major manufacturers have to give production employees training or 'appreciation' courses in the use of SPC. This was the case even though not all employees needed to use SPC in their work. As Rutherford argues, training in quality control is also necessary since many production employees are now being given quality control responsibilities as central quality control departments are being cut back. Rutherford cites a direct example of buyer intervention in supplier training, at a Rover supplier of electrical harnessing. Here, in fact, it was a Japanese equipment supplier to Honda and Rover which was now the key factor in the training programme. Some twenty-five direct operators, skilled craft workers and engineers had been sent to Japan for training lasting up to two months. In addition, the firm had adopted all of the equipment manufacturer's training programme, including a five-day induction course for new employees. As Rutherford concludes, the production process in areas supplying Rover had been reorganized by the Japanese firm, significantly increasing management control of the work-place (see also, Marinaccio and Morris, 1991).

Further, Rutherford's work indicates that buyers are requesting front-line suppliers to undertake more formal off-the-job training and re-training. In several of his sample firms, up to four per cent of shop-floor workers were involved at any one time in some form of off-the-line training. As Rutherford notes, retraining involves the acquisition of both technical and 'cultural' skills. For instance, in several firms that Rutherford spoke to, it was clear that while semi-skilled employees were being given technical training in subjects like electronics and hydraulics, they were being given few skills that were transferable outside of the firm. In particular, SPC training was viewed by managers as culturally important, since it made employees much more aware of the need to be conscious of quality and responsibilities to the customer.

Indeed, as Rutherford makes clear, some production workers were being trained to go on visits to firm suppliers in order to raise quality awareness amongst second tier supplier firms. Further, it is apparent that some buyer firms expect suppliers to bear most of the costs of training and retraining to meet their production standards. A manager at one firm supplying to Jaguar stated that because Jaguar did not want to inspect any product coming from its suppliers, it was having to increase training in SPC and quality control techniques (Rutherford, 1990, p. 24). However, as the manager made clear, the main block to getting employees trained in SPC to Jaguar's standards was meeting Jaguar's own daily production requirements!

This problem of firms being able to get time to train shopfloor employees without disrupting production schedules has, in turn, been exacerbated by the fact that in most supplier firms there is, after almost a decade of redundancies, little slack labour. Getting time to train means that firms often have to alter shift patterns and/or have employees train after work in their own time. As Rutherford shows, one firm he visited was utilizing Ford's SPC interactive training videos which alone represented almost eight hours of off-the-line training for each employee. In addition to the videos, there were another ten hours of off-the-line training per employee. In order to cope with the time required for training, as well as other needs (vacation, etc.), employees had to work a twelve hour shift, instead of an eight hour stint, for a quarter of the year.

There were also indications that translating training into actual work practice could be problematic. At a national level, a study by Dale and Shaw (1988), on the use of SPC by UK motor components firms, noted that a significant number of suppliers were,

> not devoting sufficient time in thinking through the issues related to the introduction and application of SPC with too great attention (being) given to the mechanisms in using this technique, whilst the underlying logic has been overlooked. (1988, p. 30)

This included a number of cases in which people not directly resonsible for control of the production process were filling in SPC charts, thus undermining one of the principal reasons for SPC, that is, operator controlled quality.

For instance, in the supplier firms visited by Rutherford (1990), there were a number of instances where SPC training had not led to the desired results. For instance, in one firm, a central quality control department had to be reintroduced because operators were either 'too bored' to do the requisite number of SPC checks, or they tended to reset machines before they did SPC, so they were always within acceptable quality limits. In another firm, workers interviewed by Rutherford noted that with increased production pressures, it was sometimes impossible to do more than half the prescribed number of SPC checks.

Moreover, these findings are reinforced by international research, especially the study by Gorgeu and Mathieu (1989) of the French automobile and aerospace industries. Their study of the French system indicates that auto and aerospace manufacturers have exerted pressure on first tier suppliers to change intra-organizational practices to fit in with the emerging ethos of supply. As they indicate, 'partnership' consists in applying management methods that are prescribed by buyer firms, whereby a total reorganization has often been required of the supplier. In this sense, implementing the 'partnership' concept has entailed important changes in personnel strategy including: longer term personnel management; a major expansion of training programmes for all work grades; a gradual change in the content of blue collar work; and, a breakdown in job demarcations. In particular, the new onus on quality, state of the art technologies, and responsive supply, is generating demands for highly skilled personnel, where even a semblance of process control is being devolved to unskilled workers who previously were excluded from any formal management responsibilities.

The end of adversarial contracting?

While it is increasingly evident that particular variants of obligational-style contracting are emerging in parts of British industry, it is also clear that the processes of adoption and adaptation of the relational model is highly uneven, both within and between industrial sectors and firms. Indeed, there is an emerging body of research which questions the extent to which 'best practice' is being adopted by British industry, noting that the practice of relational buyer-supplier relations is the exception rather than the rule. In adding to this debate, this section of the chapter provides a corrective to the commonly held view that best practice buyer-supplier relations is rapidly diffusing through British industry.

One of the initial difficulties, in the change from competitive to collaborative buyer-supplier relations, is the imposition of psychological and operational strains upon suppliers. Indeed, it poses similar problems for the large non-Japanese buyer firms trying to adapt to cooperative relations. For instance, the later case study of IBM, one of the more enlightened and 'Japanese' western companies, is instructive in so far that its purchasing managers have found it extremely difficult to adapt to a new ethos of openness with suppliers. In particular, suppliers are expected to adapt to the new ethos of collaboration, after years of operating in a system in which trust was the last thing that they expected. Moreover, the trauma of the shift from 'competitive' to 'collaborative' contracting goes further than merely one of managerial organization and culture. It also has important ramifications at an operational level for the supplier, in terms of its production organization.

Further, research by Appleby and Twigg (1988) indicates that adversarial practices are still a feature of buyer-supplier relations. In particular, many suppliers remain unwilling to invest in 'customer-specific' technologies, primarily because buyers still utilize a general policy of paying for design and tooling but then reserve the right to place business with the lowest cost supplier. This generates costs and uncertainty for suppliers, with the majority, in Appleby and Twigg's survey, expressing a preference for the Japanese model with suppliers paying for design work, owning their own tooling, but being guaranteed a long term contract.

In part, this position is reflected in the findings of the WMIDA report, which suggests that a limitation of one key industrial sector, the British automotive supply industry, is its traditionally reactive, rather than proactive, stance, coupled with a poor record in introducing and using state of the art CADCAM machines (also, see Rawlinson, 1990). Further, a study by Turnbull, Oliver and Wilkinson (1990) shows that the structure of the UK automotive industry mitigates against a 'tiered' system of component supply or the ability of British motor vehicle manufacturers to organize their suppliers into neat 'pyramids'. More revealingly, research by Bessant *et al.* (1984) notes that, in addition to structural impediments of the type identified by Turnbull *et al.* (1990), the utilization of a just-in-time system has proved to be largely negative in so far as the proximity of suppliers is usually used to support the inefficiencies and lack of control of the major motor vehicle manufacturers.

Similarly, Turnbull's (1989) survey research of 50 West Midlands suppliers to the motor vehicle industry, reveals the extent to which 'new partnership' arrangements are failing to come to fruition. Foremost, Turnbull points to the difficulty of 'continued mistrust' between buyers and suppliers, with the continuation of many of the 'old-style' adversarial relations. In Turnbull's sample, there was an inability, on the part of the motor manufacturers, to control production and scheduling effectively, and a deliberate policy to off-load stock onto suppliers. Further, while the majority of suppliers in Turnbull's sample reported a closer working relationship with major buyers, it was also clear that most firms were finding little improvement in some of the most vital elements of buyer-supplier relations. This was particularly apparent on the question of scheduling with the frequent complaint that,

> vehicle manufacturers would 'front load' their schedules (i.e. unexpectedly request production normally distributed over 3 months to be brought forward), and one supplier cited a recent case when 2 months production of a 3 month schedule was requested in the first week of the schedule!　(p. 10)

Turnbull also points to the lack of commitment by motor manufacturers to 'partnership sourcing', in contrast to their public pronouncements. This echoes research carried out by Helper (1989), whose investigation of 328 auto suppliers in the United States shows that suppliers are sceptical about a buyer's commitment to them. For instance, while contract length and customer switching costs suggest that buyer commitments are increasing, suppliers argue that the talk about increased cooperation means that they have acquiesced in the short term to buyer demands for low prices, high quality and JIT, with no real foundation for mutual benefit having been established. However, there is a divide of opinion, between mediocre suppliers who are being squeezed out of their first tier role, and those who are being given more responsibility for design and sub-assembly in return for the promise of a long term relationship.

In a similar vein, Turnbull (1989) argues that very few suppliers in his sample conceived of any new 'partnership'. Many of the suppliers Turnbull talked to actually castigated their major customers on the question of scheduling with the most frequent complaint relating to buyers' requests to bring forward schedules at short notice. This observation is echoed by a string of research which suggests that new partnership arrangements tend to recreate patterns of dependence which dilute the true spirit of collaboration. For instance, while major automobile manufacturers claim to be developing long term relationships with suppliers, the Rover Group has indicated that they have been forced by financial constraints to go for single source suppliers. Their marked reluctance to go down the single-sourcing route relates to some obvious constraints with this form of industrial organization, including a potential problem of over-dependence.

While the evidence suggests that manufacturers are making some efforts to transform adversarial relations, Turnbull offers a word of caution about the apparent popularity of 'preferred supplier status' and new 'partnerships'. From his investigation of the auto industry, it is clear that manufacturers are still pre-occupied with short term financial performance, and short term methods of work reorganization like job intensification. As Williams *et al.* (1987, 1989) note, while such transformations have been an important condition for low cost production, they have not been sufficient to ensure competitive success. Turnbull makes a similar observation about auto manufacturers in that,

> Rover and many Ford cars continue to be plagued by a reputation for poor quality and reliability which illustrates both a failure to address many of the important non price determinants of competitiveness and a neglect (until more recently) of buyer-supplier relations. (1989, p. 13)

This also relates to the key difficulty facing buyers of controlling production schedules, and creating the conditions for a responsive and workable JIT system. The question, of course, is why JIT is failing to come to fruition in the majority of cases. In Turnbull's study, a host of related factors were important in preventing the development of a fully fledged JIT system. For instance, while two-thirds of his sample reported having to deliver parts on a JIT basis, less than 20 per cent actually operated a JIT system themselves.

These findings are similar to Lamming's (1989) analysis of structural changes in the European automotive components industry. While JIT is claimed as a reality by all assemblers, policies differ in the implementation of the systems. For instance, the use of remote warehousing is a common practice designed to overcome the problems of delivery at distance. While companies like Toyota use this system to 'insure' long distance JIT deliveries, Lamming's research reveals that European producers tend to utilize the system to shift the inventory burdens onto suppliers. In this sense, Lamming concludes that company philosophy and practices tend to define the particular operational forms of JIT, rather than utilizing pure forms of JIT to transform costly corporate practices.

This echoes the research findings of Nishiguchi (1989), who is forthright in questioning the extent to which JIT systems are being developed between buyers and suppliers. From a study of 54 automobile component plants in Japan, the United States, and Europe, Nishiguchi concludes that the US and European suppliers are not only lagging behind Japan in frequent small-lot delivery, but, more vitally, in producing the right quantities at the right time. Thus, rather than achieving a JIT system, Nishiguchi's research shows that non-Japanese buyers and suppliers are tending to build up substantial inventories out of which small quantities of parts are delivered to assembly plants on a JIT basis. In substantiating these observations, Nishiguchi's research shows that each supplier plant in the US has an average inventory of 8.1 days of production (in-process and finished products combined), compared to 16.3 days of production in Europe. These figures compare with the figure of 1.52 for Japan.

Not surprisingly, Nishiguchi argues that the so called JIT system in Europe and the US bears little resemblance to synchronized manufacture, with little regard to the objective of eliminating buffer stocks on both sides. Nishiguchi makes a telling observation about the European system of supply, in noting that,

> they manufacture in large quantities in one lot and lavishly stock them between processes . . . Out in the field I frequently cannot but develop an impression that many European manufacturers are working in warehouses. There are so many piles of in-house materials (and in-house rejects!) scattered everywhere in the plant that I find it difficult to follow the flow of operations.   (p. 3)

Morris (1989a) makes a number of similar observations with regard to the adoption of JIT practices by Japanese owned plants in a range of Canadian industries, including metal manufacturers, electronics producers, and automobile companies. From his findings, he indicates that JIT systems were operated by half of the firms (5 out of 11 companies interviewed), with one more saying that they intended to introduce a JIT system in the near future. In the main, the JIT systems being operated were of the daily, rather than multiple, delivery variety.

It is also pertinent to ask the question of 'what's in it for suppliers'? While front-line, tier one, suppliers are increasingly being guaranteed a larger slice of contracts made available by buyer companies, a number of researchers have argued that the development of a single-sourcing system is actively undermining smaller businesses. This is because, for large national contracts, small firms do not often possess the production capacities to meet the required quantities and consistent throughput. While a system of single sourcing may actively diminish opportunties for some (smaller) firms, a key issue is the extent to which suppliers, as a whole, are benefitting from a move towards relational contracting ties. Published research tends to indicate a mixed picture.

For instance, the requirement by buyers for suppliers to develop new quality standards is enforcing changes in working methods and technologies, implying better organization, more formalization, and new personnel strategies. As Gorgeu and Mathieu (1989) note, the introduction of quality assurance and management systems is creating a whole plethora of related changes, including operator self-checking according to strict requirements, and the emergence of quality management functions. Similarly, there is some agreement that a growing emphasis on quality and process control is encouraging some suppliers to improve their competences, and to invest not only in production and testing equipment, but also in training and personnel programmes.

3   CONCLUSIONS

There is some empirical evidence which reinforces the perception that British industry is involved in a reappraisal and reorganization of buyer-supplier relations. However, the evidence indicates that the transformations are concentrated in particular industrial sectors, and, within these, in specific 'leading edge' companies. Similarly, attempts to develop new interchanges between buyers and suppliers, on the basis of collaborative rather than competitive relations, has led to an enormous variety of inter-organizational responses. For instance, while Imrie and Morris's (1988) survey indicates that work decentralization is a more substantial part of industrial organization than five years ago, it also shows that production is still largely conducted in-house, with firms tending to subcontract relatively small amounts of production-related work. These findings concur with previous research, that service subcontracting is widely practised in manufacturing industry (Marginson *et al.*, 1988).

Further, while most firms are placing new demands on their suppliers by using new operations like quality assured supplies, systems like just-in-time were less in evidence, and were typically concentrated in the automobile, engineering, and electronics sectors. It is also apparent that the reforging of buyer-supplier links in the UK motor components sector has had important direct and indirect effects on the labour practices of supplier firms. In particular, the development of PSS and JIT delivery systems puts increasing onus on supplier firms to increase training and lower the risk of industrial disputes. Buyer firms have, in some instances, intervened in both the industrial relations and training policies of supplier firms and continue to have other significant, albeit indirect, influences on these policies.

However, although certain trends can be identified, the lack of substantial empirical data on buyer-supplier relations prevents any extended insights into the phenomenon. This deficiency is compounded by a number of methodological difficulties connected to the study of work decentralization. Foremost is the problem of defining the object of research. Holmes (1986) notes that the term 'contract' is often used interchangeably with 'subcontract', creating all sorts of confusion as to the actual nature of buyer-supplier relations. For instance, in the clothing industry a direct order for a quantity of clothes is usually regarded as a contract between two independent concerns, whereas, in the car industry, any contract to a supplier is viewed as a subcontract (TGWU, 1983). We came across similar confusion and ambiguity in our own research.

Empirical advances are similarly hindered by the different scales at which explanatory propositions can be made about buyer-supplier relations, and the appropriate scale at which to do empirical analysis (Taylor and Thrift, 1982). For instance, Scase and Goffee (1982) note that work decentralization is the outcome of changes in the structure of monopoly capital and argue for empirical analysis to be done at the level of the macroeconomy if changes are to receive documentation. Whereas the macroeconomic level forms one scale of analysis, it is not wholly appropriate to most empirical questions connected to buyer-supplier relations. For instance, questions about the intra-organizational changes in supplier firms are only clearly answerable at the level of the individual firms themselves. Moreover, although different scales generate different types of empirical questions, this in no way helps link the empirical data. The question of linking scales surely requires more intellectual input by researchers.

In adding to the existing stock of empirical research, the rest of the book outlines an empirical analysis of changes in buyer-supplier relations in the British motor vehicle and electronics industries. In particular, two interrelated questions have informed the research, which was carried out from January to October 1988. First, we were interested in providing some detailed documentation of the extent to which leading multinational companies were adopting and developing obligational contracting ties with their suppliers, and investigating how and why such systems were being developed. Thus, the first bunch of empirical issues were very much concerned with a 'buyer's perspective' and their specific problems and opportunities in attempting to develop new systems of inter-organizational control.

Towards this end, we decided to interview the managing directors, and purchasing managers, of four 'leading edge' multinational companies (Nissan, Lucas, IBM, and Sony), all noted for their commitment in developing relational-style buyer-supplier relations. The companies were also chosen on the basis of their diverse responses and strategies in developing new supplier linkages, providing a contrast, for example, between Lucas's attempts to persuade a 'traditional' workforce to accept new systems of quality and that of Nissan attempting to transfer work practices from Japan to Britain. However, while interviews with four contrasting buyers formed the initial part of our research, we then followed this up with a second stage involving interviews with a sample of each buyer's tier one suppliers.

We interviewed 38 first tier suppliers, divided between the four original equipment manufacturers. Interviews were usually conducted with the managing director and/or purchasing manager, and discussions were wide ranging in content. We asked a whole series of questions relating to the supplier's involvement with buyers as a whole, and, in particular, their involvement with the buyer (or buyers) that were the focus of our study. Questions were asked about how and why supply relations were developed, the conditions and regulations underpinning them, and the extent to which the relationships had been changing over the last five years. In this way, we tried to develop a detailed picture of the contrasting interdependencies and relationships between a closely defined group of buyers and suppliers. We now turn to a detailed discussion of the empirical results of these investigations.

4 Nissan Motor Manufacturing UK: Best Practice Under Pressure

1 INTRODUCTION

The decision, in the early 1980s, by Nissan Motor to locate in the UK provoked unparalleled interest. The company were the first Japanese auto producer to locate in the EEC; and the planned investment of £617 million (by 1992) is the largest Japanese EEC investment to date (although it will be eclipsed by the planned £840 investment of Toyota). It also promised 3 500 direct jobs and many more in spin-off job creation at a time when unemployment rates in the UK were at an all time post-war high. The Nissan investment, however, represented more than a major investment and large job generation. It was the first test as to whether the Japanese manufacturing and management techniques, used to such effect in Japan, could be transferred to the UK automotive industry. Could concepts such as total quality control and just-in-time production be utilized to such effect in the North East of England as they are in Oppama? How would the various actors – British managers, workers and suppliers – respond to this challenge?

This chapter is divided into eight sections. The second will give a brief summary of the history of Nissan Motor and the company's competitive position in the 1990s. This competitive position has had an important role in the internationalization of Nissan's activities which are described in the fourth section. The third section reviews the development of Nissan's buyer-supplier links in Japan, which has influenced the development of the supplier base in the UK. Sections five to seven deal solely with the operations of Nissan M.M. UK. Section five outlines the development of the project and the wider aspects of work and production organization at the Sunderland plant. Sections six and seven focus on the buyer-supplier relations between Nissan and its component suppliers, six giving Nissan's perspective and seven that of its suppliers. These two sections are based on interview material from the company and its suppliers.

2 NISSAN MOTOR INTO THE 1990s

Nissan originated in the 1930s as an acronym for the holding company that owned it (Cusumano, 1985; Goto, 1989; Halberstam, 1987). It developed during that decade from the merger of the automobile components department of Tobata Casting with a factory formerly owned by DAT Motor, and gradually came to be known as Datsun. Nissan is credited with having started the Japanese automobile industry in the 1930s with production of trucks and by the late 1930s had became Japan's first 'mass producer' of automobiles (Cusumano, 1985). It also had early profitable links with Ford and General Motors for whom it made components and parts, and from which it acquired skills and expertise. The company also gained from confiscating Ford's assembly machinery and employing many of Japan Ford's employees in 1939.

Nissan's early strategy was to concentrate upon technology transfer from the USA and Western Europe. This was distinctly different from Toyota, its main rival from the 1930s until the present, which concentrated upon copying Western engineering and production methods through the recruitment of top Japanese university engineers. Nissan's approach brought it close links with the US owned Graham Paige Company in the 1930s and collaboration with the British firm Austin in the 1950s. This period marked the development of the sub-contracting relations, described later in the chapter, which became so critical for the development of Nissan and the other Japanese motor manufacturers. Nissan subcontracted up to 70 per cent of the Austin car (by value) and suppliers therefore played an important role. Firms such as Hitachi took a leading part in the production of major components such as carburettors, springs and shock absorbers.

Cusumano (1985) has argued that overall the reliance on links with foreign companies was detrimental to Nissan in the 1950s, in that Nissan relied upon Graham Paige and Austin too extensively for its engineering and design expertise. Certainly, despite being the first Japanese autoproducer in the market, by the 1950s Nissan had fallen behind Toyota. It gained a short period of ascendancy in the years 1960 to 1962, largely due to Austin's assistance, but thereafter Nissan again fell behind Toyota and has never been able to catch up.

A last point in the historical analysis of Nissan is that they and, indeed, all of the Japanese automobile manufacturers, were considerably assisted in their early decades of development by the Japanese government. An exemplar would be the limits on foreign participation in the Japanese automobile industry, including a ban on foreign direct investment, which lasted from the 1930s to the 1970s, by which time these firms were

TABLE 4.1   *Domestic production and distribution facilities
of Nissan Motor Company Ltd*

Location	Products and/or operations	Employees	Area (000 m2)
Oppama plant	President, Bluebird, Auster, Stanza, machine tools	7200	1835
Zama plant	Sunny, Langley, Liberta Villa VW, Santana, machining, tooling	6400	852
Murayama plant	Laurel, Skyline, Leopard, March forklifts, machining & tooling	6000	1352
Tochigi plant	Cedric, Gloria, Pulsar, EXA, Langley, Liberta Villa, axles, casting, forging	8100	2992
Kyushu plant	Pickup trucks, Safari, Silvia, Terrano, engines, axles, KD parts	4500	1744
Ogikubo plant	Aerospace equipment	950	131
Mitaka plant	Textile machinery	450	84
Sagamihara parts centre	Automotive parts distribution	900	413
Honmoku Wharf	Shipment of vehicles for export, packing of KD components	500	330

SOURCE, Robertson, 1988.

established as world class manufacturers and the western motor industry was in a position of retreat.

By 1988 Nissan was the world's fourth largest motor manufacturer, behind General Motors, Ford and Toyota. It produces 2.7 million vehicles per annum with a turnover of £19 billion, operates in 21 countries and employs 55,000 people in Japan. It has eleven major domestic affiliates, principally involved in the manufacture of specialist vehicles. The component producers will be covered in the later section on the supplier network. The two affiliates involved in specialist manufacture are Nissan Diesel Motor Co. Ltd. (heavy and medium diesel trucks, buses, industrial and marine diesel engines) and Nissan Shatai Co. Ltd. (passenger cars and commercial vehicles). The latter assembles cars for Nissan including the 300 CX model (Robertson, 1988). The company has seven production plants and two parts and distribution centres (see Table 4.1).

Nissan's reputation in Japan has been of a 'hibernating elephant' (Williamson, 1989). Since 1984, both domestic and export sales have been declining and while the whole of the Japanese motor industry was struggling, largely due to the appreciation of the yen, Nissan was performing worse than average, with extremely poor labour relations (Ishizuna, 1990). Its market share, for example, fell from 20 per cent in 1984 to 17.5 per cent in August, 1988 (Williamson, 1989). With the exception of Honda, Nissan is also more export orientated than its immediate competitors, particularly Toyota. Some 55 per cent of Nissan's production is exported compared to 40 per cent in the case of Toyota. This, in part, explains Nissan's greater imperative to internationalize given the appreciation of the yen and growing trade barriers.

The poor performance of Nissan in the 1980s culminated in 1986 with the company making its first operating loss. As a response to this worsening trading position, the company launched the '88 plan' in 1985, aimed at cutting costs and improving product quality. This plan has been successful, at least insofar as the company has returned to profitability: profits increased 121 per cent in 1988 after an upturn in the Japanese home market produced many domestic sales, and this was assisted by cost cutting and the increasing profitability of overseas plants (Wagstyl, 1989). Productivity increased by 45 per cent in the years 1985-1988, but profits still only remained 60–70 per cent of those in the peak years (Done, 1989D). In 1989, however, there was a significant increase in the volume of vehicles produced, with a 147 per cent increase after three years of decline; exports similarly increased (Economist Intelligence Unit, 1989).

3 NISSAN'S BUYER-SUPPLIER RELATIONSHIPS IN JAPAN

As Chapter 1 illustrated, the Japanese automobile industry has a pyramidal structure with an automobile original equipment manufacturer (OEM) at its apex and various tiers of suppliers. The industry consists of eleven automobile OEMs, about 1400 parts suppliers and 10000 plus subcontractors (Dodwell Marketing Consultants, 1986). The 1400 parts suppliers supply approximately 75 per cent of the parts and sub-assemblies with the remainder – engines, axles, and so on – produced in-house. Five hundred of the parts suppliers are first tier according to the criteria of scale of operation and level of technology and are heavily involved in joint product development.

The development of Nissan's supplier network started in the mid 1950s, when Nissan and the other Japanese automakers were faced with a choice of making components in-house, creating additional subsidiaries or recruiting suppliers from existing firms in other sectors such as the former aircraft industry. The last option, and to a lesser extent the second, proved the least taxing in capital requirements and the quickest to implement (Cusumano, 1985). Moreover, despite fast growth rates and high profitability in the 1950s and early 1960s, the automakers were very wary about investing in vertical integration. Management at Nissan and Toyota realized that there were few benefits to be accrued from vertical integration if suppliers could produce components of equal or better quality than they could in-house.

Nissan and Toyota operated different strategies in supplier development; Toyota relied mainly on creating subsidiaries in specialized factories which were later detached whereas Nissan required assistance from the Industrial Bank to recruit suppliers on an *ad hoc* basis. However, both had a policy of cooperation with suppliers, offering them technical, managerial and even monetary assistance. This policy of nurturing was in part prompted by the general shortage of automobile part makers in the 1950s and 1960s.

Each OEM now has between 150 and 300 suppliers which are comprized of subsidiaries of the OEMs, affiliates, independent suppliers and, occasionally, affiliates of other OEMs. The OEMs form 'Kyoryokukai', or supplier organizations, which meet regularly in order to plan procurement and supply. The majority of suppliers are dedicated to one OEM, 74 per cent in the case of Toyota suppliers and 72 per cent in the case of Nissan, although this is more prevalent in the case of the two largest OEMs than the others. Forty-five firms supply to both Nissan and Toyota; Sumitomo Wiring Systems, for example, supply wire harnesses in varying quantities to Honda, Nissan, Toyota, Isuzu and Mitsubishi (Dodwell Marketing Consultants 1986; Marinaccio and Morris, 1991).

Nissan followed the example of Toyota in setting up a supplier organisation in 1949, which was reconstituted in 1958 as Nissan Takarakai, or the 'treasure association'. It is principally composed of affiliates and now includes 105 companies which primarily supply to Nissan. In 1966 the Shoho Kai, or 'goodwill forum', was formed, comprising of independent companies, most of which supply to other OEMs, notably Toyota (see Figure 4.1). Toyota, by contrast, only has one supplier organization, Kyohakai (Cusumano, 1985; Dodwell Marketing Consultants, 1986).

Dodwell's (1986) identify four types of supply sources in terms of strength of affiliation with OEMs; in-house production, affiliated suppliers, second sources and independents. Closely affiliated suppliers tend to be engaged in key components and parts such as transmissions or electrical/electronic components. Second sources often carry out labour intensive components and parts production, such as wire harnesses. Independents specialize in parts which require large production volumes, such

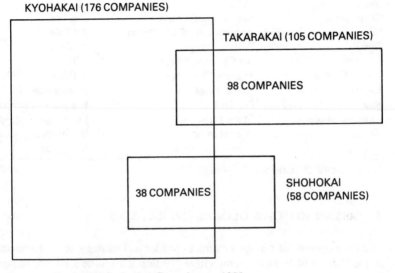

Source: Dodwell Marketing Consultants, 1988

Figure 4.1 Supplier organisations to Toyota and Nissan

as brakes, glass, batteries or tyres. Exemplars in Japan would be firms such as Akebono Brake, NTN Toyo Bearing or NHK Spring.

Three major trends have emerged in the Japanese auto component supply sector in the late 1980s. First, OEMs are encouraging their suppliers to diversify their OEM base in order to achieve greater scale economies. Key Nissan suppliers, for example, typically have a dependence of 90 per cent plus whereas the figures for Toyota are much lower. Secondly, the 'second division' automobile manufacturers such as Mazda and Mitsubishi are moving towards parts sharing and, thirdly, Japanese suppliers are following their OEMs in internationalizing production. Dodwell's, quoting the Japan Auto Parts Industry, estimate that there are some 187 overseas manufacturing affiliates, but this is clearly a gross underestimate as the numbers in North America alone exceed this (Florida & Kenney, 1991; Mair *et al.*, 1988).

Nissan has four in-house parts production plants in Japan, producing engines, axles, transmissions and other key components. Beyond this the immediate supply structure of Nissan Motor includes some 163 companies. The largest of these are shown in Table 4.2.

TABLE 4.2   *Key Suppliers to Nissan Motor*

Name	Product	Status
Ikeda Bussan	Seats	Affiliate
Kanto Seiki	Meters, Plastic Parts	Affiliate
Nihon Radiator(Calsonic)	Radiators, Air Conditioners	Affiliate
Atsugi	Pistons, Pumps	Affiliate
Tsuchiya	Air Cleaners, Filters	Affiliate
Aichi Machine	Engines, Transmissions	Affiliate
Riken	Piston Rings	Independent
Nok	Oil Seals	Independent
Akebond Brake	Brake Parts	Independent
Yazaki	Wire Harness	Independent
Kayaba	Shock Absorbers	Independent

Source: Dodwell Marketing Consultants 1986.

4   NISSAN MOTOR'S GLOBAL OPERATIONS

The development of Nissan's overseas production strategy needs to be set in the context of Nissan's competitive position within the Japanese motor industry, and in particular its position *vis-à-vis* Toyota. For example, three factors predicated Nissan's search for global production; strains on operating profits in the Japanese market, a greater dependence on exports than Toyota and its position trailing Toyota as the second biggest Japanese motor manufacturer.

In 1987 overseas production at Nissan's six major foreign bases was running at approximately 37000 units per annum, compared to the 220000 units in Japan, or under 15 per cent of overall production. The company aims to increase its overseas percentage to 25 per cent by the early 1990s, and the latest plan is to reduce exports from 1.41 million units in 1985 to around one million in 1992, while doubling imports into Japan, including USA and Australian-made Nissans and Volkswagon Passats produced by Nissan. The ratio of exports to locally produced cars overseas is set to fall to 1 to 1 from the present 2 to 1 (Thomson, 1989a).

Nissan's overseas strategy started in 1957 with a production arrangement for knock-down kit manufacture with the Yue Loong Motor Company in Taiwan, and the first overseas production facility started in 1966 with the Nissan Mexicana operation. Two years later the company started production in Australia (NMCA). However, while the company was active in overseas production in the 1960s and 1970s, the major developments have occurred in the 1980s, with the start of production in North America

TABLE 4.3   *Nissan overseas production facilities and output*

	1988	1992 (est.)	Late 1990s
NMMC (USA)	206000	480000	
NMISA (Spain)	76000	160000	200000
NMCA (Australia)	47000	80000	
NMUK (UK)	57000	200000	400000
MNCV (Mexico)	101000	120000	240000

SOURCES: Economist Intelligence Unit, 1989; Robertson, 1988; Williamson 1989; Various Press Releases.

(in 1985) and in the EEC (1983 in Spain and 1986 in the UK).

This internationalization strategy has been a key element in the company's wider recovery strategy and explains why Nissan has been much quicker to internationalize, particularly in Europe, compared to Toyota whose domestic base is far more secure. While the company now has twenty-four overseas plants in 21 countries, the main overseas production facilities are now concentrated in five, the USA (NMMC), Spain (L. M. Iberica), Australia (NMCA), Mexico (NMCV) and, of course, the UK (NMMUK). Of these the first and last have hitherto been the most important (see Table 4.3).

Several trends are observable in the internationalization strategy of Nissan in the 1980s:

(i)   Rapid upward revisions of production targets. In the UK, for example, initial plans to build 100000 cars were revised up to 200000, and the local content level of 60 per cent was achieved in 1988, two years earlier than originally anticipated.

(ii) Global integration strategies. Nissan Mexicana, for example, will export leaf springs, press materials, steering systems and gear boxes for incorporation into Nissan's hard body commercial vehicles built in the US. The Mexico plant will also supply engines, transaxles and windscreens to the US to be assembled into Sentra cars, and E & J type engines to Japan. Similarly Nissan Motor Iberica will export press materials and trim parts to Mexico for the Vanette model. Finally, an aluminium casting plant of Nissan Australia will supply cylinder heads, transmission cases and aluminium wheels to Nissan Japan (Robertson, 1988).

Thus relatively peripheral plants which were originally designed to essentially serve national markets are being upgraded and integrated into global-regional production complexes (Morris, 1991b).

(iii) Joint ventures and strategic alliances. Nissan, in common with other motor manufacturers, have entered into a series of strategic alliances with a variety of other producers. Included are production alliances with Daenoo and Dong-A in South Korea and in Thailand with Siam Motors and Prince Motor. By far the most important alliance, however, is with the Ford Motor Company, which spans North America, the EEC and Australia. In North America the two companies have entered a joint venture at a production facility in Avon Lake, Ohio to produce a minivan or 'people carrier'; in Spain the Barcelona plant of Nissan Motor Iberica with assistance from Nissan's European Technology Centre in the UK will design, develop and build a new four-wheel drive vehicle for sale under both companies' badges in Europe from 1993, and in Australia the two companies will collaborate to produce a medium-sized car (Done, 1989b).

Nissan, therefore, have internationalized alongside the other Japanese motor manufacturers and partly as a response to domestic competition from Toyota (Ishizuna, 1990). This explains their early entry into European production, which is the focus of the next section.

5   NISSAN MOTOR MANUFACTURING UK

In February 1984 Nissan signed an agreement with the British government to build a car factory in the UK, and one month later the choice of a location of Sunderland was made. This followed an intense period of competition between development agencies, county councils and local authorities for the project. Eventually three sites were identified, Deeside, Humberside and Sunderland, all outside traditional UK auto making areas, a conscious policy of the company (Morris, 1987).

Production did not start until mid 1986 and, in the interim, the company chose the Amalgamated Engineering Union to represent employees in the plant. The company also appointed key management and production staff, including supervisors and team leaders, who they then sent to plants in Japan for a rigorous training schedule. The initial investment plan involved £350 million to be spent to build 100 000 Bluebird cars per annum. In late 1987 a second shift was added and the company announced that a further investment of £216 million was to be made, largely to produce a second model, the Micra, by 1992. Total investment will be £610 million, of which Nissan have received £125 million in state aid. Production levels by that date will be 200 000 compared to 29 000 in 1987 (see Table 4.4). This is despite Jones (1989) claim that the moves to planned production levels

TABLE 4.4 *Nissan Motor UK Production Levels*

Years	Units
1987	29 000
1988	55 000
1992	200 000
Mid 1990s	400 000

SOURCE: N.M. UK.

have been slower than in similar transplants in North America, largely due to what he terms 'an unexciting model' which has failed to break into the fleet market. The Bluebird model will, in any case, be replaced. Further expansion is planned at both Nissan's Sunderland and Barcelona operations, and output by the mid 1990s is expected to be 400 000 units per annum at Sunderland, with the addition of a further 1500 workers, and 200 000 at Barcelona.

A key to the planned expansion of output is exports to Western Europe. In September 1988 the Sunderland plant made its first left hand drive cars and began to export to continental Europe. After a series of well publicized trade disputes with the French and Italian governments over the local content percentages in the UK made cars, which the company overcame, it is now set to penetrate overseas markets. The company proposes to export 50 per cent of its production to Western Europe. The expansion at Sunderland has also entailed a move from the assembly of parts imported from Japan to near-full manufacture. Production includes body assembly, paint shop, plastic injection moulding, engine assembly and final assembly. In 1989 they announced an additional investment of £7 million in an aluminium foundry. The company is also reported to be considering producing engine blocks and crankshafts (Done, 1989c). The scale and 'depth' of their investment reflects, in part, the need to meet 80 per cent local content requirements. The addition of these facilities meant that the plant was able to exceed 60 per cent local content (EEC) by 1988 and, by 1991, it will exceed 80 per cent. This increase is also due to a larger number of local (EEC) suppliers being used. In 1990 this number stood at 177, having increased from 67 in 1986 (Done, 1990; Nissan Motor UK, 1988).

At the end of 1988 the company added a research and development centre at Sunderland, undertaking original body and trim design and the development of Nissan vehicles produced in Europe at Sunderland and Barcelona, as well as working closely with British and European suppliers (Done, 1988). Additionally, in late 1989, the company announced a further research and development centre at Cranfield in the south east of England.

Employment levels stood at 1500 in 1988 and have risen to 3500 in 1990. The recruitment process that the company undertook was extensive and a testimony to the company's commitment to quality which is consistent with other Japanese auto transplants (Morris, 1989a). The original recruitment drive brought 25000 requests for application forms for only 470 jobs. After filling in a six page application form, at least six hours was spent selecting, testing and interviewing each applicant. A series of tests were employed, including numeracy, written and mechanical aptitude tests. This was followed by a practical test, a general discussion and interviews by Nissan supervisors.

The company places a heavy emphasis on training. In 1988, for example, some four hundred specific training courses were available varying from one day to one week. Basic training for operators lasts one month and for multiskilled maintenance technicians, four years. In one area alone, the final assembly shop, 30 000 man hours were devoted to training in 1988. In the early stages of the plant's development a number of team leaders, supervisors, controllers and engineers were sent to Japan for training for periods of between two and fifteen weeks; by 1988 some two hundred and fifty workers had undergone this training.

The Nissan approach to work and production is most succinctly expressed in the well-read, and often quoted, book by Peter Wickens, personnel manager at Sunderland, *The Road to Nissan* (1987). Indeed Wickens leaves no doubts as to the key ingredients of the culture with his subtitle 'flexibility, quality and teamwork'. Wickens identifies four key problems of work and production organization in the British motor industry (and British manufacturing generally), including employee relations; poor quality; demarcation and hence a lack of flexibility; and the quality of management.

In order to address these problems and avoid replicating them at the Sunderland plant, Wickens identifies a number of key approaches. First, is the 'them and us' adversarial approach to employee relations which Nissan are attempting to change to 'just us'. Four practices have been introduced which attempt to address this problem; open and frank communications within the company; single status; equal opportunity of promotion; complete flexibility of production. The second issue is of flexibility. Nissan management identified this as crucial to the successful operation of the plant. Included in the flexibility package are a minimum of gradings. There are, for example, only three grades of manual staff including manufacturing staff and technicians. Responsibility for quality is placed with operators and manual workers carrying out simple routine maintenance work. If an operator is unable to rectify the problem, the multiskilled craftsman comes to their assistance. Wickens argues that kaizen, or continuous improvement, adds real flexibility as it involves a commitment to continuous changes in technology, not merely a one-off set of changes.

Flexibility also works in other ways and extends notions of group loyalty and single status. It is not confined to manual workers but to white collar workers who, for example, may be asked to help on line functions if there are shortages. It also extends to numerical flexibility. A recurrent problem in the British motor industry is the early summer 'bulge' in production in order to meet the surge in demand in August associated with the registration change. Traditionally, British automakers have responded by increasing overtime and building up stocks. Nissan's solution to this problem, claimed to be virtually unique in the motor industry, has been to employ temporary workers. The emphasis on quality is maintained by giving these workers one month of training before they spend three months working on the production line.

Quality is the next key area, in Wicken's words 'above all', with a necessary commitment from everyone in the workforce. Three elements are crucial to the development of total quality control at Nissan. First, through the Kaizen meeting, secondly through the role of the supervisor and team working, and, finally, through the training programme in which the greatest emphasis is placed upon quality. However, Wickens argues for a committed and holistic approach to attaining quality standards, in noting that,

> You cannot achieve quality by sending people on courses and most of all you cannot mouth platitudes and then do everything to demonstrate that you don't mean what you say. (p. 63)

Included in this quality programme are quality circles, which are a natural way of extending the way that the teams normally work and do not need an external bureaucratic structure.

Teamwork is also a cornerstone of the Nissan strategy: 'Teamwork and commitment permeate every aspect of the Nissan approach'. (p. 75) However, the teamwork and commitment are contingent upon common terms and conditions of employment and flexibility. Nissan's approach is to recognize the role of individuals but to stress that individual contributions are best harnessed through teamworking. This is reflected in the Nissan-Amalgamated Engineering Union (AEU) agreement. Lessons learnt from Nissan in Japan and the Nissan plant at Smyrna Tennessee illustrated to Nissan's UK management that the five minute meeting at the start of each day was crucial and also borrowed and developed the concept of the 'Kaizen workshop' from the NUUMI (Toyota-General Motors) plant in California.

Nissan, Wickens argues, had little choice but to accept unionization at the Sunderland plant and, indeed, were not fundamentally opposed to doing so. As such they accepted a single union agreement with the AEU. The union is one of three key actors on the Company Council, the others being the company and the employees. The Company Council acts as a consultative forum, it is part of the in-house grievance system and is responsible for negotiating salaries and conditions.

Wickens' analysis of the role of the union at Sunderland is, however, at best extremely selective. It ignores, for example, the wider view of unions in the Nissan Motor Company. The US plant at Smyrna, Tennessee, for example, is cited throughout the book as a role model and yet little mention is made of it in this chapter, and no explanation given as to why Nissan placed a non-union plant in an anti-union 'right to work' state. Moreover, no mention is made of the efforts in the early 1950s by the company to break the democratically majority elected union in Japan and replace it with a company union (Cusumano, 1985; Halberstam, 1987). Finally, if the Nissan-AEU agreement is so good, why are unionization rates at the plant so low? Could it be because the company rooted out possible union activists in its exhaustive recruitment process, or is it because the agreement is so weak from a union perspective that employees see little to gain from joining?

The union agreement has not been the only area of criticism of Wicken's book or the wider developments at the Nissan plant. Early academic criticism came from The Centre for Alternative Industrial Strategy at the Polytechnic of Central London (CAITS, 1986) and Crowther & Garrahan (1988). In later reflections on the plant both of these groups have tempered their criticisms somewhat. In Garrahan's latest work with Stewart (1989), for example, based on interviews with line workers at Nissan they argue that,

> While workers talked of the line tempo and sheer physical character of the plant as intimidating, they also often felt that work at Nissan was preferable to other forms of mass production experiences.   (p. 1)

They go on to argue that,

> Where they (Nissan line workers) show positive feelings these were inspired by the way they did their work, that is by the work culture at Nissan, including the 'togetherness' features of team working'.   (p. 2)

The interview material they present, however, contradicts this tone, with descriptions of team meetings where line workers who had made mistakes were shouted at, quality circles acting as a one-way communications process where line workers were told what to do, team working being seen by line workers as a basis of survival, and a general picture of work intensification and management by stress. Despite high unemployment rates in the surrounding locality Garrahan and Stewart claim turnover rates of up to 20 per cent at the Sunderland plant and Williamson (1989) ascribes the high injury rates to this intensified work pressure.

Management at the Nissan plant at Sunderland are clearly attempting to introduce what Womak *et al.* (1990) would call 'lean production' or what Oliver and Wilkinson (1988) term 'Japanization'. Included would be notions of total quality management and just-in-time production, and hence a flexible workforce. A key contribution to such a strategy is the introduction of a new form of supplier relations, which are analysed in the next section.

6 BUYER-SUPPLIER RELATIONS AT NISSAN MOTOR UK: NMUK's POLICY

As we have seen, in 1988 Nissan's local content stood above 69 per cent which will increase to over 80 per cent as on-site manufacturing functions are increased and the company makes greater use of local suppliers. These figures need qualification, however, on two major counts. First, where is local and secondly, how is local content measured? The 'local' in this context equates with the EEC and therefore includes continental suppliers. Early Nissan suppliers, for example, included the West German firms Blaupunkt (car radios) and Bosch (wiper arms and blades). Giving evidence to the Select Committee, Nissan representatives noted that the British components industry was extremely uncompetitive in a number of areas including stampings, metal assemblies, wiring components and injection mouldings (Trade and Industry Committee, 1987).

The second issue of what constitutes local content has proved far more contentious. Nissan's method of calculation, agreed with the British Government but which has caused problems with the French and Italian governments, is on value. Two variables are included, the ex-works sales price of the vehicle and the total import bill for non EEC source material, including freight, and the difference between the two is the EEC content.

In 1990 the company had 177 suppliers with production units in the EEC. By full production the company aimed to spend £450 million per annum on components in the EEC, but in 1990 this was revised upwards to £600 million by 1992 (Done, 1990). Key terms are the need for a 'rationalized supply base', compared to the profusion of suppliers which has been typical of the British motor industry, a 'nucleus of suppliers' with whom Nissan will have a long term relationship with and who will receive a growing amount of business as car volumes expand. Nissan will achieve this through a single sourcing policy for components, with very few exceptions such as tyres, and through dealing with a relatively small number of key tier one suppliers.

While the EEC is the spatial definition of local content, 72 per cent of the value of local content is purchased in the UK; the UK has 120 of the 177 EEC suppliers (de Jonquieres, 1989). Within the UK the West Midlands is the prime source of component suppliers, by value, although component suppliers are located throughout the UK (see Table 4.5). Significant component supplies are still imported from Japan, including gearboxes and engines. There are no plans to transfer gearbox manufacture to the UK, since Nissan estimate that volume will have to increase to 600 000 units before it is economic to do so; engine assembly is, however, being moved, even although the basic castings will still be imported.

Given a long term commitment to suppliers, and the policy of single sourcing, supplier choice is made according to a number of strict criteria. A technical and financial assessment is first made and if the supplier is credible Nissan investigates the engineering and quality capabilities of the firm. The supplier must also portray the necessary 'soft' skills, including its 'attitude'. In reply to a question about supplier efficiency, Ian Gibson of Nissan summarizes the company's attitude:

> Our concern is perhaps slightly different from the usual one. Clearly we are concerned about external quality indicators such as repair rates, failure rates and cost to us. Those are important considerations. But we are at least as concerned about the insides of their businesses, that is, about their production systems, their production reliability, their in-house quality problems as well as their quality problems to us, if any. We are concerned about their internal productivity measures, their internal productivity investment plans, their internal labour relationships. In many ways we are at least as concerned about their business as a business as we are about ours. When I talked about efficiency, I was really including all those indicators. People should look at world-wide productivity improvement rates of 9–10 per cent per annum, because this is what happens elsewhere. They should look at failure rates of parts per million, not parts per thousand. As long as they see those targets and

they are going that way, that is fine.   (Gibson, in Trade and Industry
Committee, 1987, p. 80)

Ian Gibson has also made clear Nissan's strict policy on pricing, urging
them to adopt 'negative pricing' by increases in productivity (Gibson, in
Garnett, 1987). This is part of Nissan's policy of bringing down price
margins and achieving productivity improvements in suppliers. Nissan are
seeking productivity improvements of double figures by suppliers each
year. The company thus avoids suppliers with poor industrial relations
records. Clearly, with reduced inventories and just-in-time supply, Nissan
are extremely dependent on suppliers and any disruption due to industrial
relations conflicts at supplier plants would upset production considerably.

The company sees its supplier development policy as a long term
strategy. As its representatives point out, Nissan in Japan took fifty years
to develop its supplier base. An imperative is that suppliers are efficient and
a considerable emphasis is placed upon collaboration, which is both time-
consuming and costly. This function is undertaken by Nissan's Supplier
Development Team, including two Japan-trained engineers. Its remit is to
work with suppliers while having no internal responsibilities. Its objective
is to improve suppliers' productivity and quality and to pass on Japanese
ideas. One example would be in the beneficial effect of the SPC programme
which Nissan has introduced to its suppliers. The company maintains that
UK suppliers are as efficient as their West German suppliers and operate
under the same quality standards.

The technical and financial assessment is adjusted from firm to firm but
generally takes several weeks and meetings (up to six). Suppliers are also
encouraged to pass on Nissan 'best practice' to their suppliers. Nissan
attempts to enter into close collaboration with its suppliers, involving
them in regular meetings. During the selection and development period
and design period and trial builds engineers and buyers spend several
days per week with suppliers. Similarly, quality control staff spend a
considerable time monitoring quality and delivery in the first six months.
Once confidence has been built up the company withdraws from close
monitoring. At this stage Nissan accepts quality assured supplies and prime
responsibility for design and development of the part is transferred to the
supplier.

The company have a declared policy of close technical collaboration
with their suppliers. While the majority of 'pure' research and development
will remain in Japan, the company has located a Nissan Technical Centre
at Sunderland which is concerned with design and development, with particular reference to building-in components. Suppliers will work closely

TABLE 4.5   *EEC based suppliers to Nissan*

Company	Location	Components
ASC (UK) Ltd	Carlisle	Seat belts
Avon Rubber PLC	Trowbridge, Wilts.	Radiator hoses
BSG International (British)	Chichester	Door mirrors
J.Burns-Glynwed Engineering Ltd	Romford, Essex	Rear parcel tray, spare wheel covers
Corrello	Birmingham	Lighting
J. Cotton (Colne) Ltd	Colne, Lancs.	Roof insulation
Continental Tyre	Spennymoor, Co. Durham	Tyres
Delanair (Valeo)	Hengoed, Mid Glamorgan	Screen washing systems
DFN Engineering	Darlington	Ball stud
Elta Plastics	Stockton	Plastic trim
Firth Furnishings Ltd	Heckmondwike, W. Yorks.	Carpets
Fulton (TI) Ltd	Telford	Brake/clutch pipes
George Angus	Walsall	
Griflex Creators Ltd	Woking, Surrey	Windshield mouldings
Hardy Spicer	Birmingham	Welding joints
Hertfordshire BTR Ltd	Dunstable	Weather strips
Jonas Woodhead	Newton Aycliffe	Springs
Ikeda Hoover Ltd	Washington	Seats, door finishes, headliners
W. Lander & Sons Ltd	Birmingham	Battery rods
Linpac Mouldings Group	Southend	Front and rear bumpers, instrument panel, plastic injection mouldings
Llanelli Radiators (Calsonic)	Llanelli, Shildon, Co. Durham	Cooling System, Vehicle heat systems
Lucas Electrical Ltd	Birmingham	Engine management systems
Lucas-Yuasa Batteries	Birmingham	Batteries, ignition

TABLE 4.5   *(cont.)*

Company	Location	Components
Lucas Electrical	Burnley	Switchgear
Lucas Braking System	Pontypool	Brake hoses
Magneti Morelli	Birmingham	Alternators
Melton Modes Ltd	Bolton	Centre ventair duct, Engine air duct
Morgan Soft Trim Ltd	Halesowen, W. Mids.	Sunvisors
Nissan Yamato Engineering	Washington	Pressings
Pianoforte Supplies Ltd	Warwick	Bodyside mouldings
Pilkington Brothers PLC (Triplex)	Kings Norton, W. Mids.	Glass
PPG	Birmingham	Paint
The Primographic Co Ltd	Abergavenny, Gwent	Vin plate and asbestos warning labels
PSM Fasteners	Walsall	Specialist nuts, bolts and screws
Reydel Ltd	Northampton	Gaiter
Schlegel (UK) Ltd	Coalville, Leics.	Boot seal
Shellard Clifford	Birmingham	Wheels
S.P. Tyres UK Ltd	Washington	Tyres
Stadium	Hartlepool	Dash trim
Supra Chemicals & Paints Ltd	Warley, W. Mids.	Insulators
Tallent Engineering	Newton Aycliffe	Transverse linx
T.I. Nihon	Washington	Exhaust systems
Valdbim	Blyth	Cast engine brackets
Williamot Industrial Mouldings Ltd	London	Reservoir tanks and heater ducts
TRW CAM Gears	Bristol	Steering systems

SOURCE   NMUK, 1988; Peck, 1988; Turnbull, 1989; Authors' Survey.

with this centre, but will be responsible for design, development and quality. The rationale of such a policy for Nissan is that suppliers are best placed to develop products, a view which contrasts with traditional practice in the UK motor industry where the motor manufacturer drew up all of the specifications without consulting suppliers. The implication for suppliers, however, is that they will require a substantial R & D capacity and commitment. The influence of Nissan pervades supplier companies and even extends to their suppliers. In the case of its seat manufacturer, for example, Nissan influences fabric sourcing.

The initiative for choosing suppliers stems largely from Nissan, although a large number have contacted the company seeking business. Unlike others of the large case study companies, notably IBM, Nissan have no policy concerning over-dependence. The company maintains that suppliers should be competitive and only uses significant firms, that is firms with extensive track records of supply.

Nissan has five EEC-based, Japanese-owned suppliers plus eight joint ventures and 25 EEC suppliers with technical agreements with Japanese suppliers (Done, 1990). While a number of Japanese companies act as suppliers to Nissan, Nissan representatives have stated on a number of occasions their policy of not encouraging their suppliers in Japan to transfer production from Japan to the UK (see, for example Gibson, Trade & Industry Committee, 1987; Goto, 1989). However, given the strong ties between the company and its key suppliers in Japan, it would be difficult for the company to ignore the request of these key suppliers. Indeed, since Gibson's claim to the Select Committee, Calsonic (formerly Nihon Radiator) acquired Llanelli Radiators for £15 million and Marley of the UK has joined a joint venture with Kanto Seiki at Washington. Llanelli Radiators plant is merely seen as the foundation for Calsonic's expansion plans in Europe (Done, 1989a). Moreover, Nippondensu another major Japanaese component producer have taken over IMI's UK's radiator division. Moreover, Robertson (1988), working on information supplied to him by the company, claims that:

> In order to maintain its quality standards and to achieve 'just-in-time' sourcing while meeting overseas requirements on local content, Nissan has encouraged many of its parts affiliates to set up component feeder plants in the vicinity of its major foreign plants.   (p. 35)

In North America, where there are 12 Japanese production plants, some 240 Japanese owned suppliers have followed the final assemblers (Florida and Kenney, 1990) and fifty of the 120 Nissan suppliers in Tennessee, for example, are Japanese (de Jonquieres, 1989). With Honda and Toyota adding production facilities in the UK, the number is likely to increase rapidly here. NMUK, however, claims no interest in taking equity shares in UK suppliers as they have in Japan. They have also been at pains to point out there is little pressure upon suppliers to locate plants close to the Sunderland site. However, the new greenfield suppliers have all located close to the Sunderland plant, Nissan Yamato, TI Nihon, Ikeda Hoover, as have a Japanese supplier to these suppliers, the Mitsui-William King joint venture, and the imperatives of the just-in-time supply system are likely to result in suppliers locating or relocating plants in the north. Calsonic, for example, have announced a new plant in Shildon, County Durham and a number of suppliers have indicated that if delivery times are made more frequent they will be forced to transfer some of their production, possibly a final assembly operation, close to Nissan. Nissan, unlike Austin Rover, have indicated that they will not tolerate warehousing of supplies close to Sunderland, as they regard this as pushing inventory costs down the chain and not as a real saving.

A fairly complex document from NMUK outlining Nissan's requirements for suppliers, indicates the progressive move to 'just-in-time' deliveries over three stages:

STAGE 1:   During the first stage of vendor supply, Nissan will obtain experience of the vendors' capability to meet delivery due dates and quantities. Deliveries will have a maximum frequency of once per day, although generally there will be a delivery pattern of once or twice a week. Vendors will also become familiar with the use of Nissan Advice Notes to ensure prompt processing of material receipt.

STAGE II: The second stage will be to maintain vendor reliability of delivery and to increase the delivery frequency, where applicable, to more than once per day, for specified quantities at agreed times.

STAGE III: The third stage will be to expand the number of parts controlled synchronously. The implication of synchronized delivery is that small quantities of parts are delivered directly to the lineside thus avoiding the need to hold other than lineside stock. It also enables Nissan to operate exclusively with lineside stock. This method, however, requires that suppliers be absolutely reliable.   (Nissan Motor UK, n/d)

The just-in-time production system is in operation within the Sunderland plant and the company is extending this system to suppliers. T. I. Nihon (exhaust systems), Nissan Yamato Engineering (pressings) and Ikeda Hoover (seats) are all on-site and supply just-in-time, as does S. P. Tyres which is located in nearby Washington. Nissan regard just-in-time supplying as daily delivery, multiple deliveries per day are termed 'synchronized delivery'. They claim that the daily delivery policy has worked well and all targets have been met.

Nissan's buyer-supplier policy represents a significant change from traditional relationships in the UK motor industry. Many of these changes, of course, have major implications for its suppliers, which is the focus of the next section.

7   NISSAN UK'S BUYER-SUPPLIER RELATIONS: THE SUPPLIER'S PERSPECTIVE

Nissan's UK supply base, as the last section illustrated, comprises about 120 suppliers. Our research included interviews with eleven of these suppliers with the aim of gaining some understanding as to the ways in which the new buyer-supplier relations impacted upon the supplier as opposed to the buyer. The sample included a cross section of firms, ranging from companies employing a few hundred people to multinationals. It also included US owned, UK owned and Japanese owned firms and firms producing products as varied as labels and engine management systems. In addition, a separate interview also took place with British Steel Corporation.[1]

An initial observation as regards the structure of Nissan's supplier network is that it is numerically relatively small: the 150 to 200 compares with 1000 plus in the case of Rover and around 840 at Jaguar. This is a function of the single sourcing policy at Nissan on all but a few components. The suppliers are divided into a number of categories. The first distinction is between suppliers and subcontractors, with the former offering research and development input into component development. A second is between 'suppliers' and 'developer source suppliers'. There are a number of distinctive characteristics of the developer source suppliers. They tend to be the larger firms who are responsible for providing 'systems' for Nissan which are essentially generic units. These larger firms act as the first tier of Nissan suppliers and assemble components of other suppliers. While Nissan maintain control over the second tier, the first tier are responsible for

---

[1] This interview took place under a separate project with Dr Paul Blyton, but nevertheless offered some insights into the quality and delivery implications for BSC.

checking quality and price of component supply. This represents an attempt by Nissan to pass the responsibility of producing automobile sub assemblies onto the first tier suppliers. Typical key sub assemblies would be braking systems and steering systems.

Apart from their size, key tier one suppliers are also characterized by having a substantial research and development capacity. This represents a move towards passing responsibilities for design and long term development of key components or systems from Nissan, and other large automobile producers, onto their major suppliers, or at least sharing the development of systems and components. The twin rationales are key specialisms and cost reduction. The large suppliers are seen as having the key specialisms and product development capabilities and are therefore better equipped to design the car producers. Moreover, with increasingly sophisticated, and therefore expensive systems, key suppliers can spread development costs over work for a number of OEMs.

As an extension to this idea, Nissan are choosing certain suppliers not only on European basis, but on a worldwide scale. This further reduces costs overall, enables large components producers to invest heavily in R & D and leads to reductions in lead-times between model design and production. Thus R & D capacity is seen as crucial for the future development of large component firms and explains why firms are divesting themselves of peripheral activities in which they cannot hope to compete technologically and also why there is a concentration of activities of the European component producers (see Lamming 1989).

This 'tiering' policy of Nissan implies that the company is attempting to partly replicate the pyramidal structure that is typical in Japan. As such they are the first motor company in the UK, and indeed probably in western Europe, to do so. Indeed, Nissan's place in the 'hierarchy' of best practice OEMs in the UK is described in a quote from Turnbull's (1989) study of the West Midlands automobile component sector, in that,

> The picture of a spectrum in the UK market with Ford (and now Nissan) at one end and the Rover Group at the other obviously merits further investigation. (p. 27)

Indeed, in our study, favourable comparisons were often made between the Nissan and Ford approaches and sometimes unfavourably to Austin Rover. A number of the firms who supplied to both Nissan and Ford had seen Nissan adopting many of the best practices of Ford and extending them, which is unsurprizing given that a number of top managers at Nissan were formerly Ford employees.

In the new model of buyer-supplier relations emanating from Nissan and other Japanese automobile companies, three ingredients are crucial; price, quality and delivery. This relegates the price component, which was central in adversarial contracting, and would suggest that quality and delivery are as important. While this is true, it should not be read that price is no longer at the centre of negotiations between OEMs and suppliers. Indeed, the responses from suppliers suggested that this remains a major area of contention between the two sides. What has changed, however, is the context in which prices are decided. Under the 'quote' system, suppliers were asked to tender for individual and sometimes short contracts and price was viewed merely as a 'bottom line' in the negotiation procedure. In the new model price is viewed in the wider context of gaining productive efficiencies for the system, which is reflected in the whole attitude of Nissan towards their suppliers and their production organization. Nissan not only calls for curtailment of prices, and sometimes 'negative pricing', but in some cases offers advice on which way firms may gain greater efficiencies, which will be discussed later.

Nissan's pricing policy, according to their suppliers, is largely achieved through price targets based on historical data. The price is expected to fall due to supplier firms gaining technical advantages and to the learning curve effect of supplying to Nissan. Several of the suppliers felt that this was the main arena of confrontation with Nissan. The historical data that Nissan draw from incorporates benchmark comparisons with major Japanese suppliers, and some of the smaller firms felt that this was invidious given that their Japanese counterparts were often much larger and were producing much greater volumes, and were, therefore, able to achieve far greater economies of scale through automation, with consequent reduction in prices.

The suppliers coped with this situation in different ways, some, for example, passed on price margin reductions to their suppliers. Others were still holding out in negotiations with Nissan, arguing that as a result of the new system dependencies were working both ways. That is, that Nissan were now extremely dependent upon them given their specialisms, the single sourcing policy and the effort that Nissan would have to undergo to develop another supplier. One argued: 'Five years ago it was a buyer's market now we have the upper hand'. Nissan's argument, according to the suppliers, was that they could achieve greater production efficiencies through the collaboration with Nissan. One supplier contrasted the meticulous effort of Nissan's (and Komatsu's) engineers and purchasing staff in breaking down the cost of components piece by piece. These efficiencies would result in greater profits for suppliers as they could pass on these efficiencies to component supply for other automobile manufacturers. One supplier even suggested that Ford, who they argued did not 'squeeze' them on price as Nissan did, were effectively cross-subsidizing Nissan.

Given the problems, however, with price negotiations, particularly among smaller suppliers, the question that arises is why certain suppliers still work for Nissan. A number of reasons explain why firms were still keen to maintain business with Nissan. First, and most important, the quality advantages that suppliers gained from Nissan contracts outweighed the problems with pricing. Even the most vociferous critics of the pricing policy saw the collaboration with Nissan as beneficial. Second, although the percentage of business that most of these firms did for Nissan, especially among larger suppliers, was relatively small, the contracts were seen as 'strategic' for a number of reasons. They were seen as strategic in the context of Nissan UK, in that the amount of business could increase rapidly as production at Sunderland rose. They were also seen as strategic in relation to Nissan's global operation, since the arrival of Nissan was perceived (correctly, as subsequent events have shown) as the first of a number of Japanese auto investments in the EEC. Finally it was of strategic importance because it conferred a cachet to these companies; Nissan joined firms such as Ford and IBM as firms to be seen to be supplying to. An attitude pervaded that if a firm was good enough to be a key supplier to Nissan then, due to the stringency of their procedures and processes, other business would follow.

The second key ingredient is the issue of quality. The suppliers were unequivocal in their praise for the Nissan quality systems and the advantages that having to work with, and adapt to, such a system had given to their own operation. The majority of firms were already committed to total quality control; this was one of the criteria upon which Nissan chose suppliers initially and a number of firms were already supplying to 'blue chip' companies such as Ford, Sony or IBM, which have their own stringent quality checks. Indeed, this was an explicit strategy of a number of the suppliers, to concentrate on products in which they had a distinctive advantage and/or to concentrate on supplying to selected companies which they regarded as blue chip. Therefore, some of the suppliers had reduced their product ranges dramatically while others had reduced the number of companies which they supplied to. One supplier to Nissan, for example, had reduced its product range from 300 to 80, deleting low value added products and concentrating upon those components and assemblies in which it had a specific comparative advantage, usually technical. It was also adding a research and development capability to reinforce this advantage. In the case of smaller companies this usually meant just stopping production of certain lines, while larger companies have been selling off whole business units and production facilities.

Despite quality-related checks already being in place, such as conforming to Ford's Q101 standard, the Nissan requirements were far more stringent with a totally new set of demands. Suppliers phrased this approach in different ways, including 'total requirements', the 'total business environment' and 'quality of service'. One firm, which had already undergone the Q101, had to totally reorganize and extend their quality controls. Nissan's demands, over and above Ford's, include:

— written instructions for operators to follow on each process.
— factory layout and conditions.
— the creation of 'clean areas' where appropriate.
— the development of a 'counter measure system', whereby if there is a fault in the process it is noted as are the counter measures used to improve it.

Nissan were pushing firms towards zero defects and providing quality assured supplies which, for Nissan, negated the inspection of incoming components. While most of the firms inspected components leaving their factories for Nissan, many had achieved significant reductions in defect rates. One for example had reduced scrap rates from 6 per cent to 0.8 per cent in two years, while another had defects at a rate of 0.1 per cent.

The methods that Nissan used to improve the quality standards of suppliers included both 'stick and carrot'. For every job that some of the suppliers carried out for Nissan, Nissan would send down big teams of engineering and purchasing staff, especially in the quality resource area. The company requires weekly reports on component parts, has long meetings with suppliers and the suppliers are checked 'frequently and randomly' and are graded according to their quality with marks out of a possible ten. Nissan also assisted suppliers with advice on how to implement total quality control and to pass on their own methods.

The suppliers, in turn, had used a variety of approaches to achieving quality. One 'soft', rather intangible but nevertheless important method, was by the induction of workers into an attitude that quality was crucial, through education and awareness programmes. Responsibility for quality is placed with workers including those on the shopfloor. As one respondent stated: 'Every operator becomes an inspector'. The majority of firms had also trained operators in SPC techniques on an ongoing basis.

The overall impression was that the suppliers, who were already aware of quality and implementing total quality control programmes, had benefitted considerably from dealing with Nissan. 'Nissan taught us an immense amount about quality which we thought we already knew', was a typical comment.

Apart from upgrading their methods of quality control, the Nissan collaboration had two further major impacts upon suppliers, particularly among the smaller suppliers. In some cases firms totally reassessed not only their quality control but their whole production system. One supplier, for example, a relatively large US owned organization, had reorganized its factory layout, introduced a just-in-time production system, a 'harmonization' programme to include single status, and a reduction in job grades from 28 to 7, and titles from 102 to 30. A number of other suppliers were introducing more flexible workforces with multiskilling and an increasing use of temporary workers.

The second impact was that many suppliers were in turn trying to pass on new production methods to their own suppliers, with varying degrees of success. One supplier was actually reducing its outsourcing due to poor quality from its sub-contractors, and while it was attempting to introduce preferred suppliers was finding it difficult because they did not have enough suppliers of sufficient status to merit the title. Nevertheless a number of suppliers were introducing zero defect programmes with subcontractors and asking them to introduce SPC.

Unlike the IBM case, suppliers were largely free to choose their own sub contractors. One exception was a Japanese owned supplier who had initially been required to use Japan-based sub contractors. The whole just-in-time system, of course, depends upon suppliers being able to exert some form of pressure upon their own suppliers. The problems which arise, however, were illustrated in the case of one supplier which had to deal with Nissan on the one hand and the British Steel Corporation on the other, and which was being 'squeezed' between the two.

In this case, therefore, and in others throughout the four case studies, it is arguable that the implications for suppliers is that just-in-time supply effectively means pushing inventory from the OEM to suppliers. This is not confined to small suppliers. In an interview with representatives from B.S.C., for example, it became apparent that while they had managed to reduce inventories, the nature of the steel producing process made just-in-time supply to motor manufacturers an impossibility, which resulted in B.S.C. holding stock as 'finished' product.

The third key ingredient of the Japanese model is delivery. True just-in-time delivery, that is, multiple small deliveries per day, has significant implications for all suppliers at a variety of levels including logistics and production planning. To date Nissan are not operating such a just-in-time delivery system for suppliers. Only a few suppliers, who are on site or located close by, operate a multiple deliveries per day system which Nissan term a 'line supply basis'. (They refer to just-in-time as daily delivery.) Of the sample firms, only the three Japanese owned suppliers on site at Sunderland were supplying multiple deliveries per day. Ikeda Hoover, for example, produce car seats and other parts for Nissan. Nissan change their products continually in terms of car style, colour and so on, in order to be sensitive to final customer demand and, therefore, Ikeda Hoover have to be similarly sensitive. They are linked by a computer to Nissan which informs them what type the next twelve cars going down the production line will be in terms of the type of seat, material cover and so on. Ikeda Hoover work to four hours notice of what is necessary, termed a 'four hour window'. The maximum stock holding of Nissan is between six to twelve seats. In order to plan production, Nissan gives Ikeda Hoover four month output targets, which are reassessed at intervals of two months, one month and one week.

A similar situation exists at Nissan Yamato Engineering which produces small body pressings for Nissan. They supply Nissan with multiple deliveries per day, at an eventual rate of forty eight deliveries per day. Few other suppliers operate such a system. Nevertheless the frequency of deliveries from suppliers to Nissan is far greater than it would have been to any other UK motor manufacturer ten years ago and imposes considerable strains upon suppliers both in logistics and materials planning. At the time of interview most of the suppliers were delivering to Sunderland two or three times per week, although there were examples of daily delivery. Under such a supply regime it is still feasible to supply from existing plants in the West Midlands or the South of England. However, some of the suppliers who were located at long distances from the Sunderland plant – in South Wales for example – were already encountering problems with delivery, and suppliers in the West Midlands were forecasting that if deliveries became more frequent, with increasing output at Sunderland, then they too would face difficulties.

For the suppliers, two ways of coping with this problem are available. The first is to build or rent warehouses near to final assembly plants and pull off stock when required. Indeed Austin Rover have created warehouses next to their two main assembly plants at Cowley (Oxford) and Longbridge (Birmingham) in which they lease space to suppliers, as have a number of continental automakers. Nissan and some of their suppliers, however, are opposed to such an approach as it merely pushes inventory costs from buyer to supplier and creates inefficiencies in the system. Instead, a second solution is for the suppliers to build small final assembly operations close to the OEM's final assembly plant. Llanelli Radiators (Calsonic), one of the UK suppliers furthest removed from the Sunderland plant, have already announced such a unit to be located at Shildon, County Durham. Similarly, one of the US owned suppliers to Nissan has such an arrangement with Chrysler in the USA. These satellite plants are basically very small, but the key to their success is skilled assembly labour and good production planning systems. It is likely, therefore, that there will be some concentration of suppliers around Japanese automakers plants in the UK, but that they will be either dedicated to the plant, be low capital intensive plants (such as seat manufacture) or will be small satellite operations which final assemble production supplied from other UK plants. Indeed, even where plants are dedicated to supply Nissan, including the Nissan owned joint ventures, they are being encouraged by Nissan to diversify production to serve other OEMs in order to achieve economies of scale.

Nissan's solution to bad delivery schedules has been to take over delivery on an 'ex works' basis; that is, Nissan will employ a transport firm to collect parts. At the time of our interviews they had started such a practice with suppliers with poor delivery records, but several of the respondents felt that they would extend this practice at a later date to all suppliers. Nissan are not unique in this, as Toyota are reported to be considering a similar proposal for their Burnaston (UK) plant.

In terms of 'long term' contracts, this phrase was something of a misnomer. In a strict legal sense firms had more security in the adversarial system with its short contracts. No 'contract' as such exists between Nissan and its suppliers, rather the 'long term' is an attitude. One supplier (non-Japanese) described this a 'family philosophy' with suppliers. Another described the relationship as, 'we can all be better if we work jointly and look at the long term'. Contracts were seen as long term and open ended, a view supported by the amount of time and effort that Nissan had spent in developing these firms as single source suppliers and that, unless there were unusual circumstances, it would be unlikely that Nissan would look to an alternative supplier.

The new long term single source relationship offers a number of paradoxes. First, it might be expected that it could lead to complacency and lack of effort on the part of suppliers given that they are the only firms supplying that particular component and that the 'contract' is long term. This was clearly not the case, however, partly because of Nissan's ongoing vetting and performance appraisal schemes but also because these suppliers are a small group of elite 'excellent' companies who are caught up in the ethos of the new Japanese management systems. The second paradox is that the issue of dependency is reversed, now Nissan and other such large companies are extremely dependent on their single sources of supply.

With Nissan single-sourcing the vast majority of components, sub-assemblies and parts, a long term collaborative relationship would tend to occur regardless of any policy decision. However, there has been such a decision and the supplier firms all felt part of a collaborative partnership based on trust. This collaboration was generally viewed positively, and manifested itself in a variety of forms. Technical and technological collaboration, for example, existed between Nissan and suppliers. Nissan carry out initial vehicle design, load specifications etc and the supplier designs its component into the system. This allows the suppliers greater autonomy (indeed, it distinguishes suppliers from sub-contractors); but it also requires the suppliers to make considerable investment in R & D capacity, something which some of the smaller companies were doing for the first time. The supplier, in particular, is able to integrate design and manufacture, which gives them new insights and also permits simultaneous engineering, thereby shortening lead times and making savings on costs. The development of such capacity among smaller suppliers also enabled them to carry out prototype work, which in turn helps them gain new customers.

The shift of R & D work from OEM to supplier has two major further implications; first, R & D capacity is an increasingly important consideration in the selection of suppliers. Secondly, in both North America and Western Europe, a number of new relatively small companies are emerging which are dedicated to the new ethos of buyer-supplier relations and one of the characteristics of these firms is that they are technology and design driven. Exemplars from the UK would be firms such as A. B. Electronics and Race Electronics and from North America would be the Magna Corporation (Anderson and Holmes, 1989; Morris, 1989a).

This collaboration sometimes involves Nissan employees spending time working in the supplier factories, which has involved a change in culture for some of these firms. One replied, 'Five years ago we wouldn't have let Nissan or Ford people roam in a factory, now they're welcome.' In general collaboration and trust were viewed as positive, although suppliers acknowledged that confidence building is a slow process, especially when such a radical shift in systems is required. The main negative feature was that two of the smaller suppliers commented that Nissan were pressurizing them into going into joint ventures with Japanese owned suppliers, both of whom were Nissan affiliates.

Given that the new buyer-supplier relationship infers dependency on the OEMs with long term relationships, single sourcing and collaboration, it is unsurprizing that the selection process is an extensive one. No information is available on this process at Sunderland, at least in terms of the timescale, but Toyota have made the supplier vetting process one of their priorities in the build up to their development in Derbyshire. From Turnbull's (1989) research, it would seem that Nissan made a scan of all possible suppliers, sometimes without their knowledge: 'Another firm in Walsall found that it had been vetted and rejected by Nissan before even approaching the company for business . . .' (p. 41). As Turnbull goes onto argue, however, many of the West Midlands based automobile suppliers found that they didn't have the finance, quality standards, delivery times or research and development capabilities to serve the Japanese, which is a wider problem of the structure of the UK automobile components sector and the way in which it developed under the adversarial type of buyer-supplier relations.

Despite Nissan's 'scan' of the UK automotive supply sector, the initial contact between the two sides came from the suppliers in all cases. Some of the non-Japanese firms had already approached Nissan, through trade fairs for example, well before Nissan decided to locate a plant in the UK. The exceptions were the Japanese-owned suppliers, who obviously had closer links with the project than the non-Japanese companies, were dedicated suppliers to Sunderland, had no presence in the UK before the Sunderland project, and in some cases were Nissan affiliates. As one explained: 'We wouldn't exist without Nissan, we were part of the whole project of Nissan being here.' The negotiation for Nissan contracts was long and complex, and at times confusing; one firm reported that the process took over two years and some of the suppliers suggested that they were still negotiating price levels after starting supplying parts to Sunderland. Indeed, the whole vetting process was far more complex than is the norm in the UK auto industry, which is in part a reflection of the new relationship and its dependencies, but also of the meticulous detail of all of the parts of Nissan's (and the other Japanese automakers') operations. Suppliers reported that Nissan's vetting procedure amounted to an exhaustive 'audit' of their operations, taking in the expected considerations such as price, quality and quality control, delivery and reliability but also extending to the financial well-being of the company and its resources, its research and development capacity, its industrial relations record (a key consideration given just-in-time delivery), its production organization and even the general state of cleanliness and tidiness of its factories. This audit, while being a one-off procedure, is on-going in the sense that Nissan monitors supplier performance on a regular basis, particularly for quality.

8   CONCLUSIONS

Our initial point of departure was to be cynical of the new developments in buyer-supplier relations. We viewed the major tenets such as closer collaboration, trust and long term relationships with scepticism and saw it as a method whereby large firms were extending their control over suppliers. We were wary of the rhetoric and wondered if the large firms paid anything more than lip service to these notions and whether or not large firms were still squeezing suppliers even further with the new ethos of total quality control and just-in-time supply.

The findings here, and in the other companies, will suggest that our scepticism was largely unfounded. This is not to argue that Nissan and other large firms are acting in a philanthropic way, rather it is a policy of enlightened self-interest or, as one of the respondents commented, 'their motives are purely selfish'. Moreover, we would not argue that the new buyer-supplier relations do not impose considerable constraints and pressures on suppliers, particularly with just-in-time delivery and quality standards. However, a number of suppliers to Nissan argued that this was, paradoxically, advantageous to them in the longer term, in that they had to reassess their whole business and production strategies and that the efforts made to conform stood them in good stead to supply to other companies.

As a final point we should remember that these supplier firms represent the success stories. A large number of traditional auto-supply firms are being excluded, and therefore marginalized, by the concentration of companies such as Nissan on a small number of key suppliers. In addition, many supplier firms have been unable to meet standards on quality and delivery and, most importantly of all because it is out of their control, they have been unable to finance the changes to new standards and the introduction of research and development. However, it could be argued that the narrowing of the supplier band does not necessarily reduce the number of suppliers as much as might seem on first reflection: rather there is a reordering of the supplier base, with firms who formerly supplied directly to the OEMs being placed lower down the pyramid or tier structure and supplying to the large first tier suppliers, instead of to the major production firm.

5 Lucas Girling: New Practices, Old Constraints

1 INTRODUCTION

The Lucas Girling case study is unique in several respects. First, it is the only British company of the four. Second, it is an old established company which is attempting to introduce a new style of manufacturing organization in old, brownfield locations, in contrast to Sony and Nissan's greenfield operations in which they have been able to introduce new working practices. Third, and perhaps most important, Lucas are a major UK company and a global multinational employing in the UK more people than either Toyota or Nissan does in Japan. However, it is also essentially a supplier, at least in its major division, automotives. Thus, while it is a major corporation and it has a large network of suppliers and subcontractors, Lucas are caught in the middle of the supply chain between the major automotive OEMs and its own suppliers, and therefore are again unique in this sample.

This chapter focuses on the buyer-supplier relations of one part of the company, Lucas Girling, based at two sites in South Wales. Lucas Girling[1] are in turn part of the automotive division the largest of three divisions of Lucas Industries. The changes in buyer-supplier relations at Lucas Girling are part of a wider transformation in the company which amounted to a major turnaround strategy in the 1980s. These changes are outlined in sections three and four, with the latter concentrating specifically on changes in manufacturing strategy. This is preceded by a brief history of the organization. Section five concentrates on the impacts of these developments upon the two South Wales production units of Lucas Girling. Finally, the main substantive sections are six and seven, which analyse the changes in buyer-supplier relations, from the perspectives of Lucas Girling and their suppliers respectively.

---

[1] In 1988 Lucas Girling's two South Wales sites were divided into two new sub-divisions, Lucas Heavy Duty Brakes and Lucas Car Brakes. As the material, however, was largely gathered before this event, the case study will use the old name.

2   LUCAS: A BRIEF HISTORY

Lucas, unlike Sony and Nissan, has a long history extending back into the nineteenth century, having started in 1875 when Joseph Lucas patented a ships lamp. The business quickly expanded to various sorts of lamp production, but the main impetus to growth was the boom of the bicycle and their invention of the first cycle lamp. The company went public in 1897, as Joseph Lucas Ltd., based in Birmingham.[2] The company diversified in the early part of the century into motor vehicle, motor cycle and aeroplane lighting; when suppliers from the dominant German company, Robert Bosch, dried up during the First World War, Lucas expanded through acquisition to producing other components such as magnetos (Nockolds, 1976; 1978).

Lucas' major expansion occurred in the inter-war years and was a function of four factors. By far the most important was the growth of the UK motor vehicle industry; the number of vehicles in the UK increased from 100000 in 1920 to 2 million in 1939. A second factor was the increased number of components being produced, including such items as starting and ignition equipment. Acquisition was the third major factor and was, in part, an explanation for the increased variety of products. The two major acquisitions were of two London based companies, CAV which specialized in starting ignition and fuel injection equipment and Rotax, a major supplier to the aircraft industry. The fourth factor was collaboration, notably between CAV and Bosch, and between Lucas and Bendix of the US in the aircraft industry.

Between 1920 and 1939, the amount of issued capital increased three-fold, sales increased sevenfold, profits sixfold and employment increased from 3000 to 20000. During the same period there was a marked concentration of UK car assemblers, from one hundred plus to twenty, with the 'big six' accounting for 90 per centof national output. Lucas had strong ties with Morris which contributed markedly towards this expansion.

The second world war consolidated Lucas' position when the company played a major part in supplying components to the wartime aircraft industry. Sales trebled between 1940 and 1944 although profits were largely static, and employment doubled from 20,000 to 40,000. These years also marked a geographical expansion out of the traditional production areas of Birmingham (Lucas) and London (CAV and Rotax), to

---

[2] Lucas' early history is provided by the extensive company history of Nockolds (1976;1978).

the North West and South Wales. This policy was continued after the war due to government pressure to restrict pressure on the West Midlands and to increase productive capacity in the areas worse hit by the inter-war depression, such as South Wales.

Increased standardization of products, with consequent economies of scale, allowed continued expansion through the 1950s. Lucas pushed hard on OEMs with regard to standardization, pointing out the mutual advantages of lower costs. The early 1960s saw the first major push into the European market spurred by the formation of the European Community, with CAV and Lucas Girling starting overseas production units. This continued into the early 1970s; between 1972 and 1975, for example, the turnover of sales to continental European affiliates and subsidiaries trebled.

By 1975 employment in Lucas had grown to 82500 worldwide, with an annual turnover of £570 million. The company was comprised of twenty six subsidiaries and three associated companies in the UK, plus thirty six subsidiaries and twelve associated companies overseas. At this stage Lucas had grown into one of the world's leading manufacturers of electrical, hydraulic and mechanical equipment used in petrol, diesel and gas turbine engines in road and rail vehicles, ships and aircraft, as well as a wide range of industrial equipment. The company was strongly product engineering orientated, which has continued to the 1990s; in the late 1980s for example, approximately one half of the cars produced in Japan had Lucas braking technology installed under licence (Griffiths, 1989a; 1989b).

In the late 1970s Lucas began to run into operating problems. The company was becoming increasingly uncompetitive in most of its major product markets (van de Vliet, 1986). In addition, Lucas were also extremely dependent on the domestic motor car industry and in particular on its main customer, British Leyland. In 1970, British Leyland supplied 40 per cent of the UK domestic car market and 75 per cent of Lucas' total sales went to British Leyland. By the end of the decade British Leyland's market share had halved and UK car imports had increased from 14 per cent to 60 per cent.

The Lucas problem was greater than a collapse of its major market, however, as the organizational culture of the company had built up around this dependence and was based on demand led growth and thus introspective and complacent. This is perhaps best illustrated by a quote by Walter Waller, a corporate marketing director, in the late 1970s:

> Lucas is technically sound and its product base is strong. There is no serious danger to its trading position. (Walter Waller, quoted in Harding, 1989)

TABLE 5.1　*Major European automative components suppliers, 1988*

Company	Automotive sales 1988 (BN ECU)
Bosch (West Germany)	6.8
Valeo (France)	2.4
Magneti Marelli (Italy)	2.2
ZF (West Germany)	2.0
Lucas (UK)	1.8
GKN (UK)	1.8
SKF (Sweden)	1.8
T & N (UK)	1.3
BTR (UK)	1.0
VDO (West Germany)	0.8

SOURCE: Lamming, 1989.

As Van de Vliet (1986) notes, the company had become notoriously inward looking, with internal appointments to key positions and a complacent satisfaction with the 'Lucas' way of doing things prevailed. While trading profits reached a record level of £78 million in 1978, by 1980 they had fallen to £49 million. A loss of £22 million in 1981 was the first in the history of the company. While the immediate causes of the problem were due to economic recession and the collapse of the home market, there were significant problems overall in the company which pervaded all aspects of its business and manufacturing strategy. The attempts by the company to address these problems is the focus of the next two sections.

3　LUCAS IN 1990

In 1990, Lucas remains the largest automotive component firm in the UK and one of a few which are major players in European terms, in addition to its other activities (see Table 5.1). It employs some 56 000 people worldwide, with 46 900 in the UK distributed through forty manufacturing plants.

The company remains heavily technology orientated, it spends some £12 million per annum on research and development, equivalent to 6 per cent of its turnover. It is also committed heavily to training, with 2 per cent of turnover dedicated to this function although, as Rutherford (1990) has noted, this is considerably less than some of its major European competitors, notably Robert Bosch of West Germany. The company's financial health improved markedly in the late 1980s. In the financial year 1988–1989, for example, the company increased sales by 11 per cent and profits by 28 per cent, the sixth continuous year of growth (Lucas Industries, 1989).

The purpose of this section is to explain the turnaround strategies which the company employed in the 1980s, and are continuing to employ, which link the crash of the business outlined in the last section and the profitable nature of the business by 1990. Despite this turnaround, the company claims that there is still considerable room for productivity improvements, particularly in its UK plants. As a defence against granting a thirty-seven hour week in 1990, for example, the company claimed its UK plants to be 29 per cent less efficient than its own European plants and 40 per cent less efficient than Lucas plants in the US (Thompson, 1990).

Lucas carried out a five point strategy in the 1980s in order to effect a turnaround from the situation in the late 1970s and early 1980s:

(i)   A fundamental organizational change including production organization and manufacturing strategy, which has been so central to the turnaround strategy that a separate section will be devoted to it (see next section).

(ii) An industrial diversification strategy: Lucas diversified considerably away from the traditional business in automotives into the two other main activities, aerospace and industrial systems. There are, however, considerable synergies between the three divisions. Rists, for example, provides wire harnesses for all three, and switchgear equipment is also common. There are also opportunities for common technologies in sensors and engine management systems. This diversification has been achieved through concentrating resources in the automotive division (see strategy iv), and growth in the latter two divisions through organic growth and acquisitions. In 1988, for example, the aerospace division took over Epsco, a US microwave equipment manufacturer, and Utica Power Systems, also of the US. In the same year, Lucas Industries took over Bronzavia Air Equipment of France and Data Laboratories.

This industrial diversification strategy is reflected in the respective proportions that the three divisions now have of the overall Lucas business. As Table 5.2 illustrates, whereas aerospace sales nearly tripled between 1982 and 1989 and industrial systems sales increased by two and a half fold, automotive sales increased by less than 20 per cent. Thus, whereas aerospace and industrial systems only comprized one third of automotive sales in 1982, by 1989 this had increased to two thirds.

TABLE 5.2   *Lucas sales (in £ millions) by division, 1982–1989*

Division	1982	1985	1989
Aerospace	207.6	264.0	602.3
Automotive	976.0	1100.0	1307.0
Industrial	113.2	135.2	278.1

SOURCE: Lucas Annual Reports, 1982; 1985; 1989.

(iii) A geographical diversification strategy: Lucas' geographical diversification strategy dates back to the early 1950s when it started its first overseas production facilities in France and West Germany (Nockolds, 1978). This geographical spread was due to Lucas' moves towards a true multinational company and the necessity to have overseas production facilities to adequately serve foreign markets or, in the case of certain foreign markets, to serve them at all. The 1980s, however, witnessed a rapid increase in the pace of Lucas' internationalization, at a time of considerable job shedding in the UK, particularly in the Lucas heartland of the West Midlands (Gaffikin and Nickson, 1984). Moreover, it was, in the 1980s, a conscious strategy to reduce exposure to the UK because the British car industry had virtually halved between 1964 and 1980.

This geographical shift is reflected in the sales figures for UK and foreign subsidiaries. In 1982 sales from the UK subsidiaries were nearly twice those of the overseas subsidiaries but in 1989, for the first time, less than half the sales were from UK subsidiaries (see Table 5.3). In 1989, including exports from UK subsidiaries, some 77 per cent of Lucas sales were overseas.

This strategy has been achieved through a contraction of the UK base particularly in automotives, and an expansion of overseas activities through greenfield ventures and acquisitions. Between 1986 and 1988 alone, Lucas spent £150 million on acquisitions in the US market (Tomkins, 1989). Lucas overseas operations have been central to the recovery of business in the 1980s; in 1989, for example, the bulk of

TABLE 5.3   *Lucas sales (in £ millions) by geographical division, 1982–89*

Area	1982	1985	1989
UK	790.4	722.0	1000.9
Europe (Non-UK)	429.4	436.0	598.3
Rest of World		341.0	588.1

SOURCE: Lucas Annual Reports, 1982; 1985; 1989.

profits were being made from its overseas operations whereas the UK, based business remained sluggish.

The concentration on overseas expansion is partially reflected in UK and overseas employment. While UK-based employment has fallen steadily and dramatically in the 1980s, with a decline of one third between 1985 and 1989, overseas employment has steadily increased (see Table 5.4).

(iv) A product/systems concentration strategy. Alongside expansion strategies in the aerospace and industrial divisions and the geographical expansion of Lucas' production facilities there has been considerable concentration in certain parts of the business, notably the automotive division. This was part of Lucas' profit centre approach, implemented through the Competitive Achievement Plan (CAP) system described in the next section. The rationale for this policy was to concentrate resources upon areas of automotive components in which Lucas has a competitive advantage and reduce dependence on commodity-type products with a low technological content. This was an imperative, given the increasing complexity of component systems in the 1990s, and the associated costs of continuing research and development.

Between 1980 and 1988 the number of Lucas' business units declined from 170 to 130 (van de Vliet, 1986). The main divestments have been in the electric and volume instrumentation businesses; the lighting division was sold to Corello in 1987 and the dynamo and electrical generator business to Magneti Marelli, both parts of the Fiat Group. In 1989 the company sold a further part of its instrumentation business, based in South Wales, to V.D.O. of West Germany. While in other areas of the automotive business divestment has not taken place, there has been considerable rationalization of production capacity; a CAV plant in Finchley was closed and the production of fuel injection equipment for automotive diesel engines is now concentrated at Gillingham in Kent. Similarly, automotive braking production was concentrated at two sites in South Wales (Pontypool and Cwmbran).

TABLE 5.4 *Employment in Lucas Industries PLC, UK and Overseas, 1985–89 ('000s)*

	1985	1986	1987	1988	1989
UK	46.9	45.6	42.9	36.7	32.2
Overseas	18.0	18.5	19.7	22.3	23.8
Total	64.9	64.1	62.6	59.0	36.0

SOURCE: Lucas Industries.

This rationalization programme has not been an entirely negative one, however, for the obverse has been expansion in key areas, such as anti-lock braking systems, diesel injection systems and engine management systems. In 1989, for example, the company announced a five fold expansion of its sophisticated electronics based anti-skid brake system. This strategy has connections with other of the strategies, with the company supplying fuel injection systems to the German firm BMW as a result of its attempt to weaken the near monopolistic grasp of high technology components by the German components producer Robert Bosch (Griffiths, 1989b). The bulk of the expansion is due to take place in Girling's plants in South Wales, rather than at Koblenz, West Germany, because of the former's lower cost production (Griffiths, 1989a).

The crux of this strategy is, therefore, to concentrate on high value added components involving a significant degree of research and development. An examplar would be the concentration on extremely complex and technology intensive engine management systems.

(v) A strategy of joint-ventures and strategic alliances: Lucas have entered into a series of joint ventures, strategic alliances and technical collaboration deals with competitors, particularly in the automotive and, to a lesser extent, the aerospace divisions. The rationale for this policy is clear – to learn best practice in manufacturing strategy and to gain technological expertise from, mainly, Japanese competitors. Thus the company has entered into a plant-based production joint ventures in the USA with Sumitomo to produce brakes, and in the UK with Yuasa to produce batteries and Sumitomo to produce wire harnesses. The research of Marinaccio and Morris (1991) on this last venture, Lucas SEI at Ystradgynlais (South Wales), would suggest that in the short term Lucas has gained significant advantages such as increased productivity and better quality; however, the work of Pucik (1987), on similar US/Japanese joint ventures suggests that the weaknesses of the US partners has left them dependent on the Japanese partner's technology, and so vulnerable in the longer term.

Not all of Lucas' joint ventures have been entered into, however, to harness the expertise of competitors. In 1988, for example, Lucas Automotive and the Japanese company Mikuni Precision entered into a joint venture in Japan to produce fuel injection systems for diesel engines, using Lucas technology. Moreover, as Tony Gill of Lucas has made clear, this is a strategy aimed at gaining business from the three Japanese automobile manufacturers in the UK which might otherwise be lost to Japanese suppliers with close ties to those companies; that is, it is also a marketing strategy (Gill, quoted in Trade and Industry Committee, 1987).

4 WORK AND PRODUCTION ORGANIZATION AT LUCAS INDUSTRIES

As the previous section illustrated, central to the turnaround strategy at Lucas Industries was a radical and fundamental change in manufacturing strategy. An important element of this transformation was an attempt to change the buyer-supplier links at Lucas (explained in sections five and six), which in turn was a key element of the transformation of production organization. The motivation behind this new strategic approach was to regain competitiveness. As Brady (1987b) has noted, this included several elements, a product engineering strategy, a manufacturing systems engineering strategy and a business systems engineering strategy, overlain by a financial control strategy.

Each business unit in the company was required to produce a Competitive Achievement Plan (CAP) which represented a significant decentralization of resources and responsibility. These were compared to the best international competitor in each product area and the units had to make detailed proposals to close the gap. Those CAPs which the company regarded as feasible were provided with the necessary finance. Those which were considered unfeasible were sold or closed, some 130 business units were closed at 30 sites as a result (Brady, 1987b).

The CAPs had two major results. First, they attempted to change the introspective corporate culture at Lucas and secondly, they revealed that the main problems of the company were in its manufacturing methods rather than its product technology (van de Vliet, 1986). The company thus placed a considerable emphasis on a manufacturing systems engineering approach (Oliver and Wilkinson, 1988; Parnaby, 1986a; 1986b; 1987). Included are, first, a target-setting phase which included the derivation of competitive benchmarks and formulating appropriate measures of performance in all areas, including financial measures, quality measures, lead times and value added. The second phase was target achievement in order to meet the set targets. This included three main elements, the rationalization and development of suppliers, which is described in detail later in this chapter, a manufacturing strategy, and a personnel and organizational strategy.

Included in the manufacturing strategy were what Oliver and Wilkinson (1988) argue are recognizably Japanese practices, including just-in-time production, the grouping of factory machining processes into product families, cellular production or what Turnbull (1986) calls a series of self-contained mini factories within a factory and total quality control. In turn, these were matched to a coherent overall business strategy based on new market imperatives including, for example, a switch from systems designed for high volume, low variety production to ones capable of variety at short lead times (van de Vliet, 1986). Such a strategy was introduced to counter the manifold problems of excessive numbers of indirect support staff, extremely complex control systems, high stock levels and poor responses to customer demands. Clearly this had significant implications for Lucas' buyer-supplier policy which are explored in greater depth later.

As Oliver and Wilkinson (1988) note, the task force has been instrumental as a force for change. These are small, multi-disciplinary teams under the control of the local business manager who is responsible for redesigning activities. Major elements were the introduction of cellular manufacturing, including just-in-time production and kanban. They describe each cell as:

> conceived as a specific collection of resources (people, machines and support services) which are grouped together both organizationally and physically and which have clear and precise targets and objectives to meet.   (p. 48)

Such a cell structure, and indeed the wider changes in production organization, has significant implications for work organization. The cell structure lends itself to team working, and the aim is for considerable functional flexibility. This, along with other developments, has required a considerable retraining programme, elements of which continue to hamper Lucas' progress in its manufacturing strategy (Brady 1987b; Marinaccio and Morris, 1990; Rutherford *et al.*, 1989).

Non-direct staff were also affected, with decentralization of functional areas such as production engineering and quality control placed in the cells. Interestingly, however, purchasing remains centralized at Lucas Girling. One result of this business unit approach has been to cost each stage of the production process in terms of value added, with unprofitable areas of business sometimes subcontracted out (Morris, 1988b). The results of such changes has been to increase performance along a number of criteria, including stock reduction, turnover, lead times, productivity and reject levels.

Brady (1987b) cites two case studies to illustrate such improvements. The first, electronics instrumentation manufacture, in the course of one year redesigned its business into three simpler product units and two service units. The result was that average manufacturing lead times fell from seven days to five hours and non value-added activities were reduced by 60 per cent. Changeovers were reduced to five minutes maximum, in-cell work-in-progress was reduced by 99 per cent and improved quality was attained. In the second case, electro-mechanical automotive component manufacture, over a two year period stock turnover increased from 7 to 13 times, productivity increased by 30 per cent, manufacturing lead times were reduced by a factor of 5 and rejects were reduced by 79 per cent. However, as Turnbull (1986) notes, this has been at the expense of shopfloor workers, including work intensification which would seem to be confirmed by Brady's two case studies. As an element of the turnaround strategy, however, the company has clearly achieved significant benefits from it.

5   LUCAS GIRLING

Lucas Girling was the name, until 1988, of the Lucas division producing braking systems for cars and commercial vehicles. Its UK operations included plants at Bromborough (Merseyside) and at Pontypool and Cwmbran in South Wales. Overseas operations included plants in France, Spain, Belgium, West Germany and the USA. It also has significant licensing agreements; over half the cars produced in Japan, for example, use Lucas Girling braking technology. In 1988 Lucas Girling was subject to yet another Lucas corporate reorganization which split the Pontypool and Cwmbran plants between Lucas Automotive Car Brakes (at Pontypool) and Lucas Automotive Heavy Duty Brake (Cwmbran).

Girling's UK business has changed significantly from the 1960s when the emphasis was on low variety of products with high volume; due to the decline of the UK market there is a greater need to export and the increasing sophistication of motor vehicle designs has led to demands for tailor-made braking systems (Morris, 1988b; Thomas, 1988). In common with other Lucas businesses, Girling found it difficult to accommodate market changes and the business deteriorated. In part this was due to the preponderance of dedicated high volume plant and inflexible machinery, which led to production targets not being met, rising stocks and deteriorating quality (Thomas, 1988). Lucas Girling's major restructuring programme started in 1985, with a view to increasing market share and decreasing manufacturing costs. The company closed one production unit at Cwmbran and employment in the two remaining ones fell from its 1980 level of 3500 to 3060 by 1988 (Morris, 1988b).

Task forces were introduced, which in turn led to the sites being split into autonomous business units, each responsible for their own profitability. In addition there was considerable capital investment – amounting to over £30 million in five years – in new equipment, including the introduction of computer numerically controlled machine tools. Production, meanwhile, was broken down into a cellular structure with a 'kanban' control system, although Thomas (1988) claims with only limited success. This involved small batches of ten components being closely monitored at each stage of the production process by means of bar coding fed through to a centralized computer system. Final assembly is now carried out on eight short lines, contrasting with the two final assembly long-run lines previously used and demarcation barriers have been gradually removed. Total quality was promoted, and techniques such as FMEA and SPC introduced. These, and the other changes, have led to marked improvements in quality and productivity and reduced work in progress (Morris, 1988b). However, Thomas (1988) reports considerable variations between individual business units.

This section, therefore, has provided an insight into the wider change in work and production organization being undertaken at the plants, an important element of which was new buyer-supplier policies which are analysed in the next two sections.

6 BUYER-SUPPLIER RELATIONS AT LUCAS: GIRLING'S POLICY

The prime source for the Lucas case study material is face to face interviews with Lucas personnel and suppliers' personnel. However, we will also supplement this with the unpublished work of Thomas (1988), which reviewed similar themes, albeit with a different research method. At the time of our interviews with Lucas Girling, all purchasing for the two Gwent plants was carried out at Cwmbran, so this analysis applies to the overall purchasing policy of the Lucas Girling operations in South Wales.

Lucas' buyer-supplier policies must be set within a context of a large increase in the amount of work being subcontracted out. Indeed, this is the first strand of their policy. Activities such as the autoshop, presses, cold head facilities, tool room activities and the rubber plant were all stopped at Cwmbran and Pontypool and outsourced. The rationale for this policy was twofold. First, the company decided to concentrate on its own areas of production expertise and hence its core workforce. Secondly, the outsourced activities required extremely high, and increasing, levels of capital investment in order to cope with technological change and the company felt that it would be cheaper to buy in these parts and activities. Lucas Girling have, historically, been an extremely vertically integrated company. This aspect of policy is now almost complete, the level of outsourcing will not increase substantially and indeed the Pontypool operation, in particular, is virtually an assembly one.

The result of this policy was substantial redundancies at the two plants; of the 1000 overall job loss it was estimated that about 20 per cent of this was due to the policy of outsourcing. At the same time as the company was increasing its outsourcing it was drastically reducing the number of its suppliers. In the mid 1980s Lucas Girling had four hundred suppliers. By the late 1980s this had been reduced to two hundred and thirty, including 120 'preferred suppliers' and the remaining 110 on 'probation'. This had been achieved by reducing the number of suppliers per component or part from multisourcing to either single or dual sourcing. Product types, such as seals or castings, are dual sourced but individual part numbers tend to be single sourced (Thomas, 1988).

This was part of an overall Supplier Development Programme introduced in 1984–85, in conjunction with the introduction of the Stop Control System project, the SCS anti-skid braking system developed jointly with Ford. The introduction of the new supplier policy at the same time as the manufacture of the new product was not mere coincidence. As Thomas (1988) has argued, SCS provided a major challenge to Lucas Girling in two ways: first, because quality specifications were far higher and more akin to the aerospace than the automotive industry, and secondly because it allowed the company to outsource far more, and apply the systems engineering approach internally. The consequence was that only two of the one hundred components were made in-house.

Prior to the new purchasing strategy an adversarial approach had dominated, with little real attention to quality, acceptable levels of rejects, bids tendered on price, multisourcing and little collaboration. Supplier assessment was problematic due to lack of adequate quality data, a problem which still persists (Thomas 1988). Moreover, Thomas argues that the new policy of reduced stockholding was, in the short term, extremely damaging:

> The reduction of stock levels within Girling by 1985 had the effect of exacerbating many of the supply problems by revealing the inherent deficiencies in Girling's material supply systems. Without the benefit of large buffer stocks the supply of bought out parts was becoming larger.   (p. 33)

Thomas' argument implies, of course, that Lucas' development of its internal just-in-time and total quality management systems are not sophisticated and refined enough to operate at low stock levels.

In terms of the geographical spread of suppliers some 50 are overseas suppliers, representing about 20 per cent of the plant's 'spend' on outsourcing. Within the UK, the majority of suppliers are based in the West Midlands; about 60 per cent of Thomas' sample, for example, were from that region. Given that the major outsourcing is for friction materials (the major item), castings, pressings, steel strip wire and bar, rubber and plastic components, bearings, fasteners, forgings, springs and machine parts, this geographical concentration is unsurprising. However, while Sony and Nissan have a policy, either overtly or covertly, of attracting suppliers to their locales, Girling have no such policy, arguing that they do not have enough market pressure. The implication of Lucas' argument is that either the volumes of components bought in are not as great as at Nissan, Sony or IBM, or that Lucas are not enough of a blue chip company to warrant such a relocation. The major components brought in from outside the UK are castings, rubber components and cold forgings, vital components which are either unavailable in the UK to the technical specifications required or are too expensive. These are purchased mainly from continental Europe but also from Japan and the USA.

Lucas Girling's policy of trying to shift from the traditional adversarial mode of relationship with its suppliers to a more collaborative one is incremental and gradual. As the Lucas representative replied, the whole policy is:

> very much one of evolution not revolution, we have to accept that we cannot do it overnight . . . it is a five year job.

This is an acceptance of the limitations of Girling and the change process that the company is undergoing as much as a criticism of suppliers. In this regard, of course, Lucas differs radically from Nissan, and even from Sony and IBM who have been through change, in that the company is starting from a position considerably behind the other three case study companies, which should be borne in mind in the following discussion.

Quality improvements have been a major consideration in the change in buyer-supplier relationships at Lucas Girling, as part of the company's Total Quality Concept described in the last section. Indeed the improvement of quality was the main aim of the Supplier Development Programme, together with improved delivery and cost. Quality was improved to a degree at a stroke by axing suppliers with unacceptable levels of quality and delivery, although in some cases they were retained due to a lack of alternatives.

As an indication of the poor standard of quality at the Lucas Girling plants it is worthwhile quoting an unpublished internal document:

> Our 500 plus suppliers, predominantly 'B' rated by SQA [Supplier Quality Assessment], fail to conform to specifications approximately 3000 times per year.   (Lucas Girling, 1985)

The document went onto analyse why this was so. Included in the reasons were failure of purchasing to accept responsibility, acceptance of rejects, poor inventory control, lack of data on non-conforming parts, and lack of communication from Lucas to suppliers. A further reason why 'approved' suppliers supplied rejects was that 'approval' in SQA terms was not related to supplier performance.

In common with other large manufacturers Lucas have a zero defect policy which they are attempting to make suppliers conform to. To date the top 120 suppliers, the preferred suppliers, provide self-certification, or quality assured supplies, although Lucas still maintains some inward inspection with a check on one in six items. Quality standards are set down in a further document and part of the suppliers' contract is that they adhere to it. The procedure then goes on with an inspection of supplier's plant for general attitude to quality.

Following these initial stages Lucas makes a detailed study of suppliers in the areas of 'Failure Mode and Effect Analysis' (FMEA), and 'Process Capability'. FMEA is a tool introduced by Ford. It is described by Ford as:

> A process FMEA is an analytical technique which identifies potential product related process failure modes, assesses the potential customer effects of the failures, identifies the potential manufacturing or assembly process causes and identifies significant process variables to focus controls for prevention or detection of the failure conditions. It utilizes occurrence and detection probability in conjunction with severity criteria to develop a risk priority number (RPN) for the prioritization of corrective action consideration. A disciplined review and analysis of a new or revised process is promoted to anticipate, resolve or monitor process problems during the manufacturing stages of a new model or component programme.   (Quoted in Thomas, 1988)

For process capability, Lucas Girling have made extensive efforts to encourage suppliers to introduce SPC through, for example, training programmes.

The second major area of improvement which Lucas have tried to introduce is in delivery. With reduced inventories, Girling now requires suppliers to deliver more frequently and, more importantly, smaller quantities but larger varieties of components. Typically the frequency of delivery is daily which is no more frequent than previously. However, the supplier now only delivers the amount of components that will be necessary for that day's production at Girling. The result has been reduction in buffer stocks from ten to five weeks, and in some cases, a few days. The large stocks tend to be those supplied from overseas. Moreover, certain suppliers have indicated that they would be willing to supply to the plant twice or three times per day. However, Girling themselves could not cope with such frequency, as their own internal materials planning systems are inadequate.

The third key area is price, which Girling regard as crucial given that quality and delivery will be within fixed parameters. The company argues that it has not made a conscious attempt to reduce margins. This view of price as the main variable is a curious one, however, as it suggests that the other two are fixed. Delivery is, as we have seen, to a certain extent fixed by Girling's inability to take more frequent delivery, but the notion that quality is fixed goes against the ethos of one of the Japanese manufacturing practices that Lucas are attempting to emulate, kaizen or continual improvement. However, while price is important, the payment system is also seen as crucial. Girling pays on a monthly basis with a maximum of forty-five days. This has been reduced considerably in recent years, due to the increasing frequency of deliveries and to ensure that suppliers do not run into cash flow problems.

The choice of suppliers for Girling is different from the other case studies, notably Nissan and Sony, in that Girling was attempting to reduce, rather than build up its supplier base. The Supplier Development Programme split the suppliers into three broad categories: acceptable suppliers, potentially acceptable and unacceptable, according to quality and delivery criteria.

The suppliers that come through this process are continually monitored for performance on eight main criteria, including control, plant, quality, attitude, response, tooling, planning and handling. Each criteria is then marked out of ten. Interestingly, the industrial relations history of the prospective firm is not included in this list, although this is more of a monitoring process rather than a selection process. Girling has circumvented this by maintaining buffer stocks and charging the cost to supplier companies should a strike occur. This procedure also acts as a monitoring system. Suppliers are graded in two ways; first, the quality system (SQA) where firms are graded A, B or C according to quality, with the top 10 per cent being graded A. Secondly, there are the supply and development criteria including the supplier's financial situation and 'soft' skills such as attitude.

The negotiation for contracts is such that Girling have a 'call off' against schedules. Tenders are offered to nominated suppliers, a contract is negotiated, the buyers bring in samples to demonstrate the quality required and contracts are now long-term. Girling offers its commitment through a three to four year exclusivity contract, although maintenance of the contract depends on the supplier's ability to control prices and to improve component quality. Firms are asked to become 100 per cent suppliers to Girling. This contrasts markedly with the situation a decade earlier when, apart from multisourcing, contracts were only given out for four months.

Girling is attempting to offer all suppliers technical assistance. Most obviously, this is in the area of process technology, with SPC and FMEA. The company also runs in-house 'education' courses for suppliers in which it illustrates the principles and benefits to be accrued from the new system. However, in other cases Lucas went further in its assistance. One simple example was of a rubber seal company in Yorkshire which had a process of compression moulding via extrusion machines cutting rubber into specified lengths. The company never checked the settings on cutters for accuracy and Lucas identified and suggested a new system which resulted in savings of some £12 000 per annum.

In terms of product development of components, Lucas claims an open relationship with suppliers, with joint development and negotiation as opposed to tightly defined specifications. While price is extremely important, quality is also crucial because all parts are used in braking systems and are therefore safety critical. Girling is now far more involved with suppliers than it was even five years ago. With new suppliers, Girling visits and inspects regularly and with the 120 preferred suppliers buyers visit three or four times per year.

The issue of a ceiling of supply does not really apply to Girling, as all of their suppliers have a varied order base. Even in cases of suppliers where Lucas is the major client, the maximum amount supplied to Girling is 30 per cent. However, Girling respondents maintained that they would be concerned if any supplier became too dependent on them and therefore encourages suppliers to diversify and supply to other firms.

In general, the Lucas respondent felt that suppliers were favourable to the new system and extremely flexible, and the pressing current need was to restructure the procurement areas itself. However, Thomas (1988) argues that despite the enormous improvements that have been made at Girling, there are a number of problem areas, including the re-organization of the materials supply function, communications, the buyers and scheduling. He argues, for example, that the central purchasing function remained intact up until 1988, despite recommendations from successive task forces that they should be integrated into the new modules. Such integration could be assisted by good lines of communications between the customer (i.e. the user department) and the supplier via purchasing. Thomas ascribes problems in part to the difficulties that Girling have had in retaining their more able buyers, which has led to them using non-graduate staff, often former apprentices. The final problem area Thomas identifies is that of scheduling, with suppliers being expected to deal with large fluctuations in demand at very short notice. This, of course, is partly the result of Lucas themselves being a supplier who in turn have problems of unstable demand.

Girling, therefore, have made major changes in their buyer-supplier relations over a period of five years. Significant problems still exist, but this might be expected given that Girling are an old established company with an established culture, which in terms of its buyer-supplier relations included the adversarial mode of contracting.

7 BUYER-SUPPLIER RELATIONS AT GIRLING: THE SUPPLIER'S PERSPECTIVE

The supply base at Lucas Girling comprises approximately two hundred and thirty firms of which our research included ten. The suppliers were almost exclusively South Wales based and tended to be small independent firms; only two had over a hundred employees. The research of Thomas (1988) will complement this; his sample of twenty-nine firms were almost exclusively non-Welsh, being concentrated in the West Midlands, and included larger firms, varying from 10 to 1680 employees. The main disadvantage of his survey, however, is that, unlike ours, it was a postal questionnaire, and therefore prone to the restrictions of this research method as opposed to face to face interviews.

The general impression of supplying to Lucas Girling varied from supplier to supplier. The majority saw Girling as a prestigious company to be dealing with, which had positive spin-offs. Others who dealt with other major companies viewed Lucas less favourably. Two quotes from respondents illustrates this divide. The first comes from one of the largest suppliers, who also carried out work for Ministry of Defence contractors and other automotive firms such as Jaguar and Llanelli Radiators. They replied:

These are prestigious orders, you get considerable spin-offs if you work for a company like Lucas.

A second firm, which also dealt with the major Japanese companies such as Sony, had a view which contrasted with this:

Lucas are very slow and very old fashioned, especially in middle management . . . there is a continual battle between purchasing and engineers. Their approach is very much 'hands-off'.

The overall impressions of the supplier companies was, however, positive. They felt that Lucas were a good company to work with and that they had made great strides in their relationship with suppliers particularly in the area of long-term trust relationship. Only one other company had a poor view of Lucas and this was part of its reluctance to include any motor industry firms among its clients, claiming that these firms offered very low profits, wanted suppliers to carry massive stocks, wanted long credit and were highly unreliable.

The supplier firms benefited directly and indirectly from Lucas' change in buyer-supplier relations. One obvious impact is in the amount of business that suppliers received from Lucas. Several firms had grown directly as a result of Girling's policy of increasing outsourcing. Indeed, several firms had targeted large companies such as Lucas to be their equivalent of preferred suppliers, in this instance preferred customers. They had in some cases narrowed their customer base to concentrate on large prestigious orders such as Lucas. One, for example, had reduced its customer base by over 40 per cent. Typically Lucas Girling was the largest customer for many of these suppliers, with up to 30 per cent of their business dedicated to them. In certain cases firms were wary of becoming too dependent on one large customer: one firm, for example, operated what they called the '80–20' rule that 80 per cent of business should come from 20 per cent of customers.

The new quality imperative was seen as a considerable advantage by some of the respondents, as they had formerly had quality levels which were too high, or rather too expensive, for customers to accept, but which fitted well into the new milieu. In the case of some of the small engineering firms, for example, the new stringencies required the relatively high levels of investment that they had made and cut out the possibility of low cost, undercapitalized, new entrant competitors. The advantages associated with these new quality standards applied to other major customers. Other suppliers had made concerted moves to move

upmarket into specialized niches providing higher value added components.

The length of association that suppliers had with Lucas varied from four
years to twenty-three years. The experience of the latter firm was obviously
revealing in the way that it charted the changes in Girling policy. Some of
the smaller suppliers had dealt with Girling since their inception; one had
started off, for example, acting as a subcontractor on a free issue basis
and had developed into a fully fledged supplier. This company produced
30 per cent of its Girling output on a sub-contract basis, where Girling
provided the raw materials and the supplier provided the parts process, and
70 per cent on a supply basis, where they were in control of all aspects of
production.

In general, the suppliers did not view moves by Girling to improve
quality of components with hostility. There were several avenues to these
firms achieving higher quality output. Seven of the respondents singled out
heavy investment in technology, such as making extensive use of computer
numerically controlled (CNC) machine tools which had improved the
range and quality of components. A second avenue was the attainment
of benchmark quality standards; several, for example, had made concerted
efforts to achieve the British quality standard BS5750. Two comments on
this issue provide an interesting insight into the new quality demands. One
respondent felt that while this quality standard, which is demanding and
expensive for small firms, was desirable, it was not alone sufficient to
satisfy the requirements of Girling and other major firms. The second
respondent agreed with this sentiment. For this firm its implementation had
caused major problems, but had been extremely beneficial, with 'enormous
spin-offs'. However, he further added that:

> In five years time small suppliers and sub-contractors simply won't get
> jobs without it.   (BS5750)

One firm, the largest of the sample, had also invested heavily in R & D
through its parent organization, to improve quality and develop new products. In common with the suppliers to Nissan, Sony and IBM, the Girling
suppliers were often serving other customers whose demands on quality
were as strict, if not stricter, than Girling's, or who had imposed these
demands at an earlier date. Included in the sample, for example, were
firms who supplied to all of Ford's European plants and to Sony both in
Bridgend and Japan. These suppliers, therefore, had the requisite quality
standards prior to the Girling supplier development programme in 1985.
Sony and Yuasa Batteries, another South Wales-based Japanese producer,

were judged to be far ahead of Girling in their quality standards. One respondent replied: 'Lucas are O.K., but they are not in the same league as Sony.' Nevertheless, Girling were judged to have improved considerably on their previous performance.

The Ford connection was seen to be an important one by many of the suppliers, with many of the quality improvement ideas coming to them from Ford via Lucas. Indeed the previous section confirmed this in the case, for example, of FMEA.

Quality and reliability were generally seen by the suppliers to have superseded price in importance in dealing with firms such as Girling, although this is at variance with the Lucas view expressed in the last section. This new approach was in marked contrast to that used in earlier times: one small supplier reported that it had received no vetting as such when it started to supply to Girling in 1979.

Apart from investing in new technology and achieving general benchmark quality standards, a variety of techniques had been introduced, often at Girling's (or another customer's) instigation. Most had attempted to introduce SPC techniques, and several had introduced process systems charts and were introducing zero defect policies with positive results; one had reduced its reject rates, for example, from 4 to 1 per cent. Some of the suppliers had made considerable efforts to improve their quality systems. One supplier, employing only twenty staff, had seconded one of their employees to work with Girling's quality team who would later come back in-house to implement the new system, while a second, again a small firm, had one of its employees totally dedicated to the Lucas account. The suppliers themselves, particularly a few of the larger ones, were attempting to pass on Girling's quality standards to their own suppliers. One, for example, had introduced SPC techniques to its suppliers and was giving its best suppliers certificates of quality.

Thomas' questionnaire also reported on quality issues. Of his sample, 82 per cent claimed that they had introduced Total Quality Control, while 13 per cent were planning to implement it. 85 per cent of the respondents reported that Girling had encouraged them to do so. Most of the respondents claimed considerable success. In addition, 73 per cent of his sample used SPC, again largely due to Girling's encouragement, although a number doubted its usefulness in their particular production process. 60 per cent of his sample had introduced just-in-time supply to Girling, although again certain firms felt that its main impact was to transfer the burden of stockholding onto them, a view expressed by several of the suppliers interviewed in our sample. However, 55 per cent of his sample reported that their stockholding had declined while only

17 per cent reported an increase, probably partly due to the half of the sample which reported that they had introduced just-in-time deliveries for their suppliers. One negative side of this was that 82 per cent reported a substantial increase in administrative workload. Two thirds of the sample reported the use of FMEA's encouraged by Girling and other customers. Thomas concludes:

> It appears therefore that the use of FMEA has become widely accepted in the motor component industry indicating a knock-on effect from Ford through its major suppliers to its suppliers' suppliers.   (p. 68)

Interestingly, large percentages of these suppliers had introduced certain Japanese management practices without Girling's encouragement; 55 per cent, for example, used quality circles while 68 per cent used group or team working.

Apart from the reduction of rejects other benefits accrued, including the ability of a number of suppliers to provide quality assured supplies to Girling. One respondent saw this as a manifestation of a wider change in its relationship with Girling:

> We have progressed with Lucas and developed 'high trust'. Our work is not sampled by them anymore, it goes straight into their line.

All of the respondents felt that they had developed a high level of collaboration with Lucas. Several respondents also commented that Girling staff were far more 'professional' in their approach than they had formerly been. Contacts were also far more frequent, typically monthly or even weekly, including 'formal' meetings in addition to frequent communications by telephone and facsimile machine. This included collaboration on design. Two quotes, from separate suppliers, illustrate this:

> We often tell them how to save costs and improve components. This differs from the old system we now work together to improve the product for each other.
>
> We are very close with Lucas and it is more of a partnership. They come to us with their design changes and communications are good. We have inputs into the design specification and this is different from a few years ago. The process is now more of a collaboration and a lot more professional. The major buyers used to be in Birmingham, we never saw them. They are now in South Wales and face to face contact is important.

For this small firm contact was frequent with Girling, with the manager visiting the Girling plant three of four times per day to discuss issues such as scheduling.

Several firms mentioned that Girling had offered them considerable technical assistance. One reported:

> Lucas were very good to us, they gave us assistance on production and testing. While there was no financial assistance as such, if we have technical problems, we go to them for advice.

Another had been offered considerable assistance when purchasing and using CNC machines in terms of the best types to buy and subsequently how to use them to their best advantage. This level of collaboration is notable in that less than half of the sample acted as sole suppliers to Girling.

While the implementation of new quality standards posed considerable problems for suppliers, this was matched by the new demands of more frequent deliveries and moves towards just-in-time supply. One small presswork company, from Thomas' sample, described it as 'Japanese induced terror'. Only one of the respondents supplied to Girling on a true just-in-time basis, that is, multiple deliveries per day. This was being used as a twelve month experiment at Girling's Pontypool plant, with a view to extending it to other suppliers. The implementation of JIT supply is, of course, extremely complex. Lucas Girling are supplied with some thirty to forty thousand items, thus the logistical problems are enormous. Even in the Nissan and, to a lesser extent, the Sony case, where sub-systems and parts are less numerous and larger, the moves towards multiple deliveries per day have been tentative. Moreover, Girling are themselves prone to the vagaries of demand fluctuations from their customers.

All of the suppliers noted that deliveries were becoming more frequent, with deliveries varying from once per day in some cases to once per week in others. The frequency of deliveries had a number of implications for suppliers. In certain cases, particularly those firms on the second rung of the supply chain who relied on raw materials suppliers or metals producers, this meant a significant squeeze on their company. As one respondent replied:

> Basically we are Lucas' stockholders, four years ago, they held big stocks, now we do.

However the positive side of this was: 'But on the other hand, it has meant a big growth in business for us'; another commented that: 'Essentially,

JIT puts the pressure on us, . . . we are the bottom of the pile.' In other cases, suppliers had managed to keep their own inventory low, but were still burdened by inventory control. One respondent summed it up:

> We supply a sort of JIT system. We get a twelve monthly order and deliver to schedule. It is called off on a weekly basis. This has pushed inventory control onto us and caused us big headaches on planning and job loading. We need to be highly computerized to cope and have to keep a close control on our cost performance, our delivery and our quality.

Another expressed similar sentiments:

> Our supply to Lucas is not really JIT, but it is much more frequent, and we use a business workflow simulation. Lucas are fairly efficient; for example, we have a terminal to get in changed schedules and we have decreased our stock levels over time. We have a separate stockpile exclusively for Lucas Girling, but we have nevertheless decreased stock levels. Our stock turnaround is now eight times per year whereas it was twice.

However, this respondent went onto offer a cautious note:

> We do daily deliveries, sometimes twice per day, to Girling. This is O.K. for a few firms, but we would be pushed to do it for a lot. We are a single source and this often means very short lead times, we have to work all hours. JIT is part of our quality and range of service, but it puts us under immense pressure all of the time. It's difficult to achieve the right price, quality, and delivery all at the same time.

In order to respond to fluctuations in delivery, with rush orders sometimes being required with only a few days notice, some of the suppliers had extremely flexible forms of work organization. Overtime was a typical way of dealing with such a situation, in other cases workers were quickly interchanged between processes, which implies flexibility and work intensification. Clearly, in the small firms and production units which typified this sample, this would be easier to achieve than in larger firms.

Thomas' study also indicated major changes in suppliers' operations as a result of changes to Girling's requirements, although other customers had also had a major stimuli. These included major training programmes, changes in product design, and the installation of new quality control equipment.

Whereas quality of components and the frequency of delivery had become an integral part of supplying to Lucas Girling, pricing of components has become relatively less important. Only one firm, the supplier that was earlier quoted as having a very jaundiced view of supplying to the motor industry, was negative about Girling's pricing strategy, and even then the quote applied to all large companies, not Girling *per se*:

> Large firms do screw us down, they don't accept that it should be a 'win-win' situation. They're always interested in reducing their costs at our expense.

This contrasted with the majority view; all of the other firms felt that Girling's pricing policy was fair and that the payment system was excellent, as one firm put it 'one of the best in South Wales', with prompt payment of bills, in contrast to other customers such as Austin Rover. Several suppliers pointed out that large firms such as Girling were now far more willing to pay for reasonable quality and where there were a limited number of firms in the market place, the dependence was reversed.

> Lucas are very good payers, but then again they are very reliant on us.

A number of firms noted that the pricing policy had moved away from the short term 'quote' type contracts to annual price reviews, which gave them a greater degree of stability and was again an indication of the high level of trust. Contracts generally had extended with a shift from short term contracts to fairly open ended yearly rolling controls. Only one firm reported a negative pricing policy, that is prices being reduced annually, and in this case the supplying firm was initiating such a policy due to productivity gains accrued from the 'learning curve', unlike the Nissan case study where the momentum was coming from the OEM.

Major changes, then, have taken place in Girling's relationship with its suppliers. However, the suppliers, whose customers also included major Japanese electronics firms, considered that Girling were still some way behind in their quality control and organization of purchasing. This is, perhaps, an unfair comparison for a number of reasons. Girling are having to undergo a dramatic turnaround in the culture of buyer-supplier organization and are therefore having to start behind the field of Nissan or Sony. The Girling plants have existing workforces and existing cultures, issues which have to be addressed.

8 CONCLUSIONS

As the introduction noted, Lucas differ from the other case studies in a number of respects. First, they themselves are major suppliers and sub-contractors and are therefore dependent upon the policies of the firms they supply to. As the Nissan case study illustrated, supplying to companies such as the Rover Group is sometimes fraught with difficulties in areas such as scheduling.

The second difference, and perhaps the more important one, is the state of the company in the early 1980s. Unlike Sony and Nissan, which were greenfield locations, and IBM which at the time was a highly profitable and well-organized company, Lucas were in some disarray, with out-of-date business and manufacturing practices manifesting themselves in a trading loss.

Judged in this light, Lucas have made major improvements in the business strategy, in their manufacturing strategy and their supplier relationships. However, as company representatives acknowledge there is considerable room for further improvement and the company were unfavourably compared on a number of occasions by suppliers with Japanese customers, whom Lucas are trying to emulate.

6 Sony UK: Supplier Development and the Cooperative Ethos

1 INTRODUCTION

Sony's Bridgend Colour television plant in South Wales was a milestone in Japanese investment. Although not the first Japanese company to locate in Wales, it was the catalyst for considerable further investment in Wales in consumer electronics. The region now has over thirty Japanese-owned plants primarily engaged in consumer electronics, which represents the largest regional concentration anywhere in the EEC. The initial wave of original equipment manufacturers has been followed by a second wave of component suppliers. Sony remains, in employment terms, the largest single Japanese investment in the UK.

This chapter is divided into seven sections. The second will outline the company's competitive position which has had a major impact on the 'global localization' policy of the company, described in the third section. Sections four to six focus solely upon Sony's operation in the UK. Section four describes the production organization at the Bridgend plant. The buyer-supplier relations are covered in sections five and six, the former giving the Sony perspective and the latter that of its suppliers.

2 SONY TO 1990

Compared to the other major Japanese consumer electronics corporations, Sony were formed relatively late; the company did not come into operation until after the Second World War, when Masaru Ibuka formed the Tokyo Telecommunications Engineering Corporation, later to become Sony. The corporation is marked by innovation, both in a product and an organizational sense. The first technological breakthrough was in the late 1940s with a tape recorder, but the product that made Sony a world class innovator came in 1957 when Sony developed the first successful small transistor radio (Morita 1987; Quinn et al., 1988). Sony's decision to develop its own technology at that time was crucial for the company and for Japanese manufacturers generally. As Quinn *et al.* (1988) argue:

> It was a momentus change for Japan and Japanese manufacturers had to become truly independent of foreign technology, for perhaps the first time.   (p. 728)

This development also marked a new departure in buyer-supplier relations, as Sony had to lend component producers technological assistance in order to persuade them to supply the necessary components.

Two years later the company changed it's name and pioneered product innovation, including solid state and transistorized televisions in the 1960s, its Trinitron tube in the late 1960s, and in the 1980s the Walkman Personal Steroes, the Malvica camera, compact disc player, the video cassette recorder, 3.5 inch floppy disks and hand held video cameras (Morita, 1987).

The innovative nature of the company arose from attempts to compete with older established firms. The company had few relations with major banks or with government; indeed its relations with government were sometimes extremely frosty (Quinn *et al.*, 1988). Moreover, the innovative style extended to other aspects of the corporation's strategy. A later section will describe the internationalization strategy of the corporation. The company was also innovative in its personal and employment practices; pioneering single status, cellular manufacturing, team working and job rotation in the 1960s (Quinn *et al.*, 1988).

Despite Sony's earlier core competancies in consumer electronics, specializing in televisions and audio and video equipment, the company diversified away from those activities in the late 1980s. This was part of a twofold diversification programme, the second part of which – geographical diversification – is described in the next section. Thus in 1988–89, the two strong growth areas in sales were in video equipment and other products (Sony Corporation, 1989).

This diversification is reflected in the corporation's sales figures in recent years. Television sales now account for only 17 per cent of revenue, audio equipment accounts for 19 per cent, and video equipment for 36 per cent. A rights issue for £980 million in 1989 for expansion included plans for further semiconductor production, the development of high definition television in Japan and the USA, computer disk drive production – in which it is the world market leader – and workstations. This transformation has not been achieved entirely painlessly, since in the mid-1980s the company's financial performance was poor. Despite steady sales between

1985 and 1988, income fell considerably before the corporation doubled its consolidated profits in 1988–89 (Sony Corporation, 1989; Thomson, 1989b). In general, the Japanese audio producers have struggled against low cost producers overseas and a saturated home market. However, the larger groups have confounded pessimistic forecasts by moving upmarket into the new high technology areas of telecommunications and computer equipment.

Thus Sony has been diversifying into new areas such as semiconductors, computer disc drives, video equipment and high definition television. The workstation market is another area of diversification and Sony has led the Japanese challange in this market. As Dodsworth (1988) has pointed out, while this is a growing market, it is dominated by major US producers such as Apollo, Sun, Hewlett Packard and Digital Equipment. Moreover, in North America Japanese products are prone to considerable tariffs, which has led Sony to start up a manufacturing line for its NEWS workstation at its San Diego plant. However, the attack on this market is risky given the need to collaborate closely with customers and software providers, of which Sony has few outside Japan.

Perhaps the most interesting and best publicized diversification strategy of Sony has been in the 'software' market. Included in this strategy was the takeover of two American firms C.B.S. Records in 1988 and Columbia Pictures Entertainment in 1989, at a combined price of $2 billion. While this strategy may seem initially to be straight forward diversification, there is considerable synergy with Sony's existing operations. The purchase of C.B.S. Records, for example, ties in with audio hardware, including compact disc players, while the purchase of Columbia Pictures is linked with developments in high definition televisions and the camcorder. There is also the possibility of the merger of the two activities in that the purchase of the 'software' of Columbia Pictures is already designed to boost hardware sales. Sony is trying to boost sales of its 8mm video and competing with the 16mm standard of other producers, and if it controls pre-recorded films which will be on the 8mm format this will clearly help. This may prevent the kind of difficulty that Sony experienced with the VCR betamax: in that case Sony developed a technologically superior product but ultimately lost out to the JVC format, which the majority of Japanese producers accepted as the industry standard.

The twin purchases of C.B.S. and Columbia will result in approximately 25 per cent of Sony's sales being concentrated in 'software'. The Columbia purchase also fits with Sony's development of the new standard for television manufacturing high definition television (HDTV) in which applications go beyond broadcasting to printing, data transmission, medical equipment, surveillance systems and CAD-CAM. Sony, as the market leader, together with other big Japanese corporations, also seems set to dominate this market segment (Rapoport, 1988).

The corporation has also had an extensive geographical diversification policy, Sony now has plants in sixteen countries, as well as thirty affiliated firms and consolidated subsidiaries in Japan (Sony Corporation, 1989), a theme which is the focus for the next section.

3   SONY'S GLOBAL AND EUROPEAN STRATEGY: 'GLOBAL LOCALIZATION'

The overseas production strategy of Sony reflects its more general pioneering strategy in product markets and innovation as a competitive edge. The innovation in this case has been to establish overseas production bases as a way of boosting market share in comparison to more conservative Japanese competitors, although the company is following strategies employed by US multinationals such as IBM and Ford.

Sony's policy, much like Honda's, has been one of 'global localization' (see Morris, 1991a), which other Japanese electronics and automobile manufacturers have copied. The basis of this strategy is to serve local markets from the inside, much as American corporations such as General Motors and IBM have done. The new elements of such a policy, however, are that there are increasing technological, market and political imperatives to do so. In particular there is a need to serve markets from domestic production bases in order to be responsive to local market peculiarities, and there is a strong political rationale given import restraints, tarrif barriers and so on. The scale of this 'local market' is essentially that of supranational trading blocks, involving North America (including Mexico), the EEC, and Japan and the Western Pacific Rim (North and South East Asia, Australia). This has also been driven by the fact that Sony are export oriented. Indeed, they are one of Japan's most 'international' companies; only 34 per cent of sales in 1988 were in Japan (Wagstyl and Buchan 1989).

In accordance with these market and political imperatives, production is being reorganized on an integrated scale in these blocks. Sony has had three major areas of relocation and development:

(i)   *Japan and East and South East Asia*: there has been a considerable shift of production of consumer electronic products and components from Japan to other South and East Asian Countries. This is especially true of lower value added products such as consumer electronics, rather

TABLE 6.1   *Sony's European manufacturing operations*

	Location	Product(s)	Started	Employees
1	Bayonne, France	Audiocassette tape	1980	370
2	Dax, France	Camcorders Video Cassette tape	1984	210
3	Colmar, France	HiFi/C.D. Players, 8mm Video	1986	648
4	Bridgend, UK	CTV, Tubes	1974	1,700
5	Stuttgart, WG	Audio, CTV, Videos	1975	640
6	Barcelona, Spain	Audio, CTV, Videos	1982	250
7	Anif, Austria	Compact Discs	1987	248
8	Roverto, Italy	Audiocassette tape	1988	150

SOURCE: Sony Corporation.

than the newer products outlined earlier in the chapter. As part of this strategy, Sony announced in 1989 the location of a plant in Singapore to produce tubes for colour televisions (CTV) and assembly factories in Malaysia and Thailand, replacing production from Japan.

(ii) *North America*: as with Europe, Sony were the first Japanese CTV Manufacturer to locate in North America when Sony located a plant in San Diego, California in the early 1970s. This plant has been expanded considerably and now producers workstations, one of the areas in which Sony is focussing attention. It is served by a research centre at San Jose, California.

(iii) *EEC*: Sony now has an extensive European wide complex of plants which is rivalled only by Matsushita Electric amongst the Japanese producers, and which is set to grow considerably in the 1990s. The hub of the operation is the Bridgend plant, which opened in 1974. The company now has eight Western European plants spread across the UK, France, West Germany, Spain, Italy and Austria (see Table 6.1).

There is no duplication of products between plants. While there are, for example, three CTV plants, they produce different models. Moreover, there is also a strong degree of integration between plants; the Bridgend plant, for example, supplies picture tubes to the West German and Spanish plants. Similarly the Alsace plant makes components of sub-assemblies for other European plants.

The expansion of Sony's operations in Europe extends beyond the number of plants; it includes diversification of product lines – CTV's, hifi, compact disc players, audio and video cassette recorders, camcorders and video and audio cassette tapes – and it includes vertical diversification up and down the value chain. Local content levels, for example, have slowly risen to the position where they are close to 100 per cent on certain products. This has been achieved through a sometimes painful process of using local suppliers and through transferring production from Japan to the EEC.

On certain product-lines – colour televisions, for example – Sony's European plants now virtually satisfy local demand, which – in 1988 – comprised some 8 per cent of EEC market share (Rodger, 1988). The plans for the 1990s include raising local content further by transferring production of high value added components such as semi-conductors, VCR heads, optical pick–ups and magnetic tape coating.

Sony was one of the first Japanese manufacturers to locate R & D activities in the EEC. This was at Bridgend, which now has forty design engineers, with back-up from the Stuttgart plant and from Japan.

The company plans further major expansion in preparation for full EEC integration in 1992, which will include semi-conductor and telecommunications production in the early 1990s, the building of several component plants and increased research and development activity. Major growth areas are likely to be telecommunications (mobile communications), computers, robotics, medical electronics and security systems, which could be carried out by Sony alone, or by collaboration and joint ventures (de Jonquieres and Dixon, 1989). Specific plans include a $70 million magnetic coating tape plant at Dax to serve the Italian tape assembly plant and increase its local content from 50 per cent to 100 per cent; a $150 million semiconductor plant; component factories to produce video heads and drums and optical pick-ups for compact disc players to increase local content in European made VCR's and CD's; two telecommunications research and development centres in the UK and West Germany and a high definition TV research centre in West Germany (Dawkins, 1989; de Jonquieres and Dixon, 1989).

The commitment to this policy of global localization is repeated in the autonomy it gives to its international managers. In 1989, for example, Sony appointed a European and an American to its main board, the first Japanese company to do so. This is part of a strategy of a largely self-sufficient industrial *and* management infrastructure with substantial freedom to run its own affairs. As de Jonquieres and Dixon (1989) note, the essence of the plan is to transfer from Japan the functions needed to perform the entire product life cycle including design and development. As they go on to argue, this is in part a response to uncertainty about 1992 and local content rules.

This policy of global localization, therefore, is manifested in the scale of Sony's operations in Western Europe and in particular, at the Bridgend site, which is the focus of the next section.

4 THE BRIDGEND PLANT

Sony was the first Japanese colour television manufacturer to locate in the EEC when they set up a production facility in Bridgend in 1974. That plant was seen by other Japanese manufacturers as a 'test case', one which eventually led to firms such as Hitachi and Panasonic locating plants in South Wales (Morris, 1987; 1988a) in what Connor (1989) terms the 'domino effect'.

The Bridgend plant now employs 2000 workers and is the largest Japanese plant in the UK although it will eventually be surpassed by the Nissan and Toyota investments. The size of the plant is a reflection of Sony's policy of manufacturing virtually all of their European sales of colour televisions within Europe and the vertically integrated nature of the plant. Total investment at Bridgend is estimated to be approximately £95 million, with a further expansion of the tube plant, currently underway, adding £48 million. This will raise the proportion of locally (European) produced tubes close to 100 per cent .

The plant, it is claimed, is one of the most vertically integrated colour television manufacturers in the world. In addition to assembling colour televisions, the plant produces Trinitron tubes, by far the most valuable component in the television, for the Bridgend, Stuttgart and Barcelona plants, printed circuit boards, high voltage transformers and deflection yokes (Lloyd, 1989). Production output in 1990 included approximately one million TV sets, including a range varying from screen sizes of 14 inch to 29 inch. Some 75 per cent of output is exported, the vast majority to the EEC. Due to being a vertically integrated plant the workforce is large by the standards of a modern CTV factory.

The Bridgend plant has a reputation as one of the most efficient manufacturing units in the UK. Indeed, in 1989, it was chosen by the journal *Management Today*, from a survey by management consultants A. T. Kearney, as one of the five 'best factories', 'recommended for the excellence of their practice according to the criteria of operations management, quality, technology, organization and clarity of mission (Ferguson, 1989).

When Sony introduced their '1D project', in 1984, quality levels were ten times worse than in equivalent plants in Japan and thus the long term future of the plant depended on improving quality (Lloyd, 1989). In 1985, having identified the objectives and targets, plant management in Sony developed two broad concepts. The first was that of 'unit management', whereby each manager was responsible for his or her own work area or unit and that unit's target. At the time shopfloor workers also became involved and a quality circles programme ensued. The second concept was that of 'upstream action', whereby problem solving would be attempted at source to avoid recurrence; a practice of 'do it right first time'.

Developments in later years tended to reinforce these programmes and practices. One important part of the transformation was to communicate to shopfloor employees the need for quality. CEDAC diagrams (cause and effect diagrams with the addition of costs) were introduced, which gave a great impetus to the drive.

Involved in the quality campaign were a zero defects programme and total quality control. This included vertically integrating the factory, the reverse of what might be anticipated from a Japanese concern, including bringing in-house tube manufacture and printed circuit board (PCB) manufacturing. In-process checks such as SPC were introduced using frequency charts. The result of this combination of such techniques has been a seventy fold reduction in faults over four years.

Product design was a second key area. A major problem at Bridgend was in product variability but in 1984 Sony designed a 'Eurochassis', common to all products, which – with other standardization methods – led to big increases in productivity. In addition to the R & D centres, some 200 graduate engineers are employed at the plant.

The large production volumes in operation at Bridgend mean that production lines are in operation. However, in order to build-in flexibility into the system, the company has invested heavily in information technology and flexible automation. Production is carried out in cells of small teams of workers in the CTV assembly area with a minimum of component inventory using a Kanban system.

All of these aspects, of course, quality, suppliers and delivery and design, depend upon the quality of Sony's own personnel and the way that they operate within the plant. Extensive training is carried out – for example, key workers have recently been trained in Sony's plant in San Diego and a plant in Japan – on the introduction of a new tube. Skilled workers are multiskilled and all workers are salaried. The communications process includes daily team briefing, charts and reward systems.

These innovations in quality have been implemented alongside the innovative personnel practices which have become the hallmark of Japanese manufacturing organizations. All workers at the Bridgend plant, for example, have single status terms and conditions and open communications are seen as crucial, with regular weekly communications meetings taking place in addition to the quality circle meetings and the five minute meeting which starts each shift. In common with the other big Japanese manufacturers which have located plants in the UK, Sony have a single union deal with a no strike clause. Unusual, at least for the electronics industry, this deal is with the engineers union, the AEU, rather than the electricians union, the EEPTU.

As the plant moved from an assembly operation to full production, the number of European suppliers inevitably increased, from virtually none in 1973 to approximately one hundred and twenty in 1990. All mechanical components are sourced in the UK, many locally. This is seen by Sony's top management as a crucial long term strategy:

> We can't survive long term in the UK without a strong base. If we can have an infrastructure of small excellent component manufacturers around us, that is a competitive edge. (Anthony Abbot, *Bridgend's* general manager, in Ferguson, 1989)

5 BUYER-SUPPLIER RELATIONS AT BRIDGEND: SONY'S POLICY

One of the major problems of Sony's UK operation has been the development of a reliable local supply base, a difficulty which has affected quality levels at the Bridgend plant. Sony are not unique among Japanese owned companies in facing these difficulties. The Japanese electronics producers generally have voiced concern with this problem. Successive JETRO reports on Japanese manufacturing in the EEC, based upon questionnaires sent to Japanese companies, have illustrated that this is the major negative feature associated with locating a plant in the EEC (JETRO, 1984; 1987).

The latest of these reports suggests that, although Japanese suppliers are locating plants in the EEC, and despite firms such as Sony introducing supplier development programmes, significant problems still exist. Thirty-nine of the seventy-one Japanese electronics and electrical equipment respondents reported that local procurement was their greatest concern. Quality of component supply was the major problem, although delivery and price were also major issues. This has led in turn to major quality problems at the major Japanese consumer electronics plants in the UK and the EEC, with high defect rates and has necessitated inward inspection of components (JETRO, 1989). It has also made moves to increase local content more difficult, be it for reasons of overcoming EEC barriers or attempts to integrate into the EEC economy, and explains in part why Japanese companies have set up 'screwdriver assembly' operations.

The fault, of course, as with automotive component suppliers, does not only lie with suppliers *per se*, but is a function of the system in which they have traditionally operated. Trevor (1988), for example, has illustrated the vastly different relationships which existed pre- and post- the Toshiba take-over of the Plymouth plant where supplier development became a key principle of turnaround, and a similar picture emerges with Hitachi's gradual take over of the GEC plant at Hirwaun, South Wales (see also Morris 1987; Pegge, 1986; Trevor and Christie, 1988).

Whatever the case, problems with suppliers caused major operational constraints at Sony's Bridgend plant well into the 1980s (Dixon 1989; Lloyd, 1989). John Hoskins, component quality manager at Sony, is quoted as saying, 'Five years ago, quality at Sony's television plant was a 'disaster'; 30 per cent of components were rejected'. For this reason, allied with delivery problems and the fact that significant proportions of components were still being imported from Japan, stock levels of components were equivalent to fifty-one days of production (Dixon, 1989). This pattern has now been changed dramatically, with reject rates being reduced to 0.29 per cent and stocks reduced to seventeen days.

Sony, as with other large firms, classifies suppliers and sub-contractors separately. The problems of definition remain, however, as Sony's method of distinguishing between suppliers differs from the other companies in the study. Included in the sub-contractor category are a few small local companies which receive materials from Sony and make them up into various sub-assemblies; these firms include ones run by former Sony employees who have been encouraged by the parent to start their own businesses as sub-contractors to Sony.

While the Bridgend plant is vertically integrated, it is certainly not as integrated as the older UK plants such as the former Rank factory at Plymouth (now owned by Toshiba) or the GEC plant at Hirwaun, South Wales (now owned by Hitachi), where a far greater variety of components, such as transformers, were produced in-house. The vertical integration stems from two factors. First, the array of components made in-house, notably the picture tubes (which amount to over half of the value of the set) and other components such as printed circuit boards. These tend to be outsourced in Sony's Japanese factories but have been brought in-house at Bridgend due to the poor quality of boards provided by UK Suppliers.

Sony, at the time of interview, had 120 EEC suppliers, although this included Japanese distributers with a UK base. Local content, as judged by material cost, is approximately 90 per cent. Largely due to the rise in the value of the yen, there has been a gradual movement of component sourcing away from Japan in the past few years, both to other eastern and South East Asian countries, and to the EEC. Indeed, as part of the more general 'global localization' strategy outlined earlier in the chapter, in order to achieve one hundred per cent local content, Sony intends to transfer several more component supply and related factories to the EEC, including semiconductor facilities and videocassette recorder and compact disc component facilities.

The Bridgend plant is gradually moving to a just-in-time supply system, which they equate with daily delivery. Thus for bulky, relatively low-value added parts, components and supplies, the majority of suppliers are within a one hour drive time. At present the company is experimenting with Kanban deliveries from ten suppliers. Over 90 per cent of supplies are not inward inspected and thus are quality assured supplies (Ferguson, 1989). This will be assisted by the electronic data interchange system between OEM and suppliers – Tradanet – currently being introduced.

In order to overcome supplier problems, Sony have developed a threefold strategy of:–

(i)   using Japanese owned supplies
(ii) using new entrant suppliers
(iii) initiating an extensive supplier development programme.

Among the recent wave of Japanese companies who have located in the EEC in the past five to ten years, there have been a large number of electronic component suppliers or suppliers to the electronics industry (Morris, 1987; 1989b; 1991b). This includes suppliers owned by the large Japanese electronics companies as well as independents. Alps Electric, based in Milton Keynes, which produces remote control panels, was one of the first and largest, and Table 6.2 indicates the extent of this trend. A number of these plants supply to the Sony plant at Bridgend, including Alps Electric and Tabuchi. Perhaps the most interesting case is that of Diaplastics which produces major plastic injection mouldings for CTVs and which, despite being a Mitsubishi owned venture, is dedicated for the present to the Sony Bridgend plant, although it will later diversify to other customers. A feature of these OEM-owned suppliers is that, unlike in the

TABLE 6.2   *Japanese owned electronics suppliers in the UK*

Company	Location	Product(s)	Date of Location
Alps Electric	Milton Keynes	VTR components modulators, tuners	1984
Tabuchi	Middlesborough	transformers	1985
Mitsumi	South Tyneside	modulators/tuners for CTV'S	1988
Accuromm	Milton Keynes	plastic precision injection moulding parts	1988
Electronic harnesses	Llantrisant, South Wales	wire harness	1988
Kiyokuni	Telford	printer parts	1988
Matsushita Electronic Components	Port Talbot, South Wales	electric components	1988
Optec D. D.	Buckley, Clwyd	wire harness	1988
Sanyo Electric	Newton Aycliffe	electronic ranges magnetrons	1988
Sharp Precision	Wrexham	engineering plastics	1988
Omron Electronics	Telford	PCB	1988
Diaplastics	Bridgend	CTV plastic moulds	1988
Tsuda	Wrexham	VTR Plastic parts	1988
Murata	Plymouth	ceramic compositions	1990
Enplas	Milton Keynes	VCR components	1988

SOURCE: Anglo-Japanese economic Institute; Jetro; Various Press Releases.

automobile industry to date, they are far more likely to serve other OEMs. This is particularly true in the UK where the relatively low volumes of output of OEM plants, compared to Japan-based plants, precludes dedicated investment for one OEM alone.

Given the problems that UK based suppliers have had with meeting Japanese standards, the need to source greater percentages locally, and the close links between OEMs and suppliers in Japan, it is unsurprizing that these suppliers should have followed the OEMs, or even been encouraged by them to the EEC.

The second method of ensuring good UK supply links is by encouraging 'new entrant' suppliers. This has been done in two ways. First by actively encouraging employees to set up new sub-contract businesses. Such a policy has given Sony extra flexibility as demand for their products varies seasonally, with a peak in the winter and particularly at Christmas, and is also cheaper. The second method is by encouraging existing reliable firms to enter new areas of business. Otford EPS, who now supply plastic mouldings to the Bridgend plant, is one such example. Originally they supplied boxes to Sony, but with considerable assistance from Sony they developed a capacity to supply mouldings. Our supplier survey uncovered other such examples.

The final method of improving the supply network has been through developing existing suppliers, including those run by ex-employees of the firm and firms with no experience of individual component production but with a commitment to supply to Sony. The success of this policy of developing suppliers is a defect rate which is virtually zero and a 'quality assured' supply policy which means that Sony no longer has to inspect incoming components, in contrast to the mid-1980s when all components had to be inward inspected in one form or another.

Sony enters into two types of contracts with its suppliers. First a commercial contract for quantity and, secondly, a quality contract. Contracts are essentially open-ended with the proviso that, as long as standards are adhered to, then suppliers will be kept on, although the company is also aware that certain suppliers have made substantial investments in order to reach Sony's rigorous standards.

The three main issues that Sony regards as important in dealing with suppliers are net productivity (or decreasing costs), zero defects and just-in-time supply. The position that Sony aspires to is shown in Figure 6.1. The relatively small number of suppliers is part of a deliberate policy by Sony to limit its base through single sourcing of components and parts. However, it maintains a second source for parts should the main supplier fail them. While a key number of preferred suppliers are dependent on

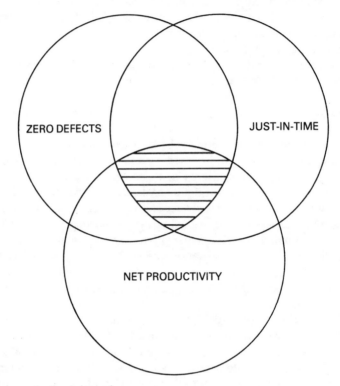

Source: Author's interview

Figure 6.1   Sony's supplier policy

Sony, the majority of these firms only supply up to 40 per cent of their output; this, however, does not represent a deliberate policy on the part of the company as it has done with IBM.

The process of choosing suppliers takes about six months, when Sony's engineering, development and quality staff undertake a review of the potential supplier. In general, Sony have found UK suppliers to be very poor in terms of quality and delivery. Often the company has been in a position of searching for potential suppliers rather than – as happened in the Nissan case, and as Sony expected – suppliers coming to them for business. Although the Sony respondent felt that the attitude among suppliers was changing, he felt that for the majority this had come too late. This also contrasted with the experience of the Sony Wega plant in West Germany, where the company has had a good response from local suppliers. This is fairly unique in the experiences of Japanese electronics firms elsewhere in the EEC and in North America. One Japanese commentator reported that a clear advantage of being located in Stuttgart was the high concentration of technologically advanced machinery manufacturers – especially in the area of precision processing – available in the city and region (Abo, in Trevor and Christie, 1988). The experience of the Sony-Wega operation has prompted Sony to encourage one of the best German suppliers, Ninka, to locate a factory in Cwmbran, South Wales.

Sony claimed to offer considerable technical assistance to its suppliers, which was confirmed in the supplier interviews. However, once a firm begins to supply to Sony, they are continuously monitored for performance in six key areas: quality, problem response, audit results, recurring faults, the zero defects campaign and paperwork. Supplier firms are regularly graded on these indicators and placed on a 'league table' of supplier firms according to their performance. Suppliers are informed of quantities required in a detailed production schedule one month in advance.

The main stress on suppliers is for good quality components and Sony has been pro-active in increasing supplier quality. John Hoskins, component quality manager at Bridgend illustrates this point: 'Rather than wait for poor product to hit us, we influence the way it is made. (Hoskins, in Dixon, 1989). This included the introduction of a 'zero defect campaign' in 1985 and it is now a condition that suppliers adhere to it. This campaign included sending quality controllers to monitor production, and applied not only to smaller suppliers such as Otford, but to larger firms such as Philips of the Netherlands, a major source of semiconductors and other electrical components (see also, Dixon, 1989).

The company, compared to Nissan, has been slow to move to a just-in-time delivery system. Even in the mid-1980s, the plant was accepting delivery weekly, but has now moved to daily delivery of locally sourced parts. Suppliers in the immediate locale – that is, South Wales – tend to be at the lower technology end of the spectrum, although this is gradually changing as new suppliers locate in the region. Elsewhere in the UK, suppliers are found in a variety of locations, ranging from Hampshire to Scotland. The company is now attempting, however, to introduce a just-in-time supply schedule, that is, multiple deliveries per day. To this end the company is trying to persuade suppliers to locate close to the Sony plant with a view to sourcing eighty per cent of local content within a fifty mile radius, or one hour drive time, of the Bridgend factory.

6   SONY UK'S BUYER-SUPPLIER RELATIONS:
    THE SUPPLIER'S PERSPECTIVE

Eleven Sony suppliers were involved in the survey, including Japanese, UK and Welsh owned firms and sub-contractors as well as suppliers. Unlike the supplier firms in the Nissan sample, the majority of these firms were engaged in relatively low value, bulky, low technology component production. Indeed Connor's (1989) study of Japanese electronics plants in Wales, which included Sony, suggested that higher valued added components were likely to be sourced from Japan and south east Asia for the foreseeable future. Even when they are sourced in Europe, these are likely to be sourced from the continent.

There are several explanations for this: first, as the previous section illustrated, Sony's Bridgend facility is now vertically integrated, one reason being that Sony have taken certain components in-house due to the poor quality of UK suppliers. However, this is not a one way process. Jenkins (1988), for example, cites the case of one of Sony's suppliers, Dove Assembly and Packing, which is run by a former Sony employee:

> When Dove Assembly's managing director worked for Sony he, along with other managers, was regularly encouraged by Sony's management to consider forming a business of their own with the purpose of supplying to Sony.   (Jenkins, 1988, p. 37)

Dove, a small company located close to the Bridgend plant, is one of a number of sub-contractors who work on a free issue basis, receiving materials and tooling from Sony and assembling for them. The large firm therefore vertically disintegrates, in that these functions were formerly carried out in-house (CRT shields and heat sink assemblies in the case of Dove), while maintaining some control and having supplier personnel whom they themselves have trained.

Second, outside of the Japanese component firms, there are now very few high technology suppliers remaining in the UK. A 1988 study, for example, showed that the largest source for components for the electronics industry in Scotland was Japan, which had overtaken the USA (Scottish Electronics Industry Database, reported in Buxton, 1988).

In common with the other case studies, three issues are critical, quality, delivery and price. The impact of Sony's quality standards upon its suppliers cannot be overstressed; without exception the suppliers viewed the collaboration with Sony to have been of tremendous value in teaching them new standards on quality. This applied to firms who supplied to the leading edge motor manufacturers – several, for example had, achieved Ford's Q101 standard – and to other Japanese consumer electronics plants in the UK. Several quotes from Sony suppliers, however, illustrate the major benefits they had received from dealing with Sony: 'We didn't think that we could set new quality standards. We already supplied to other Japanese companies but the relationship has been superb.' The respondent went on to say: 'Sony are more active and professional than other companies and their standards are very high.' Another replied: 'Sony's rigours on quality are affecting us fundamentally.' Yet another said: 'Sony are a model of quality control.'

The reputation of Sony for superb quality preceded them and proffered a significant status to suppliers. As one respondent replied: 'Sony are a superb name to have on your books.' Despite the impetus provided by Sony to improve quality standards a number of suppliers already had reasonably sophisticated quality systems in operation before being chosen as suppliers; indeed these factors would have been important in Sony's selection procedure, both with the implementation of quality controls and potential suppliers showing an attitude and willingness to change.

As we have seen, two firms already had Ford's Q101 quality standards. Others had already implemented quality improvement and zero defect programmes before supplying to Sony. The British Safety Standard BS5750 was one which firms already had or were working towards; one supplier reported that Sony was now insisting upon supplier firms achieving this standard. This has major implications for suppliers and small and medium sized firms generally, as other major firms may follow Sony's lead in insisting upon this as a 'bottom line'. Supplier firms without this standard, as a minimum, will find themselves increasingly marginalized.

Quality assurance was one part of the strict assessment of potential suppliers to Sony. The quality checks on suppliers typically included a full day process, with a review of all of the suppliers' systems which resulted in a points rating. The relationship, however, is not just a case of a one-off initial assessment but is part of an ongoing practice procedure in which Sony make continual checks on quality and are extremely willing to help suppliers to improve their quality standards and procedures. As one respondent explained:

Sony were dying to get in and have an input. For example they got us to use CEDAC charts which analyse problems via the operator.

The frequency of visits of Sony quality personnel varied from supplier to supplier, but typically was one per month, with far more frequent inter-company communications between the respective quality personnel. The performance of supplier firms is regularly monitored, with firms being assessed by scores which are combined with other indicators such as delivery.

Certain of the suppliers, presumably those with the best quality standards, were supplying Sony quality assured supplies and most were moving towards the ultimate goal of zero defects; one, for example, had a record of no component being rejected in eighteen months. One supplier described its quality assurance programme with Sony as 'integrated quality control'. Indeed for some of the suppliers, Sony had used the zero defect programme as part of a wider education in quality standards, including the organizational techniques necessary to implement quality control. To maintain Sony's quality standards also meant, in some cases, that suppliers had to invest heavily and continuously in new technology.

The move towards new quality standards has, for certain of the suppliers, meant a fundamental rethinking of their whole attitude towards production and the ways in which they conduct their business, rather than a series of minor incremental changes. The experience of one supplier, a packaging company, is a graphic illustration of this process. In 1980 the company had a very poor quality record – with final inspection, high defect rates, extremely costly scrapping of defects and few in-process checks. The respondent summed it up with the comment: 'We just hoped for the best'. The company was an early supplier to Sony, starting in the mid 1970s. The new quality demands initially seemed impossible and the supplier never thought that they would achieve them. However, ten years later these demands have largely been met by the supplier 'designing in' quality into the product than being reactive.

The turnaround started in 1982–83, when, as a previous section illustrated, Sony started to clamp down upon poor suppliers. Sony began to query why this particular supplier was producing defects in the first place, what led to such an event and gave advice on how to reschedule production runs. They questioned all aspects of the production process and introduced the firm to new accounting procedures which illustrated the enormous cost of waste. Finally, they made the introduction of a zero defects programme a condition of continued supply; the reject rate in the late 1970s stood at 10–15 per cent. However, in the context of the collaborative type of relationship between Sony and its suppliers, Sony were extremely patient in allowing the supplier to implement these changes. One firm described the change that they were having to undergo in these terms: 'Many of our customers are forcing us to change, but Sony is the most sophisticated; they organize it well in advance.' This particular firm had to change its emphasis from being production driven to sales driven.

In common with IBM, Sony exerts some influence over the second tier of suppliers, that is the suppliers' subcontractors. One respondent reported that while Sony personnel do not actually visit their suppliers, they do at least examine carefully the checks that the supplier has on its suppliers, including all records, details, files and specifications. In general, therefore, first tier suppliers were free to choose their own suppliers although they were encouraging them to implement quality standards such as zero defects with Sony's approval. Only in one case did Sony control the purchasing policy of one of its subcontractors, in this case down to the purchase of semiconductor devices from specific plants of individual firms.

Of the supplier sample, only one was mildly critical of one aspect of Sony's quality policy and this firm was generally very praising. Their criticism was that in the early days of supplying Sony had been very inflexible on certain issues of quality, but that this had now changed.

Production scheduling, and hence deliveries, is the second key area of supply. The frequency at which suppliers delivered to Sony varied from twice per day to once per week. For the suppliers with the most frequent deliveries, proximity to the Bridgend plant was important. Moreover, this was compounded in two cases by producing bulky, easily damaged parts. One of these firms was Japanese owned and had located five minutes away from the Sony plant and the second had opened a new plant in South Wales primarily to service Sony.

The frequency of delivery did pose certain problems for suppliers, notably in production planning. One supplier, for example, noted that Sony had changed their manufacturing strategy from large standard volume output to far lower volume product differentiation. Given the highly capital intensive nature of this firm's production they had formerly pursued a policy of producing in large volumes in order to achieve economies of scale, but had subsequently been forced to change this policy. Paradoxically, however, while this had posed obvious problems, it was also beneficial as it made the supplier totally reconsider its production planning. A second supplier had also undergone a similar experience, with delivery frequency falling over a number of years from three monthly deliveries to three times per week; and the firm was anticipating moving to 'synchronized manufacturing' in the near future, with multiple deliveries per day. However, the respondent again saw this as ultimately positive in that the planning, attitudes towards stock holding and work-in-progress and delivery methods all had to be reassessed and a more efficient way of working developed. In this respect Diaplastics, the Mitsubishi owned plant close to Sony's facilities, which supplies cabinets and sub assemblies, is at the leading edge, building up to three to four deliveries per day.

Not only has the frequency at which suppliers deliver to Sony increased, but the amounts vary from delivery to delivery. The crucial issue here, for suppliers, is prior knowledge of the required volume. Typically Sony gives schedules – which tend to be very accurate – to the firms one month in advance. None of the suppliers had encountered problems in the scheduling of volumes, and several were praiseworthy of Japanese consumer electronics firms – including Toshiba and Hitachi, as well as Sony – in this regard. A typical response was: 'There is far less panic in dealing with the Japanese.' All of the supply firms in turn tried to keep stockholding to a minimum. Although this varied from component to component, typical was a firm who made up the Sony order the day before it was required. Clearly this is not extending just-in-time to the level of refinement that some of Nissan's suppliers have achieved, but the difference can largely be ascribed to the different production processes.

One of the firms, who acted as a sub-contractor to Sony on a free issue basis, worked on a 'four day system', receiving components from Sony, assembling them and shipping them back within four days. The variability of demand not only required detailed planning but in some cases require considerable flexibility in terms of manpower. At least two of the suppliers made extensive use of temporary and part time workers for this purpose, while one used overtime working to adjust. Others emphasized the need to organize flexibly with skilled workers, for example, operating machines at lunchbreaks during times of peak demand.

The suppliers had a variety of perspectives on Sony's pricing policy and the evidence was confusing. Three of the firms, for example, felt that price considerations were important but much less so than issues such as service and quality. Indeed, one argued that as Sony did not compete directly on a price basis but rather a quality basis, they were willing to pay well for guaranteed quality, a policy that British companies are now starting to follow. They also argued that Japanese firms generally responded well to reasonable price increases based on increases in raw material prices. Another agreed that Sony were not so sensitive on price issues as other firms and recognized if they were in difficulty with increases in raw material prices. This, however, contrasted with their experience of other UK-based Japanese consumer electronics plants who operated a 'take it or leave it approach' with an attitude that 'inflation doesn't exist'.

Others of the suppliers argued the opposite, that they were being considerably squeezed between Sony on the one hand and large raw materials suppliers on the other. One argued that this had proved the major sticking point between themselves and Sony in the negotiation period. A second respondent argued that prices changed periodically and were very unstable, and that it was a continually moving target.

The initial contact between the two parties varied from supplier to supplier, in some cases it was Sony who made the initial contact while in others the supplier firm had approached Sony. While quality, delivery and price were the key criteria for choice of suppliers, the industrial relations record of the supplier was also important. As one procurement manager stated: 'If they are prone to industrial relations problems then, quite honestly, we should not, perhaps, bother with them' (quoted in Jenkins, 1988, p. 53). By their own admission, Sony initially had a poor opinion of several of the suppliers, but were willing to foster a relationship due to a positive attitude on the part of the supplier. In these cases the firms started as one of a number of supplier sources to Sony, although subsequently had become single sources due to a good record of supply. Another supplier had the opposite experience, having formerly been a single source to Sony for one component, but now being one of two suppliers. However, the respondent was candid about its inefficiencies:

It was obviously a reflection of our inability to respond adequately to their quality demands – they were unhappy with our process control. We were a low technology industry and we had never been put under a critical eye – we were found wanting when Sony looked at us. They said our flow line production was poor and urged us to use CAD-CAM. The final straw was when we provided an order to the Sony plant in West Germany and it was *full* of defects. It showed up our poor technical knowledge, faulty procedures etc. We lost a lot of business as a result and it shook us out of our complacency. Since 1987 we have made enormous changes, including big changes in management, an onslaught on costs and productivity and made major capital investment. Sony have been a major help to us, introducing a quality improvement programme, including BS5750.

This quote perhaps illustrates the quality gap between British suppliers and Japanese requirements, and explains the seeming reluctance on the part of Japanese producers to use British suppliers.

Time contracts, as such, do not exist between Sony and its suppliers (although normal commercial contracts do), but suppliers simply rely on the several months advanced orders, which one respondent termed a 'renewal contract'. That Sony and its suppliers have come to such an arrangement is a clear indication of the high degree of trust that exists between the two parties. One of the suppliers contrasted this with the traditional approach of UK firms, which it described as very short-sighted and short-term orientated. Where UK firms tended to merely seek the lowest possible price, Sony and other Japanese firms first sought good quality, then a reasonable price and once they had chosen suppliers, remained loyal, and worked in collaboration with them. This supplier's representative said: 'The big difference with the Japanese is that they look for suppliers with no intention of changing them.' The tendency towards single sourcing, the long-term relationships with suppliers and the commitment to quality is reflected in the long negotiation period spent between Sony and its suppliers; in one case, for example, of ten months.

All of the supplier firms felt that they were in a collaborative relationship with Sony, although this did not always extend to technical collaboration. One respondent described their relationship as being an extension of Sony and being committed to running units down their line. Face to face contact was seen as crucial, weekly meetings on delivery schedules and quality were common, and the suppliers were open to Sony personnel freely entering their plants. As one respondent put it: 'I wonder, sometimes, if there are more Sony people in my factory than my own employees.' Another found this intrusive in the early stages of the Sony collaboration, although Sony had lessened their presence and supplying firms, in turn, had become accustomed to the situation.

This collaboration extended in a number of cases to a close technical interchange. In these cases, Sony makes general specifications and the supplier develops the parts, regarding the supplier as the specialist with the requisite knowledge. In certain cases this included Sony lending certain tooling and machinery to suppliers.

The supplying firms, then, were extremely positive about their relationship with Sony. They benefited in a number of ways from the relationship: some, for example, were the main suppliers to Sony plants elsewhere in Europe, including the West German and Spanish colour television facilities. While the benefits went beyond the specific volumes of business that Sony gave its suppliers, these should not be discounted. The single-sourcing and the high volume of output at the Bridgend plant represented a good business opportunity for firms, especially those which had been supplying Sony from the mid-1970s.

As with others of the supplier samples, some of the supplier firms were adopting 'niche' marketing strategies of a sort, concentrating on supplying to blue chip companies. One firm, for example, had set a target of about ten leading-edge customers and would grow as they did, particularly as the volume of imports declined. This was not untypical, and often firms also supplied to other Japanese consumer electronic plants. Because of its cyclical nature, firms were also anxious to serve markets outside of consumer electronics, including automotives and office automation and computers.

Significant advantages were perceived from dealing with Sony, including the consistency of demand and accurate scheduling and the large volumes which enabled suppliers to invest in plant and machinery. This was summed up in a quote from one of the suppliers:

> They (Sony) are *the* quality firm, Bridgend is Sony's world number one plant and therefore to crack Sony was a coup for us. We figure strongly in their expansion plans and they are invaluable to our development, especially from the publicity point of view. The long term relationship is good and we *already* know them far better than a conventional UK company.

7 CONCLUSIONS

The Sony Bridgend plant offers some interesting insights into improving quality and changing supplier attitudes. In the early 1980s Sony's local management faced two major problems. First, there was the issue of poor internal quality. The remedies for this make an interesting case study in itself. Second, and following from the first, management were caught between Sony's global policy of localization of production on the one hand, and therefore its commitment to increasing local content, and on the other hand the very poor general standard of local suppliers.

As Dixon (1989) has noted, this was not purely a problem of supply from small local companies but a general European problem, with the company experiencing major difficulties with large suppliers such as Philips. Sony has used a number of strategies to overcome this. First, it has taken in-house component and part supply which, in the 'Japanese model', would normally be outsourced; PCBs is one good example. Second, it has made use of Japanese component suppliers based in the UK which it could rely upon, and, in the case of Diaplastics for example, which it actively encouraged to start production in the UK.

The third and fourth elements of the strategy have been to develop indigenous suppliers. It has, for example, trained firms such as Otford to produce the necessary components. In the fourth case it has gradually developed existing suppliers to meet Sony's exacting standards, particularly on quality. It is clear from the supplier interviews that this was a painstaking process in some instances, and that Sony were extremely patient for the time that certain suppliers took to meet these standards. In these cases, the relationships could be described as long-term, collaborative and endowed with trust.

If the process was painstaking in the case of Sony, it was also painful for the suppliers as many had to radically rethink the way in which they carried out their business, organized production and monitored quality and delivery. The effort, however, was viewed as worthwhile from the suppliers' perspectives and all considered that they had come out of the process far more efficient and better companies.

7 IBM, UK: From Control to Collaboration?

1 INTRODUCTION

The IBM case study is of interest for a number of reasons. The company is the world's third largest corporation, and in the UK alone employs nearly 18 000 and is its third largest manufacturing exporter. Moreover, it has dominated its market at a global level in a way few other companies have managed. Even in the late 1980s it had a 70 per cent share of the European computer market for hardware, software and services. IBM has become a bye-word for certain features; its distinctive corporate culture, its innovativeness, its quality and the professionalism of the organization.

Further, at a superficial level at least, it has many organizational similarities with the large Japanese manufacturing corporations which other western manufacturers were desperately attempting to emulate in the 1980s and still are in the 1990s (Womak *et al.*, 1990). Oliver and Wilkinson (1988) for example, contend that a comparison of IBM with Japanese companies in Japan or with Japanese companies in the UK reveals remarkable similarities and that IBM are a western organization which has, for many years, done many of the things for which the Japanese companies have become renowned, although Bassett (1986) takes a contrasting position, arguing that the IBM way is the opposite of the Japanese method.

This chapter will focus on some of these arguments, and in particular on IBM's relationships with its suppliers. It will become evident that while there are many similarities with the 'Japanese model', if indeed there is such a unified model, there are also many strains which are distinctive. While the next two sections of the chapter will focus on IBM generally, the substantive part of the chapter, sections four and five, will concentrate on one of IBM's two UK manufacturing plants, Havant in the South of England. This plant produces 9335 disk files and the interview material relates to this plant alone, although by and large the practices also apply to IBM's wider policy in the UK and indeed its wider corporate policy. As in the other case studies the main research evidence is preceded by some relevant contextual material on the company, including a brief history, the strategic position of the company, the UK operation and work organization at the Havant plant.

2 IBM TO 1990

IBM was formed in 1914 through a merger of three firms in New York, Ohio and Washington, to form a time recorder and calculator manufacturer, although it was not until ten years later that it became known as IBM. The company gained its reputation as an innovator from the early days of its formation; by 1935, for example, it had introduced the first commercially successful electric typewriter (Hamilton, 1989).

This process of innovation continued in the 1950s and 1960s when IBM emerged as a world class innovator and manufacturer and came to dominate the computer and data processing industry on a global scale (Parker-Jarvis, 1990). In 1952, for example, the company launched the 701, the first production model designed for scientific calculation. In 1954 it built the Naval Ordnance Research calculator, the fastest and most powerful hitherto, and in 1956 the company created SAGE, a major part of the USA's air warning defence system. In 1957, meanwhile, IBM introduced FORTRAN, which became the most widely used computer language for technical work.

The 1960s saw a number of key breakthroughs: the company, for example, played a central role in the USA's space programme, creating the computers used to track the Mercury space vehicle. The most important product innovation at this time was, however, the introduction of the IBM System/360, the first major compatible family of mainframe computers, which was introduced in 1964. This set the pattern for the future development of the entire computer business as their design quickly became the industry standard.

In association with this innovation process was a geographical spread and the phenomenal growth of the company. IBM's policy of 'global localization' preceded that of Sony by twenty to thirty years with production units and R & D centres spread across North America, Europe and Japan. The company also rapidly increased its workforce and at the time of the formation of the European Community in 1957 employed 15000 in Europe, a figure which had increased to 100000 plus by 1987.

By the late 1980s, IBM had come to dominate the computer industry in a way that few other companies do in their respective market segments. For example, 70 per cent of all mainframe computers sold worldwide were either manufactured by IBM or run on IBM software. The company was

TABLE 7.1   *Top ten data processors, 1988*

1988 rank	Company	Data processing revenue ($bn)	Corporate R & D spend ($bn)	R & D spend as % of corp sales
1	IBM	55.0	5.9	9.9
2	Digital	12.2	1.4	11.8
3	Fujitsu	10.9	1.5	8.9
4	NEC	10.5	2.0	8.8
5	Unisys	9.1	0.6	5.9
6	Siemens/Nixdorf	9.0	4.0	10.8
7	Hitachi	8.3	2.2	4.7
8	Hewlett-Packard	6.3	1.0	10.4
9	Olivetti	5.5	0.3	4.8
10	NCR	5.3	0.4	7.0

SOURCE: Datamation.

also a major components manufacturer; in semi-conductors, for example, which IBM produce only for internal consumption, they are by far the largest producer in North America and of a roughly similar size to the Japanese giants Fujitsu, NEC and Hitachi which, of course, sell on the open market. When IBM entered the 1980s, therefore, they were in an unrivalled position in the computer industry and their dominance of the market seemed almost impregnable. During the 1980s, however, the company faced a series of challenges to its position, which is documented later.

In 1988 IBM employed over 387 000 people worldwide distributed through seventy-five thousand companies and had a revenue of $5.8 billion (IBM, 1988). It remained the predominant force in computing and data processing; in 1988 its revenue from data processing was over four and a half times its nearest rival, Digital. Moreover, the company retained its leading edge on R & D expenditure, although as a percentage of corporate sales it had fallen behind Digital, Siemens/Nixdorf and Hewlett Packard in this respect (see Table 7.1). However, while revenues were still increasing at five to seven per cent per annum, this was considerably below the industry average of fifteen per cent. Such problems, which will be returned to later in the section, included a fundamental and irreversible decline in the growth of the mainframe market to which IBM had been tied, a splintering of the computer market place into a series of niches and a change in customer whereby the purchasers are now information technology directors rather than data processing departments. Technological improvements, for example, together with more powerful software and changes in the use of computers, has led to IBM being challenged by younger dynamic firms which have successfully exploited new market niches (Cooke and Wells, 1990). That is to say, these smaller young firms such as Digital and Sun Microsystems have entered into growing market niches, while the market segments that IBM have dominated, particularly mainframes, have seen a large relative decline in importance.

Despite IBM's pre-eminence in the global computer industry, the company faced an increasing number of challenges, both at a corporate and technological level, in the 1980s. While specific factors, such as technical problems and a shift towards leasing rather than outright purchases, were partly to blame for this poor growth rate, as Cane (1989) has pointed out, the underlying problems were more fundamental:

> IBM's present predicament, however, is only the tip of the iceberg. The fact is that profound long-term trends in the industry are choking the engine which powered IBM's growth, leaving it vulnerable for the first time in twenty-five years.

The challenge to IBM's main market segment started in the 1970s with the rise of mini- and midi-computers, particularly with DEC's unified VMS operating systems (Cane and Kehoe, 1988). In the 1980s the challenge has come from the phenomenal growth of the personal computer (PC). As a consequence, between 1975 and 1985 mainframes, as a percentage share of worldwide shipments by US manufacturers, dropped from 83 per cent to 36 per cent, while personal computers gained a 20 per cent share of the market from a zero base. This, of course, was a relative shift as output increased overall by five-fold in dollar terms. However, between 1988 and 1993 the business and professional PC market is expected to quadruple while the scientific and technical PC market will triple.

IBM has made a number of forays into these new market growth areas. Included in this was the purchase of Rolm, in anticipation of the technological convergence of computer and telecommunications, which proved a major drain on resources and was subsequently sold, at a loss, to Seimens in 1988 (Dixon, 1988; Oram, 1988b). A second example was the RT PC workstation introduced in 1986 which gained only 1.8 per cent of the world market in 1989 while other workstation producers were taking market share from IBM in other areas (Verity, 1990).

Allied to these hardware developments have been developments in software systems. Up until the early to mid-1980s, IBM dominated operating systems because of its predominance in hardware. That is, IBM virtually imposed its operating systems as the industry-wide standards, with customers 'locked in' to IBM operating systems. IBM was at this stage operating in a near monopoly situation and was therefore accruing monopoly-type profits. This situation was further compounded by other firms developing IBM 'clones' which used IBM standards. In the 1980s there was considerable movement to create compatibility between computers of different manufacturers – that is, 'open standards' although this has developed into a battle between the two main systems, Unix International (led by AT&T and Sun Microsystems) and the Open Software Foundation (IBM and DEC) (Cane, 1988). This is a crucial commercial battle, as systems and software are now the highest value added part of the computer industry (Greene-Armytage, 1990). These various commercial battles, plus the rise of the Japanese producers – Fujitsu, NEC, Hitachi are the world's second, third and fourth largest mainframe producers – have led to a considerable shake-out of the computer industry, and in particular the US industry (Rodger *et al.*, 1990).

IBM has not been the worst hit of the firms in this process, which is unsurprising given its size and market share. Nevertheless, following a reduction in profits in the early 1980s and a collapse in 1986, the company adopted a three year restructuring programme which incorporated cutting staffing levels, the elimination of bureaucracy, worldwide decentralization, collaboration with software and systems houses and a concentration on market specializations (Cane *et al.*, 1990). IBM has reduced its workforce from 407 000 to 373 000 in 1990, as a result of a big corporate restructuring programme (described by the company as the biggest in thirty years), which included the closure of five manufacturing plants in the USA (IBM, 1988; Oram, 1988a). The two major features of this corporate restructuring were first, a much greater emphasis placed on marketing and service functions, and second, a reorganization into seven main lines of business: Applications Solution; Programming Systems; Communication Systems; Enterprise Systems; Applications Business; Personal Systems and Technology Products.

The 1980s also saw the continued shift of IBM towards global production, or at least to continental production. The Greenock plant in Scotland, for example, is the European source for PS/2 machines while the Havant and Hursley plants in England are world sources for 9335 disk files and PS/2 colour monitors respectively. The final, major, development at IBM in the 1980s has been the growth of strategic alliances. In this regard IBM are no different from the other major computer hardware manufacturers or for that matter other major industrial organizations (Cooke and Wells, 1989). IBM's alliances have operated on a number of levels which, in general, have excluded links with other hardware companies. These include links with software houses such as Microsoft; links with telecommunications companies, notably Siemens; standards agreements and, finally, market-specific alliances in which IBM uses other organizations to achieve greater market penetration, including dealership alliances (Cooke and Wells, 1990; Oram and Fisher, 1988).

All of these factors had led to the company being forced to seek the new relationships with its suppliers, which are examined in sections four and five.

3   IBM IN THE UK

To understand the way in which IBM UK operates, the wider organisation of IBM worldwide and in Europe must be developed (Cane *et al.*, 1990). As the last section indicated, IBM has introduced a policy of global localization to its operations for the past thirty years. Thus products manufactured in a single plant may act as a single source of that product for IBM globally, or at least on a regional basis (in this case for Europe). The same is true for research and development activity, with individual research laboratories being responsible for product development in a number of product areas at a regional or worldwide basis.

The main activities of IBM UK are concentrated on three sites. IBM UK has two manufacturing plants, one at Greenock in Scotland which produces keyboards and information display systems for personal computers, and at Havant, Hampshire in southern England which produces the 9335 disk files and finance industry systems. The main product development operation is based at Hursley, near Winchester in the south east of England, which is responsible for research into communications programming products, low-cost disk storage, graphic products and advanced display technology. In addition to these three main sites, the company has its UK headquarters at Portsmouth, close to the Havant plant, and over sixty enquiry, education, marketing and software development centres located throughout the UK. In total the company employed some 17 700 in the UK, in 1986. The result of this global and European integration policy is that IBM is a major exporter both of semi-finished and finished products, and is the UK's third largest equipment exporter.

IBM's manufacturing methods are based on the ethos of total quality management, and yet this has been arrived at independently from the influence of the large Japanese manufacturers, although, as the later sections on buyer-supplier relations will illustrate, IBM are now seeking to emulate elements of Japanese best practice. Just-in-time production was introduced in the 1980s, under the guise of 'continuous flow manufacture' (CFM) and, together with quality, has been the key element in IBM's manufacturing strategy (Caulkin, 1988; Doran, 1986; Hewitt, 1989). In the years 1982 to 1988, due to this policy, revenues from the Havant plant have increased fourfold, defects have been cut by a factor of ten and multiplied inventory turn three times, while the manufacturing cycle is one-fifth (Caulkin, 1988).

The productivity improvements have largely been a result of the quality improvement programme. This programme, termed EXCEL, started at the end of 1980 in response to a view that Japanese competitors, in particular, were achieving higher standards of quality. Indeed, Japanese manufacturers were used as a benchmark for best practice. Responsibility for the programme was with functional managers and the programme included induction into the new techniques which would be used, such as quality circles. An intensive communication programme followed with the message that quality was the number one priority (Doran, 1986).

What emerged was that major problems were often inadequacies in the manufacturing support process, or in product design, and therefore engineering and support service staff were included in the process, as were procurement buyers and procurement and manufacturing engineers. The important elements were pressure for better service from manufacturing operatives and peer pressure to emulate quality improvements in other parts of the Havant plant. Customer visits were also introduced to gauge the level of satisfaction with products.

In order to measure quality improvements, the EXCEL team set quantifiable annual targets for improvements, such as reductions in failure rates, which were widely communicated. The procedure led to a considerable re-evaluation of the manufacturing philosophy. As Doran (1986) comments:

Over the whole 1981–1983 period, the thought-processes induced by this programme clarified Havant's strategic goals and made them more attainable. One clear conclusion was that the guaranteed way of avoiding defects in a particular activity is to stop it. Over the years, the total process had grown to include many activities which added no real value. The long-term goal was essentially to be the high-quality, low-cost producer in the industry. One element of the strategy to achieve this is the avoidance of waste – whether in defects or unnecessary activities.   (p. 98)

Among the innovations and benefits were cross-functional cooperation, visible and public display of targets and an increasing responsibility for quality of manufacturing operations. The second phase has involved pilot projects for continuous flow manufacture, with an emphasis on employee motivation and organizational improvements rather than the introduction of flexible automation.

These two phases encompassed a series of ten techniques introduced at the Havant plant (Ward, 1987), including waste elimination; flexible manufacturing; more effective asset utilization; reductions in work in progress; group technology; mixed mode assembly; kanban control; a zero defect drive; 'management by sight' and multiskilling and teamworking. Supplier integration was to be part of the overall strategy.

Closely allied to this drive for greater quality and just-in-time production, and essentially facilitating or easing its introduction, were a series of employment and industrial relations practices which on the whole were fairly unique in a UK context. These included employment contracts, selection, induction and training policy, payment and reward systems, consultation and communications and industrial relations practices (Brady, 1987a; Oliver and Wilkinson, 1988; Peach, 1985). IBM, for example, has a *de facto* lifetime employment policy, although this has been sorely tested in the 1980s as the company cut back its workforce. Such a policy is maintained by a tight manning policy, flexibility and job rotation. The practice is also assisted, of course, by the subcontracting policy which is described later in the chapter.

Given IBM's reputation as a blue chip employer, its long term employment policy plus its favourable payment rates, it is unsurprizing that the company is not short of applicants. It thus uses a careful vetting and screening procedure, followed by an induction process which acts as a socialization procedure to the company's strong culture. The payment and reward systems at IBM are equally unusual in a UK context. A system of individual rewards pertains with fierce competition for promotion and motivation maintained by publicly displayed performance indicators (Spiridion, 1987). Communications are encouraged by the company's open-door policy, with grievances the responsibility of immediate superiors. In addition there is an anonymous communication procedure termed 'speak up'. Oliver and Wilkinson (1988) maintain that a combination of such practices as the reward systems, selection procedure and its consultation and communications channels militates against attempts to unionize.

IBM, therefore, is a highly distinctive company in terms of its production organization. An integral part of this package is its relationship with its suppliers, which will be discussed in the next section.

4 BUYER-SUPPLIER RELATIONS AT HAVANT: IBM'S POLICY

The age of IBM's Havant plant – it was opened in 1968 – has meant that the buyer-supplier policy has changed considerably over the years, and in the last five to ten years in particular. IBM is also fairly unique in a UK context, in that while many of their buyer-supplier policies have affinities with the so-called 'Japanese model', they were introduced independently of Japanese influence and before the Japanese model became in-vogue. However, while IBM, alongside Ford, could be regarded as offering an example of 'best practice' in the field of buyer-supplier relations, this does not deflect from the fact that the firm is now undergoing a gradual transformation in its buyer-supplier relations.

The changes at IBM represent, in some ways, a culture change for the company. The tradition at IBM up until the 1970s was of self-sufficiency; we have seen, for example, that the company is the world's largest producer of microchips, for its own consumption. The introduction of personal computer production, however, marked a change in orientation for the company, with a shift to relying on outside suppliers (Evans and Doz, 1989). The most visible change at IBM Havant is the amount of work being subcontracted out. While all key technologies are being kept in-house, cable harnesses and assemblies and 'buffer' work such as mechanical operations, plastics and castings are now increasingly subcontracted out including high level assemblies. In times of emergency this work would be called in as IBM maintains its innovative technology and ideas within the company. Keyboard manufacture is one example of this.

The plant is increasingly moving, therefore, to an assembly rather than a manufacturing operation, whereby the company gets its machines built outside the plant and merely tests products and puts the IBM label on them. The nature of the product manufactured at Havant has meant that the plant is not as vertically disintegrated as IBM's other UK plant at Greenock in Scotland. Moreover, the company is extremely wary of letting its technology out, particularly 'card' technology. In order to avoid this, the company has a policy of splitting the machine into small parts and giving the different parts to different sub-contractors to make up. Nevertheless some 75–80 per cent of machines 'produced' at Havant are now manufactured by sub-contractors.

IBM representatives were explicit about the advantage of sub-contracting on such a scale. The company increasingly sees itself as a 'marketing organization', with a greater emphasis on placing resources into selling products. Sub-contracting is clearly seen as a way of pushing expensive overhead costs onto the sub-contractor and the company, in an attempt to reduce inventory, will attempt to put more work out. Sub-contractors have, for example, been used to reduce or at least restrict, the number of IBM's own workforce. As an overall indication of the increase in subcontracting IBM's total UK spend on sub-contracting increased from £720 million to £920 million in the year 1986–1987 alone (the 1980 level stood at approximately £120 million), while in the same year the total number of UK suppliers to IBM fell from 6720 to 4796 (IBM, 1987).

While the amount of work subcontracted out is increasing relatively slowly, what is important is that the method of sub-contracting out is changing. First, the supplier base, in common with other large firms, has been declining. In the mid 1980s, IBM's Havant supply base comprised of approximately one thousand firms; by the late 1980s this had been reduced to 570 firms. This total of 570 was comprised of two levels, including 70 preferred suppliers who were certified Category A (the top category), with the remainder in categories B and C. These included firms approved to the British Safety Standard BS5750 *plus* an IBM approved standard. The rationales for this decrease was first one of costs, and second, the ease of control of a smaller number of suppliers. The third, and most important rationale, is that the company is placing different demands on sub-contractors. With IBM's corporate strategy turning towards customer orientation and sensitivity to changes in market demand, IBM now needs to respond far more flexibly, and suppliers also need to be flexible. Thus, the final rationale for decreasing the number of suppliers has been to create a manageable pool of suppliers able to respond flexibly to IBM's demands.

The major changes in IBM's buyer-supplier policy dates back to 1982–83. This change in policy was part of the wider EXCEL programme described earlier in the chapter, which attempted to increase quality performance at Havant. As part of this quality drive, procurement buyers and engineers embarked on a programme to radically improve the quality and delivery of purchased parts and, in turn, suppliers were drawn into the programme (Doran, 1986). At this stage there was an engineer and buyer assigned to each product group, but the company is now moving towards vendors who are self-supporting. The majority of work outsourced used to be done on a free issue basis with some 75 per cent plus of work was put out on this basis. By the late 1980s, however, the firm was simply subcontracting work out.

All of these moves represent, to an extent at least, a relinquishing of control by IBM over its suppliers. Previously suppliers had been tightly controlled, but gradually IBM is moving towards giving more autonomy to suppliers. This, however, is not a simple progression. It represents a considerable shift in corporate culture from secrecy and control to openness and greater autonomy which members of IBM's purchasing department had some difficulty in coming to terms with.

The degree of control is still, in some ways, considerably greater than in the other case studies. IBM extends its preferred list of suppliers several tiers down the hierarchy. Thus the grade A and B suppliers have 'nominated' lists of suppliers who they must purchase from. This is a throwback to an earlier policy; up until 1980, IBM would buy large amounts of individual components, such as wires and cables, which were 'free issued' to sub-contractors. While the company no longer does this, it maintains the sources of supply and insists that sub-contractors now buy directly from them. Interestingly the numbers in this pool of second tier suppliers has been maintained. Therefore, while there has been a reduction in the number of overall suppliers to IBM Havant, there has also been a reordering of the tier structure.

The company also maintains control through its rigorous evaluation process in choosing suppliers, which takes up to six months. This includes all of the usual checks such as quality, delivery, price and so on, and includes also the industrial relations record of the supplier and their financial viability, right down to the individual security of suppliers. Although the company is in a position of contracting its immediate supplier base, it does investigations of new potential suppliers.

IBM have in the past had a maximum ceiling of output bought from each supplier. However, with an increasing amount being outsourced to fewer suppliers, IBM has relaxed its '15 per cent-of-output maximum to IBM rule' and now has no upper limit, although the company reviews the finances of suppliers to ensure that overdependency does not occur. The majority of the suppliers to IBM Havant are UK based, some 75 per cent, with the remainder spread globally. The latter group, however, includes a considerable number of Japan-based suppliers, largely electronics based components which are either not available in the UK, are too expensive in the UK, or are not up to the requisite quality standards.

As with the other case studies the three main issues of the buyer-supplier policy at IBM Havant are delivery, quality and price. The majority of suppliers operate on a daily delivery basis to Havant, although on certain components multiple deliveries per day are made. This fits with the manufacturing strategy at Havant of 'continuous flow production', which is akin to just-in-time production. The company has gradually been moving towards a just-in-time supply system since 1975 and suppliers have had to adjust to IBM passing inventory down the line by, in turn, pushing it out to their suppliers. This policy has not resulted in firms relocating closer to the Havant plant, although there is a network of supplier companies in Hampshire. However, it has led to significant reductions in work in progress at the plant.

Quality is the second major issue in supplier development. Included in this notion of quality is support service provision and IBM has sought suppliers who can provide good technical support. The company started a major quality control drive in 1975 which was extended to suppliers. This included a zero defect policy which, by implication, has been passed onto suppliers. The top quality suppliers are those in the grade A category. While IBM still has inward inspection this is restricted to certain components; category A suppliers, for example, are expected to delivery quality-assured supplies and in general the company is pushing quality inspection back to its suppliers.

IBM's respondent had little to say on IBM's pricing policy. However, he confirmed that IBM have a policy of prompt payment, settling all accounts within thirty days. Suppliers are also expected to adopt such a policy with their suppliers. Contracts are fairly open ended, although the company claims no direct policy with contracts as they are essentially maintenance contracts. However, IBM has a *de facto* longer term relationship with its suppliers which is reflected in the company giving its suppliers one year forecasts of demand for parts in order to give them stability. The respondent implied declining margins for sub-contractors, reflecting IBM's more competitive market, although he denied that the company was in any way 'squeezing' suppliers.

The reduction in the number of suppliers and the increased amount of work being outsourced imply greater collaboration with suppliers (see, also, Hewitt, 1989). This is certainly an innovation at IBM, given that previously the company maintained a culture of secrecy with suppliers, not imparting information on new product developments or long term scheduling. This, however, has changed, with IBM realizing that in order to develop long term, high trust relationships, in which the emphasis is on partnership, then they have to be more open with suppliers. This change in emphasis, however, has not been without its problems, as the respondent noted there have been personnel and attitude difficulties in changing from a culture of secrecy to openness. As an illustration of the move to collaboration, however, IBM representatives are heavily involved with suppliers, with engineers and buyers often visiting supplier companies on a weekly basis, and at least once a month.

In summary, IBM's policy towards suppliers has, within a UK context, been one of best practice, with close control of suppliers and strict grading controls. As company representatives admit, however, these policies came under scrutiny in the 1980s and the company has been open to adopting best practice from, notably Japanese, competitors, and in particular has made significant strides toward reducing supplier numbers, introducing just-in-time supply and improving quality. This, of course, has significant implications for suppliers, which will be the focus of the next section.

5 BUYER-SUPPLIER RELATIONS AT HAVANT: THE SUPPLIER PERSPECTIVE

The IBM supplier sample included six firms, the smallest of the suppliers samples. The relatively small number was a manifestation of the general culture of secrecy that seemed to pervade the company and was one which permeated to suppliers, some of which were quite willing to discuss certain details of their relationship with other of their customers but were unwilling to discuss these details when they related to IBM. A recent article on IBM echoed this:

> The same goes for suppliers. Ask Timex or Lithgow Electronics, for example, which supply printed circuit boards and other components to IBM's PC factory in Greenock, Scotland, what it is like dealing with the corporation and there is no reply. They fear that any comment may be misinterpreted.   (Hamilton, 1989, p. 49)

The sample firms were relatively large, ranging from several hundred employees to several thousand, although in the latter cases these firms had a variety of different businesses and a wide customer base. The components supplied varied from plastic mouldings and electronic sub assemblies to complex metal fabrications.

Included in the sample were several specialist sub-contract firms, that is, firms dedicated to specialist sub-contract as opposed to OEMs who use only spare capacity to carry out sub-contract work for other firms. This has been one of the major features of sub-contracting in the electronics industry, creating a situation similar to the motor industry and allowing in several successful new entrant firms. It is also associated with the general trend of 'hollowing out', which is particularly prevalent in the high technology parts of the electronics industry such as computer hardware manufacture. Given the highly dynamic and changing nature of the industry OEMs in this sector are eshewing heavy investment in machinery and, to a certain extent in component R & D, by sub-contracting and passing these costs on to specialist supplier firms. The suppliers amortise such costs by spreading the load of investment over a number of OEMs who they

TABLE 7.2   *Electronic contract manufacture in the USA*

	1986	1992 (est.)
Total market	$17.7bn.	$27.7bn.
In House	85%	80%
Domestic Suppliers	11%	14%
Foreign Suppliers	4%	6%

SOURCE: Gnostic Concepts Inc.

supply to, while the OEMs 'hollow out' and become essentially R&D, marketing and service organizations, with limited assembly functions (Morris, 1988a;b). The market niche opportunities for such specialist supplier firms is illustrated by Table 7.2 which shows that in a substantial growth market, increasing proportions of work are being sub-contracted out. These specialist suppliers have significant advantages over their OEM competitors who are essentially capacity contractors.

It is difficult to quantify if such a practice is occurring in the UK, but evidence from leading firms in this field, including IBM, and the phenomenal growth of firms such as A. B. Electronics and Race Electronics would suggest that this is the case (see Morris, 1988a;b).

All of the supplier firms were positive about their relationship with IBM. One of the respondents, for example, saw IBM as a role model. The firms viewed IBM as a select company to supply to and most had a policy of concentrating upon blue chip companies. One for example reported that, 'we have supplied IBM since 1983, we identified IBM as a customer that we wanted'. Another firm supplied to only twenty-five companies which included six main companies including IBM and the major Japanese consumer electronics producers. A third firm had only nine customers, another of which was Nissan. For several, IBM was the single largest customer. While some had reduced the number of firms they supplied to, two had reduced dependence on single firms after nearly going bankrupt in the early 1980s after their major customers had themselves gone bankrupt in one case and pulled out of the UK in another. One had made a conscious policy decision to diversify out of the automotive components sector into electronics supply, claiming higher profit margins in the latter.

In addition to 'key customer concentration' the firms had also engaged in policies of what might be termed 'key specialisms', that is, concentrating to a certain extent upon market niches in which they specialized. One, for example, had reduced its product range from 300 to 80 at a time of a rapid overall turnover expansion. This was a result of having to engage far more in product specialization to meet customer demands, including investing in R&D capacity, and due to the wider changing nature of the supply industry in the global arena. This included product development worldwide being done by single sources as a result of a cost reduction strategy on the part of OEMs to reduce lead times. Indeed, all but one of the supply sample were extremely research-led organizations.

The term 'full service organizations' was one which a number of the suppliers used to describe themselves, demarcating themselves from sub-contractors. Such 'service' included elements of good quality, delivery and reasonable prices. In this, the key variables that were important to supplying IBM were similar to those used by the other three case study firms. While IBM were influential in all three areas, the supplier sample firms were also influenced by other major customers. One, for example, noted the key influence of its major Japanese customers, particularly in the introduction of 'just-in-time' supply and inventory control, comparing it to their previous situation when they had 'stores the size of the factory'. Another saw Ford as the leader in driving quality assuredness.

The majority of the supplier firms already had their own quality programmes installed prior to supplying to IBM. This reflected the fact that most had only relatively recently started to supply to IBM, in most cases in the 1980s and in one case as recently as two years prior to the interview. Despite this, one supplier described its position 'as sub-contractors we are never right, therefore we must be responsive and give the best service'.

All had some form of quality standard, including BS5750, and all supplied to IBM on a quality-assured basis, as part of what one described as 'integrated quality control'. One supplier typified the approach to quality. It had introduced a two pronged attack by first placing great strategic emphasis on process and quality planning and, secondly, by introducing an educational and awareness programme for all workers to instil the notion of 'quality of service'. They had introduced SPC as far back as 1981 and 50 per cent of their workers had been trained in its use. This had major benefits on performance and quality. This firm viewed IBM, together with Ford, as the leading firm on quality. Another went further in asserting that 'IBM have the most refined quality system of all, including the Japanese and Ford, but the others are catching up'. One supplier, however, comparing IBM to Sony, commented on their very good working relationship with IBM, but contended that managers at Sony's Bridgend plant had greater autonomy than managers at IBM Havant, and were therefore easier to deal with. IBM's quality managers were said to be constrained by the company's corporate culture. One of the firms described the procedure of dealing with IBM on the issue of quality in the following way:

IBM came down with a multidisciplined team and quality inspectors, they did a detailed survey . . . IBM have their own independent standards. They suggested minor changes, mainly managerial.

As a condition of the supplying to IBM, all of the respondents have to take part in a zero defect programme and produce quality plans which are subject to approval. If problems arise over quality in supply, the supplier firm is required to produce 'corrective action reports' to IBM, a standard ongoing requirement. Quality is continuously monitored by IBM for defect levels, information is passed onto IBM for analysis and control charts are developed and used. As an illustration of the quality levels now required to serve firms such as IBM one of the firms had a reject rate of five parts per million.

Only one of the firms viewed delivery to IBM at Havant as a major issue. Typical delivery frequencies were four to five times per week, although one delivered to the plant at Havant on a daily basis, which it saw at the maximum frequency from its plant in the north of England. The respondent doubted any moves to agglomeration and relocation to a site closer to Havant, pointing out that as they supplied to a variety of customers, economies of scale would preclude such a move. One Welsh supplier to IBM's plant in Greenock has, however, been forced into a relocation. Formerly the company had been delivering on a daily basis to Scotland from South Wales, but the introduction of 'direct line feed' (or just-in-time supply) has led the company to open a second plant on a greenfield location in Ayrshire to serve IBM Greenock.

The supplier based in the North of England described its supply relationships to IBM as 'store at the door'. IBM built three transport containers for the company, all of which are constant operation, one at the supplier, one at IBM and one in transit. The supplier had moved from weekly supply gradually to daily supply over a five year period, and had managed the transition by drastically increasing its own throughput. In 1984, for example, its stock turnaround was four times per year but by the time of interview had increased to twenty four times, with all of the increase based on reduced machine set-up times.

Such a system relies on extreme flexibility on the part of the employees in supplier firms, and all of the suppliers were reliant on workforces which were flexible both functionally and numerically, in addition to close production planning. Several relied heavily on an extensive use of temporary and part-time workers or by using a multifaceted operation. Several were trying to increase the flexibility of their response by incorporating their own subcontractors into the process. This included trying to improve delivery from suppliers, but this had proved problematic. One of the suppliers had attempted to circumvent these difficulties by forming offshoot satellite sub-contractors. Senior employees were encouraged to set up their own firm and act as suppliers in a similar way to the Sony case. The sub-contractors acted as a buffer for the parent organization and were part of a policy of maintaining the 'leanness' of the parent. The parent encouraged the satellite by placing orders and by giving technical assistance to it; thus four satellite firms had been set up, each employing between 30 and 50.

Another of the suppliers had invested heavily in flexible automation. One supplier in the north of England, for example, had started such a process in 1982 by introducing CNC machines and now had eight robots. The majority had also invested in EDI link-ups to IBM, which they saw as a prerequisite for supplying to IBM, and others, in the 1990s. Ease of delivery is, of course, also greatly facilitated by good scheduling procedures on the part of the parent organization. The responses from the suppliers on this subject were mixed. One respondent for example, described a system of six month orders which were updated constantly and were extremely accurate. By contrast, however, a second respondent described the procedure in this way:

> We do a blanket order, to schedule. IBM are very poor at scheduling. They are not as organized as firms in the auto industry. They recognize it, they need to be more open. We do some forecasts but they are extremely volatile. Nissan, by contrast, build to schedule. Partly this is due to market fluctuations, but part of it is a question of organization, which they are trying to change. We just have to cope, we do a three year rolling plan, budget for it and judge IBM historically. This is a better way of predicting volumes than their schedule.

In general, the supplier firms concurred with the view regarding the relationship with IBM as long term. One respondent explained that this was a necessary outcome of the move to relying on specialist contract assemblers, as IBM, and other firms, no longer have the capacity in-house.

One supplier confirmed IBM's policy of nominating second tier suppliers; IBM picks the supplier and negotiates a price with it, therefore the supplier buys at a set price from a nominated supplier which inevitably reduces the scope and autonomy of the supplier. Price was not viewed as an important factor by any of the suppliers; indeed several suppliers regarded that this had diminished as an issue over time. One respondent argued that:

If you want quality assuredness, this will actually decrease costs. Therefore, the foremost factor is quality, then delivery performance, then engineering expertise, then price. If the first three are correct, this will be reflected in the price.

Despite price being of minor importance in comparison to quality and delivery, several firms noted a continuous squeeze on margins. However, IBM's reputation for extremely prompt payment of bills was also commented on favourably.

All of the supplier firms acted as a single source of their particular component to IBM. With some of the suppliers, IBM ensured that the supplier only supplied a certain percentage of its output to them – 25 per cent was the figure mentioned – in order to ensure that suppliers did not become overdependent on them. In one case, however, the figure had risen to 40 per cent. This particular respondent argued that while the increase ran contrary to IBM's policy, it was an inevitable consequence of single sourcing and an increase in the overall level of business.

The process of becoming a preferred supplier to IBM was described as exhaustive. The negotiation took up to 3 to 4 years and involved an extensive audit of the supplier, including its manufacturing capability, its quality systems and its industrial relations record. IBM require full process information, information on the performance of the process and even information on the functional operation. Virtually every part of the supplier's operation has to be approved – for example, operators have to undergo a series of tests and show their work to IBM representatives for approval, and IBM representatives are involved in the vetting and approval of certain staff changes.

Such procedures imply a high degree of control by IBM over its suppliers. This was contrasted with Sony and involved an extremely tight documentation of procedures and practices. It was described by one respondent:

> We see IBM as a unique pattern and approach . . . it doesn't conflict with our interests. If you want to work for IBM you have to meet their requirements.

In comparing this approach to Sony's this respondent replied:

> IBM's input is much higher and much more in evidence. However, we're now starting to see changes with IBM, they're much less secretive now.

The last comment alludes to a greater degree of knowledge-sharing and collaboration between IBM and its suppliers, with a shift to a higher trust relationship. It required suppliers to be extremely open with IBM, a position only recently reciprocated. As one respondent replied:

> We discuss and share – we give them a break-down of our material, labour, overhead costs and profits and projections – in fact all of our books are opened up to IBM.

All of the suppliers commented on the degree of technical assistance given to them by IBM, but there was little evidence of collaboration on R & D. Moreover, the moves to a long term trust relationship were unfavourably compared to the relationships that some of these firms had with Japanese plants.

In conclusion, the suppliers all judged the winning of supplier status to IBM as a key account to a blue chip company. Some of the suppliers had won such contracts after years of trying. What emerges from the interviews was that IBM have a unique relationship with suppliers which, while superficially similar to Japanese style buyer-supplier relations, has emerged separately and therefore has many differences.

The keynote characteristics of IBM's policy are quality, control and formality. All of these characteristics are bound into the fairly unique culture of the parent organization. IBM's quality procedures, for example, were described by a number of suppliers as the most sophisticated in the UK, including Japanese-owned plants. The degree of control is also perhaps unique in its intensity, which is exemplified in IBM choosing and negotiating with second tier suppliers. Again, all dealings are extremely formal, even compared with the Japanese companies, and particularly on specifications. While being unique, IBM's policy does, however, work in a dynamic. There are indications that IBM is moving, within the constraints of a strong corporate culture, towards a more high-trust and open relationship with its suppliers.

6 CONCLUSIONS

The IBM case study differs from the others in a number of respects. First, IBM is itself a fairly unique company, dominating as it does the world computer industry, even if this dominance was severely challenged in the 1980s and will continue to be challenged in the 1990s. Second, IBM Havant is a relatively old site with established tradition, even if, because of IBM's well-developed managerial system and strong corporate culture, it has avoided many of the problems that are associated with trying to bring about organizational change on such a site.

Despite Oliver and Wilkinson's (1988) assertion that IBM have many of the characteristics of the large Japanese corporations, IBM seem to have been consciously emulating Japanese best practice in a number of respects. Their EXCEL quality programme, for example, was largely stimulated by the much higher quality standards of rival Japanese producers and a desire to be *the* high quality, low-cost producer. In the field of buyer-supplier relations also, IBM seem to be attempting to emulate a number of features of the Japanese model, including sourcing greater proportions of work from suppliers, reducing their supplier base, implementing just-in-time (or continuous flow manufacture), and developing long-term high-trust relationships with suppliers.

In this, IBM are no different from other UK and US manufacturers. They differ, however, from companies such as Lucas that are virtually abandoning their systems of buyer-supplier relations, because IBM are 'grafting on' some of these solutions to a sophisticated system of buyer-supplier relations which is essentially their own. While these already had many similarities with the Japanese model – for instance with regard to quality and the payment of suppliers – in other ways they were fairly unique and distinctive to IBM, particularly on the issue of control.

It was evident from the responses of suppliers that not only was a change occurring, but that IBM were successfully implementing this change. However, as both IBM and their suppliers representatives maintained, this was an introduction which caused considerable strains, particularly with regard to the movement from an attitude of secrecy to one of openness with suppliers.

8   Beyond Adversarialism: the Advent of New Supply Practices?

1   INTRODUCTION

The 1980s have witnessed the development of a number of innovations in industrial organization, characterized by some new and different forms of supplier relationships, including long term contracts, joint ventures, high technology cooperative agreements, and dedicated supplier arrangements. It is also apparent that, in response to heightened levels of global competition, companies are being forced to reappraise interlocked systems of quality and process control, stocking, delivery, and related inter-industry transactions. In particular, British and European producers are now much more aware of the potential cost savings and control to be gained from developing obligational-style buyer-supplier relations, although there is evidence that many producers are a long way off from developing the requisite systems, even in our four case study firms.

As Oliver and Wilkinson (1988) note, there is almost an evangelical flavour to many of the writings about changes in industrial organization, and a widespread acceptance that the implementation of new supplier practices is crucial to the future of British manufacturing. In noting this, they quote an example from Lucas' managing director who considers JIT production to be 'fundamental, and when completed there can be no other improvement since it completely tailors a manufacturing strategy to the needs of the market' (Parnaby, 1987, quoted in Oliver and Wilkinson, 1988, p. 299). This echoes Pais (1988), the former Vice President of General Motors, who argues that 'the implementation of a new philosophy, a bold new vision of a restructured manufacturing base, is beginning to pay off' – evoking the notion that the break with past practices is more or less complete – heralding a new era of competitiveness and profits. In contrast to this, others note the ideological appeal of the 'new philosophy' while doubting that there is any real coherence between manufacturers in the development of systems which require a more or less complete overhaul of British manufacturing practices.

In trying to contribute to the debates characterized by these contrasting views, the case studies in Chapters 4 to 7 offer a number of insights into changing buyer-supplier relations in two of the more highly disintegrated industrial sectors – motor vehicles and electronics. One of the purposes of this concluding chapter is to synthesize the case material, in order to compare and contrast some of the similarities and differences in buyer-supplier relations between the case studies. In doing this, we divide the chapter into two sections. The next part provides a discussion of the extent to which new practices are evolving between buyers and suppliers. We critically consider the divergence in practices between the different cases, and seek to explain why different forms of supply practices are emerging. We also focus on a number of important relationships, including the role of price, quality, collaboration, supplier development, and JIT practices, including delivery. The second part of the chapter briefly generalizes some of the findings to the wider context of British industrial organization, and concludes by discussing the interdependence between supplier relationships and industrial policy (see Hirst, 1989; Tomlinson, 1989).

2   THE DEVELOPMENT OF NEW SUPPLY PRACTICES?

The cases provide a flavour of the changes in buyer-supplier relations in some of the leading multinational companies in the British economy. In particular, the cases are instructive in highlighting the diverse patterns of buyer strategies in developing a supplier base, and in demonstrating the difficulties facing buyers in moving towards a system of relational contracting. A unifying feature of all the cases is the clear rejection of many of the features of adversarial buyer-supplier relations, although, as the Lucas – and to a lesser extent the IBM – case clearly demonstrated, some buyers are finding it more difficult than others to set up and implement the requisite systems of supply. It should be reiterated, however, that three of our firms are unusual in that they are a self-selecting sample which are at the leading edge of moves from adversarial to obligational contracting. In particular, Chapter 2 considered the theoretical possibilities of the development of organizational innovations based on the proliferation of external economies of scale and the formation of new flexible forms of industrial production.

At a theoretical level we would not wish to characterize these developments as part of a flexible specialization thesis. While there are moves towards agglomeration, these are often top down (by 'importing' sub-contractors for example), and the regions in which these plants are located, particularly South Wales and North East of England, could hardly be characterized as innovative milieus (although this is not to deny the emergence of small flexible firms). Moreover, the emergence of new buyer-supplier relations does not herald a 'new era' of cooperation. The large firms are not, for example, introducing these new forms of relationships out of a sense of altruism. While the study did not address working conditions in supplier firms, the supplier interviews were littered with references to being flexible. The implications for workers in such firms are highly flexible hours regulated by working to order, and for some at least, 'peripheral' work contracts – part time, temporary and so on. To return to the theoretical frame, we would place these changes firmly within a neo-Fordist framework.

The case studies also provide some insights into the key aspects of buyer-supplier relations, namely price, quality and delivery. In Chapter 3, for example, we considered a range of empirical research which suggests that non-price criteria, as the basis for 'make' or 'buy' decisions, are still of lesser significance than price. In particular, it appeared that the maxim of production at 'the lowest price, highest quality, and the best delivery', is one of the emerging business 'ethics' of the 1990s. This was clearly the case with Nissan, who are attempting to utilize a 'negative' pricing system by inducing increases in labour productivity. However, their method is quite different to the practices of many British, 'adversarial-style', producers. In particular, Nissan utilizes price, not as a 'bottom line' threat, but as a measure of efficiency and 'continuous improvements' in processes and labour utilization. In this way, price is integrally locked into the wider structural context of intra- and interorganizational productive relations and into the whole ethos of total quality management. This contrasts with the position adopted by Lucas, who regard quality and delivery more as fixed parameters, with price as a fluctuating variable. However, as our interviews with Lucas's suppliers indicated, while quality of components and frequency of delivery have become more important to Lucas, the price of components has become less so. Indeed, certain of Lucas's suppliers maintained that they had benefitted significantly from offering better quality components and a slightly higher price.

Moreover, in Chapter 3, our review of empirical research tended to reinforce a certain cynicism of the new developments in buyer-supplier relations. While one of our original notions was to be sceptical about the apparent development of relational contracting, and especially what many perceive to be 'buyer rhetoric' in espousing the virtues of the obligational model, the findings from our case studies confirm a major break with past buyer-supplier practices. In particular, the onus on new methods of collaboration and the primacy of quality considerations were referred to, time and again, as a 'working partnership', in contrast to the state of adversarialism in the early 1980s. However, most tier one suppliers acknowledged that there was generally an insistence on the part of buyers that certain changes be made, a position typified by one supplier who noted that,

> We get the orders and we deliver on a lead time. We make the boxes straight away and deliver by quickly pushing things through the process . . . this is what we are being forced to do . . .

Despite these covert pressures, most suppliers did feel that the outcome was worthwhile, citing a reduction in defects, increased process control, and enhanced profits. Indeed, certain of the suppliers, to Sony in particular, were initially convinced that they would never conform to all of Sony's specifications on delivery, price and quality. The rigorous demands of this schedule had in some cases brought about a fundamental re-evaluation of production methods and great gains in quality standards. Indeed, this was perhaps the key feature of the interviews, the transfer of quality standards in production from OEMs to suppliers.

The case studies also provide some insights into the key problems facing buyers of controlling production schedules, and the extent to which workable JIT systems are an emerging feature of British industrial organization. As noted in Chapter 3, a plethora of research is sceptical about the implementation and utilization of JIT, while our own work tends to suggest that the flexibility inherent in JIT is not being wholly utilized to achieve the objectives of coordinated delivery and stock reduction, even in firms at the leading edge such as Sony, IBM and Nissan. The case of Lucas is instructive in showing that the new demands of more frequent deliveries were proving to be difficult to implement. While Lucas's suppliers noted that deliveries were becoming more frequent, the majority felt they were being burdened by inventory control. Also, the success of JIT systems is obviously linked to stability both in the buyer and the wider supply chains. As Rutherford (1990) notes, this relationship extends to the point at which, given the heightened dependency of buyers on suppliers, buyers are now significantly concerned with industrial relations in supplier firms, and with related supplier labour practices.

The cases also confirm much previous research which suggests that levels of personnel, technical, and management assistance are all on the increase between buyers and suppliers. For instance, while Nissan have a declared policy of close technical collaboration with all their suppliers, their underlying rationale is premised on the notion that collaboration should involve forms of 'supplier sovereignty'. As far as Nissan are concerned, they tend to regard 'sovereignty' as circumscribed practices, although, like the other buyers we interviewed, they acknowledged the real economies to be made by devolving product and process control to their suppliers. This, of course, places a further onus on suppliers, in that they have to develop some form of R&D capacity. Indeed, for key tier one suppliers (particularly in the motor industry), a major product and process development capability is becoming a pre-requisite for supply to the OEMs.

It is also important to consider the extent to which new collaborative practices between buyers and suppliers represent more than suppliers paying lip service to their buyer partners. One of the commonly espoused notions is summarized by Pais (1988), who uses the analogy of a supplier and a buyer as an extended family. In noting this, he argues that,

> this kind of thinking involves levels of trust never experienced before in the (automobile) industry. It involves degrees of interdependence never experienced before . . . more general ground floor cooperation and, all in all, it has put new meaning in the word 'integrate'. (1988, p. 31)

The use of an extended familial ideology to characterize new supply relationships is something of an irony, given the virtual break-up and disintegration of extended family ties in Western societies. Indeed, this metaphor is richly symbolic of the ideological underpinnings of Pais' thinking, and serves to direct attention away from some of the real conflicting objectives, and effects, of contemporary buyer-supplier relations.

Some of the case material also indicates a greater reliance of buyers on developing an indigenous and/or localized, supplier base. This was particularly evident in the cases of Sony and Nissan, with the former quite prepared to spend lengthy periods of time setting up new technologies and processes in their chosen suppliers. Indeed, whether or not the OEMs were attempting localization of suppliers – Sony, for example, openly admitted they were, Nissan denied it – the rigours of just-in-time delivery schedules were leading to supplier firms relocating plants nearer the OEMs, even if this was only in the form of satellite plants. Certainly, the Japanese-owned supplier firms which have followed Nissan and Sony to the UK have shown a marked preference for locations close to the OEMs.

It is also apparent that there is great diversity in the form and content of buyer-supplier relationships. For instance, Nissan used affiliates in which it has equity investments as a way to secure access. The other case study buyers tend to retain legal independence from their principal suppliers. Nissan justify equity shares in a number of ways, especially in offering a short-cut to technologies and specialized activities.

Moreover, it is clear that Preferred Supplier Status (PSS) is a feature of buyer-supplier relations in all four case study firms, unlike the situation ten years ago. For instance, as our case study of IBM indicated, in 1978 they clearly multi-sourced and only gave suppliers short term contracts of up to four months. Now, more security is built into the relationships, with the company extending its commitment to its suppliers of up to three or four years ahead on the basis of exclusive supply contracts. This is slightly surprizing given IBM's traditional reticence to change some of its established practices with suppliers, but clearly shows the way most multinationals are developing towards a relational model. Also, the development of PSS has a number of positive spin-offs, not least in creating some stability for tier one suppliers who make the grade. The long term relationship is, however, necessitated as a *quid pro quo* for the increased demands placed upon suppliers.

For instance, there was consensus, between the suppliers we interviewed, that the creation of longer-term business ventures was enabling them to invest with fuller confidence in the future, partly because of the 'protective ring' placed around them by their dominant suppliers. Also, PSS was held up as providing some suppliers with access to international markets, with a selection of our supplier interviewees gaining preferred status to international branches of buyers they supplied to in Britain. As Otford EPS, supplier to Sony Bridgend and Sony West Germany, argued, 'this is where the real pay-offs are generated'. However, the cases also show that PSS is fraught with difficulties, especially for buyers trying to find an adequate supplier base in Britain with which to develop a responsive series of networks. As the cases of Sony, and to a larger extent, Nissan illustrated, companies have been frustrated in developing a localized PSS system due to the dearth of good quality supply companies in Britain. This would seem not only to be confined to the case study firms, but to be a wider feature of the UK supplier base, particularly in the electronics industry.

Moreover, while research suggests that the volumes of work being put-out by buyers is increasing, the utilization of a PSS strategy by the leading multinationals is a clear sign that a disproportionate number of suppliers are reaping the benefits of a closer relationship with buyers. However, as many suppliers mentioned, this seems to be creating a widening gulf between the different categories of suppliers, with many businesses now finding it harder to gain contracts at the more lucrative end of the supply chain (that is, as tier one suppliers). It was also apparent from the cases that suppliers were being encouraged by their buyers to consolidate their specialist services, through the adoption of the latest technologies, skills, and knowledge. In particular, those suppliers who had achieved PSS seemed to share a number of common features.

Foremost, it is apparent that some of the specialisms required by buyers have been putting pressure on suppliers to concentrate on a narrow product base, and to retreat from a prior position of diversified production. A number of examples were cited by the cases we investigated, noting that while a diverse product base could initially stimulate business, it could not sustain growth or development. It was also outlined that 'product narrowing' was the main method of developing a 'preferred customer' base, or serving the specialist needs of buyers. In this way, product development in suppliers, over the course of moving towards a relational supply system, has been heavily led by market demand. This process has been characterized by the replacement of low technology products with high technology, high yielding ones, orientated towards market niches.

As we have already intimated, the development of new buyer-supplier relations cannot be seen as a process wholly initiated by buyer firms. In many ways, suppliers have been active participants in stimulating the downfall of many facets of the adversarial system. For instance, generalizing from our studies, it is clear that many suppliers have consciously adopted a policy of concentrating their output on 'leading edge' customers. In this way, suppliers in our sample were developing what we consider to be a 'preferred buyer status' policy, characterized by a number of strategic changes made by suppliers towards their customers. For instance, as we have already noted, the majority of suppliers we interviewed regarded the contraction of their customer base as essential in establishing a basis for stability and profitability. In particular, suppliers noted the importance of targetting resources to those customers most able to generate higher returns, contract stability, and volume orders. It was also clear that the tier one suppliers in our sample had actively pursued a policy of attaching themselves to buyers who required volume, high value-added products, with the attitude that one had to make the customer reliant on you, your skills, and technologies. As one manager of a supplier said,

> our strategy has been to make our big customers reliant on us so that they think of us as their best supplier, not in price terms, but the service and quality we provide.

This finding is a neat reversal of the popular wisdom which suggests that supplier firms tend to be subservient to their buyers, and dependency operates one way. For many of the suppliers we spoke to, their positive attitude towards developing quality service was reflected in the longer term ties they were developing with their buyers, and the admission by the buyer firms that once they had developed a supplier it was extremely costly to pull out of the relationship and start again.

In concluding this section, the cases indicate the uneven development of buyer-supplier relations and the persistence of certain elements of adversarial contracting. In all the cases, price is still 'the bottom line' whatever the rhetoric about 'quality' and 'delivery'. We did not really discover fully-fledged JIT systems in operation, but more a 'knock-on' effect down the supply chain. Similarly, despite the commitment to zero defects and total quality there were few examples from our interviews of suppliers having come close to the ideal. Further, while it is argued that the new relationships indicate a new era of cooperation between businesses, it is clear from our research that the evolving systems of supplying are more to do with enhancing corporate control and competitiveness, perhaps heralding a new phase of corporate reorganization and growth. In this sense, suppliers are part of the evolving global, corporate economy.

3   STRATEGIC IMPLICATIONS OF CHANGING BUYER-SUPPLIER RELATIONS

While recognizing the importance of supplier relations as an integral input into the competitiveness of industry, it is less clear how government policy should respond in providing a dynamic context for the development of relational-style contracting. It is clear that the present Conservative administration has forsaken an active industrial policy, by stressing the rights of company managements to manage free from the 'interfering state'. In this 'hands off' scenario, government policy envisages economic recovery and growth through the effects of freeing markets and promoting competition. However, as Hirst (1989) argues, an active industrial policy is required because of the relative failures of British industry in developing new products, and the relinquishing of both domestic and export markets to overseas competitors. Hirst, echoing our own observations in Chapter 1, also notes that an industrial policy is needed to step in where British management has failed, and that,

> without an external stimulus and assistance from appropriate public bodies, firms will respond with caution born of failure, a response

that locks them into a risk averse defence of given market shares . . .
industrial decision-making has to be a central public policy concern, not
merely aggregate levels of demand and investment. (p. 273)

Certainly, at an EEC level, there has been recognition of the importance
of the small and medium sized enterprise sector, generally, and given
the importance of subcontracting to this sector, wider issues of changing
industrial structure. These Small and Medium Sized Enterprises (SMEs)
are not seen as operating within a vacuum. This has manifested itself in
the creation of the SME Task Force (DGXIII) and a series of EEC-led
initiatives to gain greater understanding of the new industrial order and to
spread awareness (see CEC/EC – Japan Centre for Industrial Cooperation,
1990).

At a more general level, what emerges from this study is that supplier
firms which do not adopt new quality standards, new technology such as
Electronic Data Interchange (EDI) and a capability to undertake research
and/or development work will be pushed further and further down the
tiering pyramid and run the considerable risk of marginalization.

Similarly, economic advisers, governments and agencies are increasingly
concerned with developing indigenous suppliers as a part of economic
development. Despite this, companies like Sony and Nissan felt that
British quality standards fell far below their own rigorous measures.
This clearly implies that any industrial policy must have three strategic
elements in utuilizing a supply based as a mechanism of local, regional
and national economic development. First, the national benchmarks of
quality must be significantly raised to match and exceed those utilized by
'best practice' corporations. Second, there is a need to develop information
and training networks throughout the UK to verse would-be suppliers in
what is expected of them. Finally, a higher level of localized intervention
is required to encourage the development of local supply networks and,
in doing so, to encourage spatial agglomeration and localized centres of
supply excellence.

However, the extent to which any of these developments will occur is
dependent on the realignment in the British state away from centralist
principles which emphasize the market as an instrument of industrial
policy. As many of the supplier respondents indicated, lack of direction,
information and knowledge is at the heart of a supply system which still
fails to match the highest standards.

Bibliography

ABERNATHY, W., CLARK, K. B. and KANTROW, A. (1983) *Industrial Renaissance: Producing A Competitive Future for America*, New York: Basic Books.

ACAS (1988) 'Labour flexibility in Britain: The 1987 ACAS Survey', *ACAS Occasional Paper*, 41, ACAS, London.

ACKROYD, S., BURRELL, G., HUGHES, M. and WHITAKER, M. (1988) 'The Japanization of British Industry', *Industrial Relations Journal*, 19 (1): 11–23.

AGLIETTA, M. (1979) *A Theory of Capitalist Regulation*: The US Experience, London: New Left Books.

AGLIETTA, M. (1982) 'World capitalism in the eighties', *New Left Review*, 136, 25–36.

AMIN, A. and ROBINS, K. (1990) 'Not Marshallian times', unpublished paper, Centre for Urban and Regional Development Studies, University of Newcastle-upon-Tyne, Newcastle.

ANDERSON, M. and HOLMES, J. (1989) 'New forms of industrial organisation in the automobile industry: the case of Magna International', paper presented at the Annual Meeting of the A.A.G., Baltimore.

APPLEBY, C. and TWIGG, D. (1988) 'CAD diffusion in the west Midlands automotive components industry', unpublished paper, Centre for Industrial Studies, Wolverhampton Polytechnic, Wolverhampton.

ATKINSON, J. and GREGORY, D. (1986) 'A flexible future: Britain's dual labour force', *Marxism Today*, 30 (4): 12–17.

BALL, M. (1989) 'The economic record', in M. Ball, F. Grey and L. McDowell (eds), *The Transformation of Britain: Contemporary Social and Economic Change*, London: Fontana.

BASSETT, P. (1986) *Strike Free: New Industrial Relations in Britain*, London: Macmillan.

BERGER, S. and PIORE, M. J. (1980) *Dualism and Discontinuity in Industrial Societies*, Cambridge: Cambridge University Press.

BESSANT, J., JONES, D., LAMMING, R. and POLLARD, A. (1984) *The West Midlands Automobile Component Industry: Recent Changes and Future Prospects*, West Midlands County Council, Economic Development Unit Sector Report, No. 4, Birmingham.

BIM (1985) 'Managing new patterns of work', report of the *Organisation of Work Panel, BIM Social and Economic Affairs Committee*, British Institute of Management, London.

BOYER, R. (1987) 'Labour flexibility: many forms, uncertain effects', *Labour and Society*, 12, 107–29.

172

BRADY, T. (1987a) *Education and Training in IBM United Kingdom Ltd.*, London: NEDO.

BRADY, T. (1987b) *Education and Training in Lucas Industries*, London: NEDO.

BRAVERMAN, H. (1974) *Labour and Monopoly Capitalism*, New York: Harvester Press.

BRESNEN, M. (1990) *Organising Construction*, London: Routledge.

BURAWOY, M. (1979) *Manufacturing Consent*, London: Routledge.

BUXTON, J. (1988) 'Japan top source for Scottish electronics sector', *Financial Times*, 7 November, 11.

CAITS, (1986) 'Flexibility – who needs it?', CAITS, Polytechnic of North London.

CANE, A. (1988) 'IBM set to join rivals in agreeing common software', *Financial Times*, 9 June, 3.

CANE. A. (1989) 'Why IBM is feeling a little blue', *Financial Times*, 2 October, 25.

CANE, A and KEHOE, L. (1988) 'IBM goes into battle to regain middle ground', *Financial Times*, 20 June, 21.

CANE, A., ORAM, R., KEHOE, L. and RODGER, I. (1990) 'Small earthquakes: IBM slightly hurt', *Financial Times*, 21 April, 21.

CANE, A., RODGER I., ORAM, R. and KEHOE, L. (1990) 'IBM's worldwide lesson from Europe', *Financial Times*, 2 May, 12.

CASTELLS, M. (1988) 'The new industrial space: information technology manufacturing and spatial structure in the United States, in G. Sternlieb and J. Hughes (eds), *America's New Market Geography: Nation, Region and Metropolis*, New Brunswick: Rutgers University.

CAULKIN, S. (1988) 'Britain's best factories; IBM', *Management Today*, September, 76–8.

CEC/EC-JAPAN CENTRE FOR INDUSTRIAL CO-OPERATION (1990) *EC Fact Finding Mission on Subcontracting in Japan*, CEC: Brussels.

CENTRAL POLICY REVIEW (1975) *The Future of the British Car Industry*, London: HMSO.

CENTRAL STATISTICAL OFFICE (1987) *Monthly Digest of Statistics*, August, London: C.S.O.

CHANDLER, A. (1977) *The Visible Hand*, Cambridge, MA: Harvard University Press.

CLARKE, S. (1989) 'Overaccumulation, class struggle and the regulation approach', *Capital and Class*, 36, 59–92.

CLUTTERBUCK, D. and HILL, R. (1981) *The Remaking of Work: Changing Patterns of Work and How to Capitalize on Them*, London: Grant McIntyre.

COASE, R. H. (1937) 'The nature of the firm', *Economica*, 4, 386–405.

CONNOR, P. J. (1989) 'Japanese Investment in the UK', unpublished MBA dissertation, Cardiff Business School, U.W.C.C.

COOKE, P. (1988) 'Flexible integration, scope economies and strategic alliances: social and spatial mediations', *Environment and Planning D:*

Society and Space, 281–300.

COOKE, P., (ed.) (1989) *Localities*, London: Unwin Hyman.

COOKE, P., ETXEBARRIA, G., MORRIS, J. and RODRIGUES, A. (1989) *Flexibility in the Periphery: Regional Restructuring in Wales and the Basque Country*, Cardiff: Regional Industrial Research.

COOKE, P. and WELLS, P. (1989) 'Strategic alliances in computing and telecommunications', paper presented to ESRC symposium, Regulation, Innovation and Spatial Development, U.W.C.C., Cardiff.

COOKE, P. and WELLS, P. (1990) *Strategic Alliances in ICT: Learning by Interaction*, Regional Industrial Research Report No. 4, University of Wales College of Cardiff.

COYLE, A. (1984) *Redundant Women*, London: The Women's Press.

CROSS, M. (1986) 'Time to change', *Industrial Society*, December Issue, 14–15.

CROWTHER, S. and GARRAHAN, P. (1988) 'Invitation to Sunderland: corporate power and the local economy', *Industrial Relations Journal*, 19, 1, 51–9.

CUSUMANO, M. A. (1985) *The Japanese Automobile Industry: Technology and Management at Nissan and Toyota*, Cambridge (Mass): Harvard University Press.

DALE, B. and SHAW, P. (1988) 'A study of the use of statistical process control in the automotive-related supplier community', *Paper No. 8801, Department of Management Sciences*, UMIST, Manchester.

DALY, A., HITCHENS, D. and WAGNER, K. (1985) 'Productivity, machinery and skills in a sample of British and German manufacturing plants', *National Institute Economic Review*, February, 48–62.

DAWKINS, W. (1989) 'Sony to begin output of magnetic tape in France', *Financial Times*, 19 September, 9.

DE JONQUIERES, G. and DIXON, H. (1989) 'Sony plans to increase European investment in preparation for 1992', *Financial Times*, 31 July, 16.

DE JONQUIERES, G. (1989) 'Coping with local sensitivities', *Financial Times*, 13 October, 22.

DICKENS, P. and SAVAGE, M. (1988) 'The Japanization of British industry? Instances from a high growth area', *Industrial Relations Journal*, 19 (1): 60–8.

DIXON, H. (1988) 'IBM to take loss on Rolm sale', *Financial Times*, 30 December, 13.

DIXON, H. (1989) 'Pulling back from a quality disaster', *Financial Times*, 6 October, 18.

DODSWORTH, T. (1988) 'Sony leads slow-off-the-mark Japanese into workstation market, *Financial Times*, 18 March, 36.

DODWELL MARKETING CONSULTANTS (1986) *The Structure of the Japanese Auto Parts Industry*, Third Edition, Tokyo, Dodwell Marketing Consultants.

DONE, K. (1988) 'Nissan plans UK design centre', *Financial Times*, 15 March, 48.

DONE, K. (1989a) 'Japanese springboard', *Financial Times*, World Car Industry Report, 6.

DONE, K. (1989b) 'The complicated global square dance', *Financial Times*, World Car Industry Report, 14.

DONE, K. (1989c) 'The changing climate of investment in Britain, Financial Times, 5 July, 8.

DONE, K. (1989d) 'Car wars after the yen shock', *Financial Times*, 12 May, 12.

DONE, K. (1990) 'Nissan to buy more European car components', Financial Times, 26 June, 30.

DORAN, P. (1986) 'How to achieve performance', *Management Today*, April, 94–100.

DUNNING, J. (1986) *Japanese Participation in British Industry*, Beckenham, Kent: Croom Helm.

ECONOMIST INTELLIGENCE UNIT (1989), 'Update on Nissan', *Japanese Motor Business*, 42–69.

THE ECONOMIST (1988) 'Japanese foreign direct investment: Walkman factories don't walk', March 12, 76.

EDWARDS, R. (1979) *Contested Terrain: The Transformation of The Work Place in the Twentieth Century*, London: Heinemann Educational Books.

EVANS, P. and DOZ, Y. (1989) 'The dualistic organization', in P. Evans, Y. Doz and A. Laurent (eds), *Human Resource Management in International Firms*, London: Macmillan.

FERGUSON, A. (1989) 'Britain's best factories', *Management Today*, November, 68–73.

FLORIDA, R. and KENNEY, M. (1991) 'Japanese foreign direct investment in the US: the case of the automotive transplants', in J. Morris (ed.) *Japan and The Global Economy*, London: Routledge.

FREIDMAN, A. (1977) *Industry and Labour*, London: MacMillan.

FROBEL, F., HEINRICHS, J. and KREYE, O. (1980) *The New International Division of Labour*, Cambridge: Cambridge University Press.

GAFFIKIN, F. and NICKSON, A., (1984) *Jobs Crisis and The Multinationals: The Case of the West Midlands*, Birmingham: Birmingham Trade Union Group.

GARNETT, N. (1987) 'Supplier companies urged to adopt Japanese philosophy', *Financial Times*, 5 May, 15.

GARRAHAN, P. and STEWART, P. (1989) 'Working for Nissan', unpublished paper, Sunderland Polytechnic.

GERRY, C. (1985) 'The working class and small enterprises in the UK recession', in N. Redcliff and E. Mingione (eds), *Beyond Employment, Household, Gender and Subsistence*, Oxford: Basil Blackwell.

GORDON, D. M. (1988) 'The global economy: new edifice or crumbling foundations', *New Left Review*, 168, 24–64.

GORDON, D. M., EDWARDS, R. and REICH, M. (1982) *Segmented Work, Divided Workers: The Historical Transformation of Labour in The United States*, Cambridge: Cambridge University Press.

GORGEU, A. and MATHIEU, R. (1989) 'New organizational practices in manufacturer-supplier relationships in the French automobile and aerospace industries, *Proceedings of the Third international APROS Colloqium*, Australian National University, Canberra, November.

GOTO, M. (1989) 'The internationalization of Japanese business in a Japanese perspective', paper presented to Business International Conference, November, London.

GOUGH, J. (1986) 'Industrial policy and socialist strategy: restructuring and the unity of the working class', *Capital and Class*, 29, 58–81.

GRAHAM, I. (1988) 'Japanization as mythology', *Industrial Relations Journal*, 19, 1, 69–75.

GREATER LONDON COUNCIL (1985) *The London Industrial Strategy*, London: GLC.

GREENE-ARMYTAGE, J. (1990) 'Programmed for product success', *Observer*, February 25th, 47.

GRIFFITHS, J. (1989a) 'Lucas Automotive will increase production of anti-skid brakes', *Financial Times*, 10 August, 4.

GRIFFITHS, J. (1989b) 'Today's fashion is tomorrows risk', *Financial Times*, 7 September, 15.

HAKIM, C. (1987) 'Trends in the flexible workforce', *Employment Gazette*, 95, 549–60.

HAKIM, C. (1990) 'Core and periphery in employers' workforce strategies', *Work, Employment and Society*, 4, 157–88.

HALBERSTAM, D. (1987) *The Reckoning*, London: Bloomsbury Press.

HAMILTON, S. (1989) 'Culture shock hits big blue', *Business*, September, 44–52.

HANDY, C. (1984) *The Future of Work*, Oxford: Basil Blackwell.

HARDING, R. (1989) 'Lucas Industries PLC', unpublished mimeo, Science Policy Research Unit, University of Sussex, Brighton.

HARRISON, B., (1989) 'After the crisis? The struggle for economic dominance in the age of flexibility', unpublished paper, MIT, Cambridge, MA.

HARVEY, D. (1988) 'Flexible accumulation through urbanization: reflections on post-modernism in the American city', *Environment and Planning D: Society and Space*, 6, 3.

HELPER, S. (1989) 'Changing buyer-supplier relationships in the United States: results of survey research', in *Proceedings of IMVP International Policy Forum*, Cambridge, MA: MIT.

HEWITT, D. (1989) 'Developing self-supporting suppliers', *Purchasing and Supply Management*, August, 34–6.

HIRST, P. (1989) 'The politics of industrial policy', in P. Hirst and J. Zeitlin (eds), *Reversing Industrial Decline: Industrial Structure and Policy in Britain and Her Competitors*, Oxford: Berg.

HIRST, P. and ZEITLIN, J. (eds), (1989) *Reversing Industrial Decline: Industrial Structure and Policy in Britain and Her Competitors*, Oxford: Berg.

HOLMES, J. (1986) 'The organization and locational structure of production subcontracting', in A. Scott and M. Storper (eds), *The Geographical*

Anatomy of Industrial Capitalism: Production, Work and Territory, Hemel Hempstead, Herts: Allen & Unwin.

HOLMES, J. (1988) 'Industrial restructuring in a period of crisis: an analysis of the Canadian automobile industry, 1973–1983', *Antipode*, 20, 19–51.

HYMAN, R. (1988) 'Flexible specialization: miracle or myth', in R. Hyman and W. Streeck (eds), *New Technology and Industrial Relations*, Oxford: Basil Blackwell.

IBM (1987) *IBM UK Review*, London: IBM UK Ltd.

IBM (1988) *IBM Annual Report*, Armonk, New York: IBM Corporation.

IMRIE, R. F. (1986) 'Work decentralisation from large to small firms: a preliminary analysis of subcontracting', *Environment and Planning A*, 18, 949–65.

IMRIE, R. F. (1989a) 'Industrial restructuring, labour and locality: the case of the British pottery industry', *Environment and Planning A*, 21, 3–26.

IMRIE, R. F. (1989b) *Industrial Change in a Local Economy: The Case of Stoke-on-Trent*, unpublished PhD. thesis, Department of Town Planning, University of Wales College of Cardiff.

IMRIE, R. F. and MORRIS, J. L. (1988) 'Large firm-small firm relations: the changing nature of subcontracting in Wales, in the *Proceedings of the 11th Small Business Conference*, Cardiff, November, 1988, 418–37.

INTERNATIONAL MOTOR VEHICLE PROGRAMME (1989) *International Policy Forum*, Cambridge, MA: IMVP, MIT.

ISHIZUNA, Y. (1990) 'The transformation of Nissan – the reform of corporate culture', *Long Range Planning*, 23 (3): 9–15.

JENKINS, R. (1988) 'Supplying Japanese companies in South Wales', unpublished MBA dissertation, Cardiff Business School, U.W.C.C.

JESSOP, B., BONNETT, K., BROMLEY, S. and LING, T. (1987) 'Popular capitalism, flexible accumulation and left strategy, *New Left Review*, 165, 104–22.

JETRO (1984) *State of Operations of Japanese Affiliates (Manufacturing) in Europe: First Survey Report*, Tokyo: JETRO.

JETRO (1987) *Japanese Manufacturing Companies Operating in Europe: Third Survey Report*, Tokyo: JETRO.

JETRO (1989) *Current Management Situation of Japanese Manufacturing Enterprises in Europe: Fifth Survey Report*, Tokyo: JETRO.

JONES, B. (1988) 'Work and flexible automation in Britain: a review of developments and possibilities', *Work, Employment and Society*, 2, 451–86.

JONES, B. and SCOTT, P. (1987) 'Flexible manufacturing systems in Britain and the USA', *New Technology, Work and Employment*, 2 (1): 27–35.

JONES, D. (1989) 'A second look at the European Motor industry', in *IMVP International Policy Forum*, Cambridge, MA: MIT.

KAPLINSKY, R. (1983) 'Firm size and technical change in a dynamic context', *Journal of Industrial Economics*, 32, 39–60.

KEEBLE, D. (1968) 'Industrial decentralisation and the metropolis: the North West London case', Transactions of the Institute of British Geographers, 49, 1–54.

KELLY, J. (1983) *Scientific Management, Job Redesign and Work Performance*, London: Academic Press.

LAMMING, R. (1989) *The Causes and Effects of Structural Change in The European Automotive Components Industry*, International Motor Vehicle Program, Center for Technology, Policy and Industrial Development, M. I.T., Cambridge, M. A.

LIPIETZ, A. (1984) 'Imperialism or the beast of the apocalypse', *Capital and Class*, 22, 81–109.

LIPIETZ, A. (1986) 'New tendencies in the international division of labour: regimes of accumulation and modes of regulation', in A. Scott, and M. Storper, (eds), *Production, Work, Territory: The Geographical Anatomy of Industrial Capitalism*, Hemel Hempstead: Allen & Unwin.

LLOYD, N. (1989) 'How Sony in Wales matched Japanese quality levels', *Quality Assurance (UK)*, 15 (1): 20–4.

LOVERING, J. (1988) 'The local economy and local economic strategies', *Policy and Politics*, 6, 145–57.

LRD (1986) 'Flexibility examined', *Bargaining Report*, Labour Research Department, London.

LUCAS GIRLING (1985) 'Supplier Development', internal document, Lucas Girling, Cwmbran.

LUCAS INDUSTRIES PLC, (1982) *Lucas Annual Report, 1982*, Birmingham.

LUCAS INDUSTRIES PLC (1985) *Lucas Annual Report, 1985*, Birmingham.

LUCAS INDUSTRIES PLC (1989) *Lucas Annual Report, 1989*, Birmingham.

MACINNES, J. (1987) *Thatcherism at Work*, Milton Keynes: Open University Press.

MAIR, A., FLORIDA, R. and KENNEY, M. (1988) 'The new geography of automobile production: Japanese transplants in North America', *Economic Geography*, 64, 352–73.

MANDEL, E. (1975) *Late Capitalism*, London: New Left Books.

MANDEL, E. (1978) *The Second Slump*, London: New Left Books.

MARGINSON, P., EDWARDS, P., MARTIN, R., PURCELL, J. and SISSON, K., (1988), *Beyond the Workplace*, Oxford: Basil Blackwell.

MARINACCIO, R. and MORRIS, J. (1991) 'Work and production reorganisation: the influence of a Japanese company upon a "Japanized" company', *Journal of General Management* (forthcoming).

MARSHALL, J. N. (1980) 'Spatial variations in manufacturing industry demand for business services: some implications for government economic policies', *WP35, Centre for Urban and Regional Development Studies*, University of Newcastle Upon Tyne, Newcastle Upon Tyne.

MARTIN, R. (1988) 'Industrial capitalism in transition: the contemporary reorganization of the British space economy', in D. Massey, and J. Allen (eds), *Uneven Redevelopment: Cities and Regions in Transition*, London: Hodder & Stoughton.

MASSEY, D. and MEEGAN, R. (1982) *The Anatomy of Job Loss*, Andover: Methuen.

MAVIER, J. (1982) 'Capitalist regulation, overaccumulation and the collapse of the world order', *Journal of Radical Economics*, 3 (2): 2–15.

MEEGAN, R. (1988) 'A crisis of mass production', in J. Allen and D. Massey (eds), *Restructuring Britain: The Economy in Question*, London: Sage Publications.

MENSCH, G. (1977) *Stalemate in Technology*, Cambridge, MA: Bellinger.

MINGIONE, E. (1981) 'Information, restructuring and the survival strategies of the working class', *International Journal of Urban and Regional Research*, 7, 311–39.

MITTER, S. (1986) *Common Fate, Common Bond: Women in the Global Economy*, London: Pluto.

MOORE, C. W. (1972) 'Industrial linkage development paths in growth poles: a research methodology', Environment and Planning, 4, 253–71.

MORITA, A. (1987) *Made in Japan*, London: Collins.

MORRIS, J. (1987) *Japanese Manufacturing Investment in the EEC: The Effects of Integration*, Report to DGI, EEC, Brussels.

MORRIS, J. (1988a) 'The who, why and where of Japanese manufacturing investment in the UK', *Industrial Relations Journal*, 19 (1): 31–40.

MORRIS, J., (1988b) 'Towards the flexible firm: the socio-spatial implications of changes in production organization', *Planning Working Paper* no. 102, Department of Town Planning, U.W.I.S.T., Cardiff.

MORRIS, J. (1988c) 'New technologies, flexible work practices, and socio-spatial differentiation in Britain: some observations from the United Kingdom, *Environment and Planning D: Society and Space*, 6, 301–20.

MORRIS, J. (1989a) *The Changing Industrial Structure of Canadian Industry: The Role of Japanese Direct Investment*, Final Report to the Canadian High Commission, London.

MORRIS, J. (1989b) 'Japanese inward investment and the "importation" of sub-contracting complexes: three case studies', *Area*, 21, 269–77.

MORRIS, J. (1991a) 'Globalization and global localisation: explaining trends in Japanese foreign manufacturing investment', in J. Morris, (ed.), *Japan and the Global Economy*, London: Routledge.

MORRIS, J. (1991b) 'Japanese manufacturing investment in the EEC: an Overview', in J. Morris (ed.), *Japan and The Global Economy*, London: Routledge.

MURRAY, F. (1987) 'Flexible specialisation in the "Third Italy"', *Capital and Class*, 33, 84–95.

MURRAY, R. (1985) 'Benetton Britain: the new economic order', *Marxism Today* November, 28–32.

NEDO (1986) *Changing Working Patterns*, report prepared by the Institute of

Manpower Studies with the Department of Employment, London.

NEIL, G., BAXTER, L., FERGUSON, N. and MACBETH, D. (1988) 'The continuing importance of cost in supplier selection in support of JIT', unpublished report, Glasgow Business School, University of Glasgow, Glasgow.

NEW, C. and MEYERS, A. (1986) *Managing Manufacturing Operations in the UK, 1975–1985*, London: British Institute of Management.

NISHIGUCHI, T. (1989) 'Is JIT really JIT?' in the *Proceedings of the IMVP Annual Policy Forum*, Cambridge, MA: MIT.

NISSAN MOTOR UK (1988) *Company Information*, NMUK, Sunderland.

NISSAN MOTOR UK (n.d.) *Nissan Supplier Guide*, N.M. UK, Sunderland.

NOCKOLDS, H. (1976) *Lucas: The First 100 Years, Volume 1*, Newton Abbot: David and Charles.

NOCKOLDS, H. (1978) *Lucas: The First 100 Years, Volume 2*, Newton Abbot: David and Charles.

OLIVER, N. and WILKINSON, B. (1988) *The Japanization of British Industry*, Oxford: Basil Blackwell.

ORAM, R. (1988a) 'IBM in further move to reorganise workforce', *Financial Times*, 1 July, 27.

ORAM, R. (1988b) 'Crossed lines bring IBM a wrong number', *Financial Times*, 12 December, 29.

ORAM, R. and FISHER, A. (1988) 'IBM links with Seimens in US telecoms ventures', *Financial Times*, 4 December, 1.

PAIS, D. (1988) 'The changing world of buyer-supplier relations', *Transportation Research Unit Research Review*, 19 (2 and 3): 30–31, University of Michigan, Ann Arbor.

PALLOIX, C. (1976) 'The labour process: from fordism to neo fordism', in Conference of Socialist Economist's Pamphlet, *The Labour Process and Class Strategies, Stage 1*, CSE, London.

PARKER-JERVIS, G. (1990) 'Big blue's generation gap', *Observer*, 25 February, p. 44.

PARNABY, J. (1986a) 'Competitiveness through systems engineering', paper presented to Cambridge Manufacturing Forum, 'Winning in 1990', July.

PARNABY, J. (1986b) 'Education and training in manufacturing systems engineering', Paper presented to Institute of Production Engineers, PEP conference, July.

PARNABY, J. (1987) 'Competitiveness via total quality of performance', *Progress in Rubber and Plastics Technology*, 3 (1): 42–50.

PEACH, L. (1985) 'Managing corporate citizenship', *Personnel Management*, July, 32–5.

PECK, F. (1988) *Manufacturing Linkages in Tyne and Wear*, Tyne and Wear Countywide Research and Intelligence Unit, Newcastle Upon Tyne.

PEGGE, T. (1986) 'Hitachi two years on', *Personnel Management*, October, 42–7.

PIORE, M. (1986) 'The decline of mass production and the challenge to union survival, *Industrial Relations Journal*, 17, 207–21.

PIORE, M. and SABEL, C. (1984) *The Second Industrial Divide: Prospects for Prosperity*, New York: Basic Books.
POLLERT, A. (1988) 'Dismantling flexibility', *Capital and Class*, 34, 42–75.
PUCIK, V. (1987) 'Joint ventures as a strategy for competition', in P. J. Arneson (ed.), *The Japanese Competition: Phase 2*, Ann Arbor, Michigan: Center for Japanese Studies.
QUINN, J. B, MINTZBERG, H and JAMES, R. (1988) *The Strategy Process*, Englewood Cliffs, N.J.:Prentice Hall International.
RAINNIE, A. (1988) 'Your flexible friend?: Small firms in the 1980s', unpublished paper, The Local Economy Research Unit, Hatfield Polytechnic, Hertford.
RAPOPORT, C. (1988) 'Japan tunes in while Europe talks, *Financial Times*, 21 April, 36.
RAWLINSON, M. (1990) 'Subcontracting from motor vehicle related firms to small engineering firms in the Coventry economy', unpublished PhD. thesis, Department of Geography, Coventry Polytechnic, Coventry.
ROBERTSON, I. L. (1988) *Japan's Motor Industry: En Route to 2000*, Economist Intelligence Unit, Automotive Special Report No. 13, E.I.U., London.
ROBINSON, T. (1989) *Partners in Providing the Goods: The Changing Relationship Between Large Companies and their Small Suppliers*, London: 3i's.
RODGER, I. (1988) 'Japanese strive to become good Europeans', *Financial Times*, 6 June, 4.
RODGER, I., CANE, A., ORAM, R and KEHOE, L. (1990) 'Strategic testing ground for IBM', *Financial Times*, 4 May, 31.
RUBERY, J., TARLING, R. and WILKINSON, F. (1987) 'Flexibility, marketing and the organization of production', *Labour and Society*, 12, 131–51.
RUBERY, J. and WILKINSON, F. (1981) 'Outwork and segmented labour markets', in F. Wilkinson (ed.) *The Dynamics of Labour Market Segmentation*, London: Academic Press.
RUTHERFORD, T. (1990) 'Production, restructuring and local labour markets: recruitment and training in the South Wales motor components sector', unpublished paper, Department of City and Regional Planning, University of Wales College of Cardiff, Cardiff.
RUTHERFORD, T., IMRIE, R., and MORRIS, J., (1989) 'Subcontracting flexibility? Changes in buyer-supplier relations', paper presented to Fourth Employment Research Unit Conference, Cardiff Business School, U.W.C.C., September.
SABEL, C. F. (1979) 'Marginal workers in industrial society', *Challenge*, March-April, 17–27.
SABEL, C. F. (1982) *Work and Politics: The Division of Labour in Industry*, Cambridge: Cambridge University Press.
SAKO, M. (1989) 'Neither markets nor heirarchies: a comparative study of

the printed circuit board industry in Britain and Japan', paper presented to the Second Conference for the Project Comparing Capitalist Economies, Ballagio, Italy.

SAYER, A. (1989) 'Post fordism in question', *International Journal of Urban and Regional Research*, 13, 666–95.

SCASE, R. and GOFFEE, R. (1982) *The Entrepreneurial Middle Class*, Beckenham, Kent: Croom Helm.

SCOTT, A. J. (1984) 'Industrial organization and the logic of intra metropolitan location III: a case study of the women's dress industry in the Greater Los Angeles Area', *Economic Geography*, 60, 3–27.

SCOTT, A. J. (1988) *New Industrial Spaces: Flexible Production Organization and Regional Development in North America and Western Europe*, London: Pion.

SHAPIRO, R. (1985) 'Towards effective supplier management: international comparisons', *Working Paper 9–785–062*, Harvard Business School, Cambridge, M. A.

SHEARD, P. (1983) 'Auto production systems in Japan: organizational and locational features', *Australian Geographical Studies*, 21, 49–68.

SHUTT, J. and WHITTINGTON, R. (1984) 'Large firm strategies and the rise of small units: the illusion of small firm job generation', *WP15, North West Industry Research Unit*, University of Manchester, Manchester.

SONY CORPORATION (1989) *Annual Report, 1989*, Tokyo: Sony Corporation.

SPIRIDION, R. H. (1987) 'Personnel management at IBM: theory and practice', unpublished MBA thesis, Cardiff Business School, U.W.I.S.T., Cardiff.

STARKEY, K. and McKINLAY, A. (1989) 'Beyond fordism? Strategic choice and labour relations in Ford UK', *Industrial Relations Journal*, 20 (2) 93–100.

TAN, B. (1990) 'Using the supplier relationship to develop the support industry', *Omega*, 18, 151–8.

TAYLOR, M. J. and THRIFT, N. J. (1982) 'Industrial linkage and the segmented economy: 1. Some theoretical proposals', *Environment and Planning A*, 14, 1601–1613.

T.G.W.U. (1983) *British Leyland: The Next Decade*, report by T.G.W.U. with A.U.E.W./TASS, Birmingham: T.G.W.U.

THOMAS, W. R., (1988) 'An empirical study of the buyer-supplier relationship where the buyer company is adopting Japanese style manufacturing practices', unpublished M.B.A. dissertation, Cardiff Business School, U.W.C.C., Cardiff.

THOMPSON, F., (1990) 'Lucas expects 3 plants in strike ballot targeting', *Financial Times*, 5 February, 8.

THOMSON, R. (1989a) 'Nissan's action plan promises "volume imports"', *Financial Times*, 9 September, p. 35.

THOMSON, R. (1989b) 'Sony calls for $980 million to fund expansion', *Financial Times*, 27 June, 21.

THRIFT, N. (1988) 'The geography of international economic disorder', in D. Massey and J. Allen (eds), *Uneven Redevelopment: Cities and Regions in Transition*, London: Open University Press.

TOMKINS, R., (1989) 'Overseas operations help Lucas rise to £187 million', *Financial Times*, 24 October, 29.

TOMLINSON, J. (1989) 'Macro-economic management and industrial policy', in P. Hirst and J. Zeitlin (eds), *Reversing Industrial Decline: Industrial Structure and Policy in Britain and Her Competitors*, Oxford: Berg.

TRADE and INDUSTRY COMMITTEE (1987) *The UK Motor Components Industry, 3rd Report*, London: H.M.S.O.

TREASURY AND CIVIL SERVICE COMMITTEE (1986) *The Government's Economic Policy: Autumn Statement*, London: H.M.S.O.

TREVOR, M. (1988) *Toshiba's New British Company: Competitiveness through Innovation in Industry*, London: Policy Studies Institute.

TREVOR, M. and CHRISTIE, I. (1988) *Manufacturers and Suppliers in Britain and Japan: Competitiveness and The Growth of Small Firms*, London: Policy Studies Institute.

TURNBULL, P. (1986) 'The "Japanization" of production and industrial relations at Lucas Electrical', *Industrial Relations Journal*, 17 (3): 193–206.

TURNBULL, P. (1989) 'Now we're motoring? The West Midlands automotive component industry', *Japanese Management Research Unit Working Paper*, Cardiff Business School, University of Wales College of Cardiff, Cardiff.

TURNBULL, P. (1990) 'Buyer-supplier relations in the UK automotive industry' in P. Blyton and J. Morris, *Flexible Futures? Prospects for Employment and Organisation*, Berlin and New York: De Gruyter.

TURNBULL, P., OLIVER, N. and WILKINSON, B. (1990) 'J.I.T. and T.Q.C.: implications for information systems', *Technology Analysis and Strategic Management*, 1, 409–22.

VAN DE VLIET, A., (1986) 'Where Lucas sees the light', *Management Today*, June, 38–45, 92.

VERITY, J. W. (1990) 'IBM is finally saying: "In Unix we trust?"', *Business Week*, 12 February, 54–5.

VILLA, P. (1981) 'Labour market segmentation and the construction industry in Italy', in F. Wilkinson (ed.), *The Dynamics of Labour Market Segmentation*, London: Academic Press.

VOSS, C. and CLUTTERBUCK, D. (1989) *Just-in-Time: A Global Status Report*, London: IFS.

WAGSTYL, S. (1989) 'Nissan continues strong recovery', *Financial Times*, 30 May, 30.

WAGSTYL, S and BUCHAN, J. (1989) 'Sony starts to peddle dreams', Financial Times, 28 May, 29.

WALBY, S. (1986) *Patriarchy at Work*, London: Polity Press.

WALKER, R. (1988) 'The geographical organization of productive systems', *Environment and Planning D: Society and Space*, 6: 377–408.

WALKER, R. (1989) 'Machinery, labour and location', in S. Wood (ed.), *The Transformation of Work*, London: Unwin Hyman.

WARD, J. (1987) 'IBM', in C. Voss (ed.), *Just-in-Time Manufacture*, London: IFS.

WEST MIDLANDS INDUSTRIAL DEVELOPMENT ASSOCIATION (1989) *Vehicle Components Sector Report*, WMIDA, Coleshill, Warwickshire.

WICKENS, P. (1987) *The Road to Nissan*, London: Macmillan.

WILLIAMS, K., CUTLER, T., WILLIAMS, J. and HASLAM, C. (1987) 'The end of mass production', *Economy and Society*, 16, 405–39.

WILLIAMS, K., WILLIAMS J., HASLAM, C. and WARDLOW, A. (1989) 'Facing up to manufacturing failure', in P. Hirst and J. Zeitlin (eds) *Reversing Industrial Decline: Industrial Structure in Britain and Her Competitors*, Oxford: Berg.

WILLIAMS K., WILLIAMS, J. and THOMAS, D. (1983) *Why the British are Bad at Manufacturing*, Andover: Routledge & Kegan Paul.

WILLIAMSON, H. (1989) 'Back in the melting pot? Re-thinking trade union perspectives of Japanese motor industry investment in Britain and 'Japanese-style' industrial relations', paper presented at Conference of Socialist Economists, Sheffield.

WILLIAMSON, O. (1975) *Markets and Hierarchies*, New York: The Free Press.

WILSON, P. and GORB, P. (1983) 'How large and small firms can grow together', *Long Range Planning*, 16 (2): 19–27.

WOMAK, J. P., JONES, D. T. and ROOS, D. (1990) *The Machine that Changed the World: The Triumph of Lean Production*, New York: Macmillan.

WOOD, S. (1989) 'The transformation of work', in S. Wood (ed.), *The Transformation of Work*, London: Unwin Hyman.

Index

185